The Curriculum Bridge

The Curriculum Bridge

From Standards to Actual Classroom Practice

Second Edition

Pearl G. Solomon

For information:

Corwin Press, Inc.
A Sage Publications Company
2455 Teller Road
Thousand Oaks, California 91320
www.corwinpress.com

Sage Publications Ltd.
6 Bonhill Street
London EC2A 4PU
United Kingdom

Sage Publications India Pvt. Ltd.
B-42 Panchsheel Enclave
Post Box 4109
New Delhi 110 017 India

Printed in the United States of America

Library of Congress Cataloging-in-Publication Data

Solomon, Pearl G. (Pearl Gold), 1929-
The curriculum bridge : from standards to actual classroom practice /
by Pearl G. Solomon.— 2nd ed.
p. cm.
Includes bibliographical references and index.
ISBN 0-7619-3905-9 (Cloth) — ISBN 0-7619-3906-7 (Paper)
1. Curriculum planning—United States. 2. Education—Curricula-Standards—United States.
3. Educational tests and measurements. 4. Curriculum—based assessment—United States.
I. Title.
LB2806.15.S65 2003
375′.001—dc21

2003000778

This book is printed on acid-free paper.

03 04 05 06 07 7 6 5 4 3 2 1

Acquisitions Editor: Faye Zucker
Editorial Assistant: Stacy Wagner
Production Editor: Julia Parnell
Copyeditor: Kristin Bergstad
Typesetter/Designer: C&M Digitals (P) Ltd.
Proofreader: Kathleen Pearsall
Indexer: Jeanne R. Busemeyer
Cover Designer: Michael Dubowe
Production Artist: Lisa Miller

Contents

Preface

THE SECOND EDITION

In the few short years since I wrote the first edition of this book the world has changed at an unpredicted and dizzying rate. In spite of the looming crisis of war, a rapidly intensifying call for educational change was only slightly diminished. The passions and human differences that engage the population of this country as it confronts the prospect of armed conflict in far-away places, as well as the new reality of its homeland effects are similarly manifested as it confronts the prospects of change in its educational systems. Given war or peace, education is, after all, an important investment in the future.

Good investments should provide us with profitable returns. Money and time are the currencies of investments in the process of education, investments whose purpose is to protect and improve the future of society.

WHO SHOULD READ THIS BOOK

This book is for those of us who want to make an investment of time that may help us understand how to make better decisions about what students should and can learn, and how we can help them learn. It explains why there is growing mistrust of the return on the investment in education in this country; why there is a cry for new higher standards and accountability. It will prepare us to make a knowing and credible response to those who lack faith in what we do. The time spent should give us greater confidence in our ability to identify the problems and find the solutions for whatever others have found deficient or convince them to judge us otherwise. My own investment of time in preparation for this book was made because I am a teacher and know that learning and writing about what I need to do will help me become a better one.

Profitable returns on investments require more than superficial suggestions. Although a basic philosophy about what is right in curriculum is embedded in this book, it is not a philosophical treatise. It is more of an informed "how to do it." Unlike other curriculum books, it deals mostly with the present and with current needs. It does not address the specific content of different subject areas; instead it provides an overall view that can help educators and other educational decision makers as they respond to the needs of their students and the demands of policymakers for higher standards. Although there is a strong emphasis on the research knowledge that should guide us in building curriculum, the book is not a comprehensive review of the literature. It does try to synthesize and represent the thoughts of many current researchers in a manner that can easily be understood and applied to classroom practice. Therefore, those who practice and those who lead others in their practice may benefit from the chapters ahead.

WHAT THIS BOOK IS ABOUT

This book is about curriculum and the skeleton that gives it a frame and support: the standards or levels of the bar that represent what we value, what we know, and what our children need to know. A shared understanding of the meaning of curriculum and classroom practice is a good way to begin. A variety of people and institutions make educational decisions at times, but for professional educators, it is their major endeavor and responsibility. They make long-term decisions that affect many students and small decisions that are momentary, aimed at one particular student in a specific instance. The set of all school-based decisions about what and how children should learn is the *curriculum.*

Regardless of whether curriculum decisions are made by an individual teacher, a consensus of teachers, or imposed as a policy by those in authority, if they are planned and documented, they constitute the *written curriculum*. Not everything is written down, and not everything written is accomplished. The planned and unplanned decisions made, and the actions taken by teachers in classrooms (with the written curriculum and other things in mind) are referred to as the *enacted curriculum,* which is, in essence, classroom practice. The unwritten curriculum is sometimes referred to as the "hidden curriculum," but it is not hidden from classroom practice.

Embedded in the chapters ahead is a real story of three teachers as they confront the current issues that concern schools and discover what is now known about learning. Based on this new knowledge, they work together to pursue some specific strategies that will help them use the standards skeleton to build the curriculum bridge to classroom practice. And then they will look at the future. Their task will not be easy.

When educators are given the authority to enact curriculum, they have power—more than they probably realize. However, when parents and the public-at-large entrust teachers with this power over their children, they retain some rights to monitor and control what teachers do. Teachers, then, juggle constantly. In one hand are the balls that represent what they believe is best for that child and themselves, at this time, in this place. These beliefs are based on their standards, their values, their interests, their knowledge of the content of the curriculum, their knowledge of their own skills, and their knowledge of their students. In the other hand is their obligation to respect the beliefs of others who have a stake in students' futures: parents, supervisors, elected officials, and the public-at-large.

The juggling act is tricky. It demands concentration and practice. Teachers must know where each ball is at all times. Because they must respond to different students at different moments in time, they need to reflectively monitor their own beliefs. They need to listen carefully to the voices of others who can influence what they are doing, and be alert to a lack of fit. Sometimes adjustments will be necessary, but at other times their beliefs should be held firm. The rhythm, balance, and consistency are important. Skill with old moves increases with experience, but new ones make their performance better and more interesting.

In Chapter 1 readers will discover or be reminded of some of the recent history that brought us to the current crescendo of public interest in education and the trend toward the adoption of a common core of high standards and assessments that measure student achievement. The present is viewed through the comments of the public, respected educational leaders, and politicians in regard to the current status of education. They are worthy of the attention because it is important to understand the influences and controls that affect our values, effectiveness, and choices.

Chapter 2 explores these influences. Influences may not have clearly definable consequences when you do not pay attention to them. But if we are teachers, their power is related to our own needs. Our strongest imperative is to reach our students—and we struggle to do the best we can. Controls, such as high-stakes tests based on imposed standards, can have clearly definable consequences for our students and for ourselves. The cogent strategy is to make the influences and controls of a variety of stakeholders work for our purposes rather than against them.

Chapter 2 helps us gain an understanding of the underlying struggle in this country for control of public education. Beginning with the politically charged debate between federal and state governments over who should determine standards, it considers the roles of the press and big business in framing the dimensions of the discourse. It then moves to the role of local school boards and their relationship with the internal power system of supervision by school administrators, and the unpredictable power of parents. Included among the other influences addressed are the subtle pressures of peers and professional peer groups, college professors, professional writers, and because education is a major enterprise, the powerful lure of an abundance of commercial materials and new technologies.

Chapter 3 brings us to the heart of the enacted curriculum with an abbreviated discussion of what we now know about learning. The briefing on the scientific knowledge base is intended to provide us with a rationale or decision-making template for the curriculum content and instructional strategies that we classroom teachers may choose. It will help us predict more cogently what will work, and understand why some things do not work. It is in this knowledge that our true power lies. The best use of that power includes a reflective process that is progenerative, leading us continuously to self-correction and renewal. This chapter ends with a summary analysis that applies current knowledge of how learning takes place to specific suggestions for curriculum, instructional practice, and its technological applications.

Chapter 4 takes us to the creative design step: constructing our own curriculum. Once all of the influences, controls, and existing sources have been considered, the teacher is ready to identify what standards students must meet and which additional outcomes are desired (the desired outcomes may exceed the standards). This chapter provides clarification of the new terminology and compares it to the existing terms and habits of practice so that we may all speak the same new language. It offers a template to guide us as we design down from more general prescribed national or state standards to the specific outcomes we aim for with an individual classroom experience.

It is a challenge to match these desired outcomes with appropriate learning experiences for students, experiences in settings that reflect the many new understandings that we now have about how learning happens and about what keeps it from happening. Before writing this book, for example, I thought about the outcomes I wished to achieve, but knowing how learning takes place humbled my expectations for accomplishing them with just a reading activity. However, that same knowledge about learning has made me rethink the way in which this reading activity is organized. Using a metaphor of the theater, Chapter 5 takes us through the elements of the setting: grouping students and using time, space, and material props. It addresses the role of student goals in motivating and managing learning, and then explores the use of critical themes and classroom discourse.

Unfortunately, a missing element in this educational reading activity is my ability to assess its effect on my readers. Assessments produce the signals for our educational transport system, the system that takes our students from the place of not knowing to knowing. We teacher-engineers need to know where we are going, how well and how fast we are progressing, where the switches are, and, if the track is obstructed, what the alternative routes are. We also need to stop at a station from time to time to refuel, revise, and take on new passengers and new systems. Assessments guide our station breaks.

Chapter 6 compares how traditional and alternative assessments are used to tell us how our students and therefore we, ourselves, are doing with our chosen purposes. Performance assessments will be explored as an alternative or addition to short answer tests of recall of finite and unrevealing facts, measured by percentages of correct responses for predetermined answers. These measure a wider scope of newly constructed knowledge and use open-ended problems that allow for divergent solutions. This chapter looks at rubrics that identify more clearly what has or hasn't been accomplished, and do it in a way that can provide better direction for new learning activities.

Well-done assessments can be designed to discover previously unrevealed positive outcomes and undiscovered needs. They can also be used to enforce curriculum policy mandates. When assessments are high stake or bear appreciable consequences for students, educators, and systems, special care must be taken in their construction and implementation. We provide some suggestions for this care.

Chapter 7 looks at ways to increase the potential return on our investments. Ensuring a good return requires learning new skills and sharing our skills with others in a meaningful way. Engaging teachers in a more formal process of action research can help give their craft a more scientific framework—and perhaps lead to greater success. Participation in research requires professional development. This chapter examines the possible reasons for the failure of our present systems of professional development for teachers. Teacher networks and professional development schools are suggested as one possible way to meet the challenge of instructional improvement. Finally, it looks into the near future to consider how technology can assist in the research and teacher learning process, and in our communication with the public. A better approach to curriculum writing and enactment can ensure a better future for our profession, our students, and our society. When others have confidence in our ability to ensure the return on their investments it will **bring each of us the personal satisfaction of knowing we did it well!**

Acknowledgments

There are many people who have given me the confidence to proceed with this endeavor. Faye Zucker, my editor at Corwin Press, is a constant inspiration. The sharp eyes and attention of copyeditor Kristin Bergstad were important additions to the quality of this edition. Since this is a second edition, I wish to thank my many readers who have told me how useful the original work was for them. Their feedback inspired two subsequent books and this revision. My wonderfully supportive colleagues at St. Thomas Aquinas College, my students, and the many teachers and administrators I work with in the Marie Curie Center network have kept me close to the realities of teaching in today's schools; they provide rich and responsive feedback on the effectiveness of my communication and accuracy of my ideas.

For reconnecting me intimately to the intricacies of how learning happens, for providing the emotional support that intensive work demands, and for generously giving up some of the time I would have spent with them, I wish to thank my grandsons Joseph and Edward and my husband Mel.

About the Author

Pearl G. Solomon is Professor Emeritus of Teacher Education at St. Thomas Aquinas College in Sparkill, New York. She received a doctorate in educational administration from Teachers College, Columbia University. Pearl Solomon has served as a public school teacher and administrator, director and officer for professional organizations and as a consultant to many school districts, the New York State Education Department, and the U.S. Department of Education. She is the recipient of a number of special awards from the state and community for her work in science, math, health, and career education.

Recent activities include directing the Marie Curie Mathematics and Science Center and its Project McExtend network of teachers in two New York State counties. Eisenhower, National Science Foundation, and Goals 2000 grants that she authored have enabled large-scale inservice teacher training efforts as well as Saturday enrichment programs in math and science for Grade 5–12 students. Her present teaching assignments include graduate courses in curriculum and math and science methods.

Dr. Solomon is a frequent speaker at professional conferences and author of several books published by Corwin Press, including *No Small Feat: Taking Time for Change* (1995); *The Math We Need to "Know" and "Do": Content Standards for Elementary and Middle Grades* (2001), which was selected as a finalist for Outstanding Writing Award from the American Association of Colleges of Teacher Education; and *The Assessment Bridge: Positive Ways to Link Tests to Learning, Standards, and Curriculum Improvement* (2002). The first edition of *The Curriculum Bridge* was selected by *Choice* magazine of The American Library Association as an outstanding academic book for 1999.

1 Why Standards and Tests Are on the Front Page

ABOUT THIS CHAPTER

History tells us that the degree of public concern with education has varied through time. As far back as the Egyptians, Greeks, and Romans, and considering as well the carefully prescribed ritual training of youth in tribal societies, formal schooling has been the hallmark of stable human communities. It is a reciprocal relationship, however: Formal education connotes stability, but also bears the responsibility for maintaining it. It is not surprising, then, that in relatively peaceful times positive public attention is drawn to how we educate our youth and what we teach them. Interest in education grows when there are spare energies and resources to invest. In times of stress, however, attention comes again in response to negative evaluations of the readiness of youth to protect the future. If one generation is threatened, then the next must be prepared to survive. It is the natural order of life on our planet. In order to guarantee the survival of the species, a plant compromised by drought or disease will often use its diminishing energy to produce the best blooms just before it dies.

Education is about transmitting the culture so that it may survive in the next generation. Public education in this country is also about closing cultural gaps—gaps that many fear as potential sources of human conflict. Public attention to education can be constructive, but educational processes have a greater chance of success if they carefully balance the needs and standards of society with the individual needs of the developing individual. Educators must also recognize that society itself undergoes renewal and it is their responsibility to respond to and engage in the ongoing process of change (see Dewey, 1916/1973).

With this very brief, longer-range perspective of the relationship between education and society in mind, I turn in this chapter to the recent history of this relationship and to the rapidly evolving events and setting of the current time. An understanding of history and setting is crucial for teachers who must deal with these many and often conflicting influences as they make day-to-day decisions about what and how to teach, and then must deal with the consequences of these decisions. I begin in time at the middle of 2002 and look back at the previous three decades to search for an understanding of the Zeitgeist of this more recent and volatile episode in the history of American education.

AT THE TOP OF THE POLITICAL AGENDA: EDUCATION

In spite of the looming crises of an uncompleted war on terrorism and a global controversy over an impending preemptive engagement with Saddam Hussein and Iraq, the subject of education was a major agenda item for the 2002 political campaigns of the candidates for governor of New York State. This followed a national trend in the campaigns of many politicians, including that of President George W. Bush. As early as September 23, 2001, 12 days after the terrorist attacks on the World Trade Center and the Pentagon, the U.S. Congress was grappling with and making decisions on President Bush's education plan (Associated Press, 2001).

On October 10, 2001, three days after the U.S. attack on Afghanistan, 16 state governors were meeting at an IBM center in Palisades, New York, for the fourth education summit. The location is about five minutes from where I teach, but I was not invited; neither was a fair representation of other teachers and principals. President Bush was supposed to be there but did not appear; neither did nine other governors who had originally agreed to come. Michigan governor John Engler gave the rationale for their presence in these dire times, arguing that American strength can only be maintained with an educated population. "We're in a war," he said. "We want to secure ourselves from enemies internal and external. Ignorance, lack of knowledge, poorly developed skills, these are the kind of internal enemies we can do something about" (Wilson & Weiner, 2001, p. B1). Historian Diane Ravitch (2002) reiterates this need: "In response to the terrorist attacks, U.S. public schools must reclaim their vital role—preparing students to become informed citizens who will preserve and protect democracy."

Just a month before the fatal September 11, 2001, attacks, President Bush had addressed the predominantly African American National Urban League. He described the state of many urban schools as a "great and continuing scandal" and declared, "Rarely in American history have we faced a problem so serious and destructive on which change has come so slowly" (Bruni, 2001). A major agenda item for the ensuing 2001 summit conference was the problem of the ever-widening gap in test scores between white and minority students. The solution offered by President Bush and supported by both houses of Congress was new legislation requiring annual standards-based tests for students in Grades 3–8. Many state representatives were concerned about the cost of the tests. Rhode Island's Commissioner of Education Peter McWalters cited a cost of four million dollars and expressed concern that the expense would divert dollars from other needs. Conference chairman and former IBM head Lou Gerstner, however, suggested an even more costly solution to the problems presented: increasing the salary of teachers (Steinberg, 2001).

WHY THE FOCUS ON STANDARDS AND TESTS?

In an interview of national leaders (Lehmann & Spring, 1996), Donald Stewart, president of the College Board, said that educational standards are necessary because we need to answer the question, "Are we better in terms of something?" (p. 3). Former assistant secretary of education and conservative school policy spokesman, Chester Finn, added that, "standards are only meaningful if you also answer the question: 'How good is good enough?'" (p. 6). Tests with predetermined expectations or "proficiency standards" seem to answer that question.

The term *standards* has now replaced the traditional educator's term *objectives*. Both terms essentially entail a process of coming to consensus and producing explicit statements of the elements of the American culture worthy of transmission. These statements, in essence, become the structural frame of the written curriculum. There are, in addition, many unwritten components of the curriculum and variations in organization, setting, and detail that we will discuss in the chapters that follow. As clarified statements that constitute the curriculum, standards parallel traditional goals and objectives as well as outcomes. The term standard, however, has an implication of high levels of expectation and monitoring that were not commonly connected to the widely used educational objectives suggested by Tyler (1949).

Although current standards documents include both the consensus statements of "what students should know and be able to do" and statements that provide the measures of "how well they know and are able to do," the greatest political emphasis has been on the formal instruments, the tests that use the measures to monitor performance. It is the monitoring process on national and international levels that has energized the rising concerns for our education systems. And it is the monitoring process that has the greatest potential for both positive and negative educational consequences.

Roderick Paige, President Bush's secretary of education, explained the significance of mandated tests as a solution to the education gap with his remark,

> When states commit to using assessment data—and by this I mean breaking down results and holding schools accountable for the performance of all of their students—they see real improvement in student achievement. President Bush and Congress can lay the groundwork for reform, but state standards and assessments are the real mechanisms for improving student achievement. (U.S. Department of Education, 2001)

THE NO CHILD LEFT BEHIND LEGISLATION

The final "No Child Left Behind" (NCLB) legislation, a revised version of the Elementary and Secondary Education Act, was passed overwhelmingly by Congress and signed by President Bush in January of 2002. The law mandated his suggestion for state-developed tests in Grades 3–8 by 2005–2006 and also increased federal funding for 2002 to more than $22.1 billion for America's elementary and secondary schools, a 27% increase over 2001 and a 49% increase over 2000 levels. New specific directions for how federal dollars are spent—a form of sanction to provide accountability—included their use to cover the cost of mandated private tutoring and the transportation of students from failing to more successful schools.

As a measure of "performance standards" or "how good is good enough," state-determined proficiency levels must be attached to each test. With the proficiency standards as a guidepost or benchmark, schools are identified as failing if they fail to improve their test scores and move closer to the standard as judged by year-to-year progress or *Adequate Yearly Progress* (AYP). States must develop measurable objectives for improving the performance of all students, including the economically disadvantaged, and those with disabilities or limited English proficiency. The results of the tests must be disaggregated to show the performance of each of these groups separately, and 95% of each of these groups must participate in the tests. The ultimate goal is to bring every student to the proficiency level by 2013/2014.

Table 1.1 ESEA 2002 (NCLB) Sanctions

- If a school fails to make adequate yearly progress (AYP) for two consecutive years, it will be identified as needing improvement and must develop improvement plans incorporating strategies from scientifically based research.
- School districts will be required to offer public school choice (unless prohibited by state law) to all students in the failing school no later than the first day of the school year following identification. The district must provide transportation to the new school.
- If a school fails to make AYP for a third consecutive year, the district must continue to offer public school choice and provide Title I funds (approximately $500 to $1,000 per child) for low-achieving disadvantaged students in the school to obtain supplemental services—tutoring, after school services, or summer school programs—from the public- or private-sector provider selected by their parents from a state-approved list.
- Twenty percent of Title I funds at the local school district level must be used for public school choice and supplemental services.
- If a school fails to make AYP for a fourth consecutive year, it will be subject to increasingly tough corrective actions—such as replacing school staff or significantly decreasing management authority at the school level. If a school continues to fail, the school could ultimately face restructuring, which involves a fundamental change in governance, such as a State takeover or placement under private management.
- Schools that meet or exceed AYP objectives or close achievement gaps will be eligible for State Academic Achievement Awards. (www.whitehouse.gov)

Schools that fail to meet their AYP objectives for two consecutive years are identified as needing improvement and must provide students with the opportunity to transfer to better performing schools and/or private tutoring. Table 1.1 summarizes the consequences and rewards specified in the legislation (http://www.whitehouse.gov/infocus/education/) (Linn, Baker, & Betebenner, 2002).

Prior to the NCLB legislation some states had set proficiency standards based on the concept of "high expectations." Teachers and administrators involved in the process of setting these did not realize that these levels would then be attached to tests that determined fund distribution and highly public consequences for failure to make progress. Nor did they predict cash rewards for those whose schools did well! Experimental test-related merit pay systems for teachers and school administrators are under way in the states of Colorado,

Florida, North Carolina, Iowa, and others. New York City is also rewarding its superintendents and school level administrators (Goodnough, 2002).

An interesting outcome of the parameters of the legislation, which measure the year-to-year or value-added progress toward state-set proficiency levels and penalize states that do not meet the guidelines, is that states that had originally set higher levels of standards achievement as a mark of proficiency were then at a disadvantage. Individual schools that were closer to the proficiency standard in baseline measures also made less progress than those that were significantly deficient. The irony of this, in relation to the cost for NCLB sanctions, is that in a state such as New York, where low-income students scored the seventh highest in the nation on a national test, their achievement on the New York State test was less than the predetermined and relatively high state proficiency level. Federal NCLB legislation then required that 17% of the low-income students be given the option of tutoring and transportation for school transfers (Linn et al., 2002). From the perspective of rewards for performance, rather than sanctions, New York City principals, who had been promised cash salary bonuses if their schools made good progress, also were penalized if their schools started out higher up or closer to the proficiency level.

In some cases, states lowered the standards to overcome the costly requirements for failure to make progress. In Ohio, the government responded to the realization that one third of its low-income schools would require busing by lowering the state proficiency standard for schools from 70% of their students proficient to a new standard of only 42% of their students proficient. In Louisiana, students will be considered proficient when they score at the "basic" achievement level on their state's assessment. Connecticut schoolchildren will be deemed proficient even if they fall shy of the state's performance goals in reading and mathematics. And Colorado students who score in the "partially proficient" level on their state test will be judged proficient (Hoff, 2002). Even Massachusetts, which has been persistent in its requirement that students pass its MCAS (Massachusetts Comprehensive Assessment System) exam before graduation, is reconsidering its standards (Stein, 2002). The tight Massachusetts standards were backed up by special classes and opportunities to repeat the exam. Eighty-one percent of the seniors passed the test on the third try—up from 68% on the first (Rothstein, 2002; Vaishnav, 2002).

A solution to the problem of variations in the proficiency levels and content of individual state tests included in the NCLB legislation is the use of the formerly optional National Assessment of Educational Progress (NAEP) tests in addition to the state tests. The NAEP has been used primarily as a national sampling benchmark, and sometimes as a comparison to test the validity of state tests. Under the Act, all states taking money under the federal Title I program for disadvantaged students will be required to take part in the NAEP's reading and math exams starting in 2003. While the results won't play an official role in evaluating states' definitions of proficiency, researchers and others will be comparing state rankings on their own tests with those of NAEP to see which states have set high goals and which ones haven't. Inevitably, the final arbiter of states' definitions will be the NAEP (Hoff, 2002).

Linn and colleagues (2002), however, suggest that this, too, has problems. They remind us that the NAEP may differ considerably from state tests and the standards they measure, and that the national test also has very stringent standards for proficiency. Year-to-year comparisons may in themselves be questionable because groups of students in the same school and teaching conditions vary from year to year. Other possibilities they suggest for dealing with the disparity of the states' standards include comparing individual student scores and multiyear means.

Perhaps because of late or incomplete information, but also because of resistance to moving children from neighborhood environments, a surprisingly small number of parents opted for the choice to move their children from schools identified as failing in the fall of 2002. The NCLB legislation also contains specific recommendations for the teaching of reading, as well as more money for charter schools and for training teachers. It particularly states that instruction should be research based. The problem with educational research, however, is that the many difficult-to-control variables leave some questions about what works best unanswered (see Chapter 7).

President Bush was not the first to raise the issue of higher standards. The previous president, Bill Clinton, proposed big spending increases for Department of Education programs. His 1998 State of the Union speech, of which about one fourth was devoted to education, reflected his emphasis on education and his interest in national standards and assessments. Clinton recognized the need to get the support of states on this issue as he praised the state of Georgia for its academic standards and its scholarship program. He implored that the "American people respond to the challenge . . . to make American education the best in the world, to understand that it won't be done overnight, and not to be afraid of trying to reach higher standards" (Hoff, 1997, p. 1).

Responding to critics of the move to national testing in his opening remarks to the 2001 summit conference, Chairman Gerstner (2001) said, "But if you listen closely, what you hear is a pathetic willingness to sacrifice an entire generation, and deny them their shot at a better chance, a better future, and a better life." I am sure he was also concerned about future generations. Education is about transmitting the culture from generation to generation. Public education in this country is also about closing cultural gaps; gaps that many fear as potential sources of human conflict. But, why all the interest at this moment in time? What is the American people's attitude toward education? Why are American businessmen concerned? Are the problems as serious as the critics make them appear? Are the proposed solutions valid? What do the educators think? Can we make our schools better?

Economic Influences and Some Words of Caution

Businesses, facing a shortage of technologically proficient personnel and challenged by the need to provide training for growing numbers of employees in what they deem the basic skills, rally to support the feelings of mistrust of the public education enterprise. Politicians pick up on the issue. Governors and the president make the improvement of education a major part of their agendas. Delaine Eastin, the California state superintendent of public instruction, takes her responsibility with a global perspective: "The reality is that we not only need to be able to compare across our nation—which we get in a hit-or-miss way through things like the SAT or ACT scores—but we need to be able to compare across the globe, so that we know that California's children can compete with the German and the French and the Japanese children" (Lehmann & Spring, 1996, p. 3).

Leaders of the business community and governors emerged from the education summit meetings with agendas for raising and equalizing standards across the country, and assuring accountability for them through federally legislated measures. This agenda was based on juxtaposed concerns about this country's economic health, employment needs, and reports of disappointing performances of our students on state and international competency tests.

In a report prepared for the National Alliance for Business, Nelson Smith (1996) quotes the cost to business for continuing and remedial education and expresses the opinion that it is "an expense that business should not have to bear" (p. 5). Examples of costs given in the report included: 10% of $75 million spent by MCI for basic-skills remediation, $700,000 spent by Polaroid for basic English and math, $1,350 per employee annually spent by Motorola. The author also cites, as evidence of the growing need, an American Management Association report that whereas in 1989 only 4% of American businesses provided remedial training, by 1994 "the figure had jumped to 20%" (p. 5). Smith continues with references to the hidden costs to business, to the overall costs to taxpayers for remedial education, and to the ultimate costs to the public for the consequences of poor academic and readiness-to-work skills: welfare and delinquency. The remedy the report suggests for all of these ills is higher standards and vigilance on the part of business leaders.

A report by former astronaut John Glenn, "Before It's Too Late" (2000), underscored the poor performance of the nation's students on the tests and listed four reasons why students needed to be competent in math and science: the interdependent global economy; the need for math and science in everyday decision making; national security interests; and the value of knowledge in our common life, history, and culture.

Common sense tells us that this is a serious condemnation of the educational enterprise by powerful people who are not professional educators. Their focus is mainly on the measured negative results, without regard to the many unmeasured positive outcomes. After all, how did this country achieve its technological superiority? More critically, the non-educators limit their analysis of causes for problems to the lack of a common core of criteria for promotion and graduation—and then they suggest measurement of this common core with assessments that in themselves may present problems. This proposed solution to existing problems in the education of our children completely overlooks the compounding and defeating affects on the process of education created by the societal and economic problems it hopes to defeat. It neglects the realities of an issue that is of equal concern to most educators: the issue of equal opportunity to learn. Once more, it suggests that schools bear the burden for the correction of societal ills while it offers little in the way of respect for the educators who must bear this burden.

An interesting report on schools in Japan may cast a light on the danger of using the process of education to promote societal and economic interests without consideration of the periodic and sometimes drastic variations in these interests. A recent epidemic of disruptive student behavior in the traditionally effective and disciplined Japanese school systems has been related by some to a failing economy and lack of parent support for systems they formerly relied upon. Whereas in previous Japanese economic periods hard work guaranteed a job and success, in changing economic circumstances it no longer does (French, 2002). The state of the American economy is now precarious. Will it change what we think is important? Will our singularly educated population be prepared to deal with disappointments not of their own making? Will they be open-minded to alternatives?

THE MEDIA INFLUENCE OPINIONS ON STANDARDS

A vigilant media recognizes the sensitivity of the American public to any threat to its economic and military dominance and increases the intensity of its coverage. It casts broad-brush aspersions on conscientious teachers, who begin to feel less confident, more resentful and resistant. It makes Boards of Education, concerned about their constituent's support, more vulnerable to the temptation to make hasty and ungrounded decisions. What is wrong with what they are doing? Why do outsiders see national standards as a solution to the problems?

Mortimer Zuckerman (1996, p. 128), the editor-in-chief of *U.S. News and World Report,* asks if we are content as a nation to be second, third, or fourth, and if we place greater importance on the self-esteem and happiness of our children than on what they know and can do. He accepts the financial constraints of a growing population and costs, but insists that we need to get better results at the same time. Zuckerman makes a very valid point about the mobility of our population and identifies higher and uniform national standards as the needed solution. "Science does not change because it is taught in Oregon or Florida." He decries the "dirty little secret" that we already have informal national standards in that we all use similar lessons and textbooks, and then argues that these represent minimal competency rather than the higher levels expected by other countries. Zuckerman also presents the underlying agenda that many educators suspect in his prediction, that "higher standards are the key to inducing performance-based innovation and performance-based assessment of teachers and administrators."

The press substantiates its position with the views of both noted scholars and grassroots proponents. Diane Ravitch of the Brookings Institution is quoted in a *New York Times Magazine* article (Mosle, 1996b). She notes that "nations that establish national standards do so to ensure equality of education as well as higher achievement because they make explicit what they expect children to learn to insure that all children have access to the same educational opportunities" (p. 47). Another *New York Times Magazine* article by Mosle (1996a) tells the story of Michael Johnson, an urban principal, whose school curriculum is based on preparation for the standardized tests he sees as gatekeepers for his students. He is glad that his teachers forced him to take subjects that seemed irrelevant and believes that his kids want direction.

Mosle cites from author Lisa Delpit, who in writing about African American students says that they "need skills, not fluency. . . . I'm sick of this liberal nonsense" (1996b, p. 42). It is this notion of greater equity that originally popularized the idea of standards among minority populations and aligned them with the conservatives. But leaders among these populations are suspicious of the more subjective performance assessment measures that have now been attached to new standards (see Chapter 6). They believe that standardized tests are fairer and that minority children need the "hard skills" they measure.

The media also carefully follow the opposing reactions generated by the shifted emphasis on HSSB (high-stakes, standards-based) tests. When the Massachusetts State Board of Education declared that the state MCAS exam would be required for graduation by 2003, headlines reported the protests in May of 2000. A petition with 7,000 signatures called for the law's repeal.

Protestors included the National Association of Colored People and the American Civil Liberties Union as well as teachers, parents, and students from urban school districts (Cochran-Smith, 2000). Apparently, what the legislature saw as a way to improve the instruction of minority students by holding teachers accountable, they saw as a device that "punishes students." Students nicknamed the MCAS as the "Massachusetts Conspiracy Against Students."

In response, the Massachusetts Board of Education reviewed findings from a task force and ordered the creation of an appeals process so high school students who narrowly fail the state exam could still receive diplomas. Education Commissioner David Driscoll reasoned that an educationally sound and fair appeals process for the graduation requirement would be essential to determining competency with integrity (Hayward, 2001). Recent resolutions by the Massachusetts Association of School Committees have called for local district rights to confer diplomas, and the refusal of several districts to comply with the state regulation has resulted in a federal court case (Vaishnav, 2002a).

Somehow, we may have missed the boat on the communication of what is good about our schools, and what is needed. Can negative reports and mandated HSSB tests be turned into useful mechanisms for productive change? Although the test results seem valid, the recommendations for ameliorating the problem are grounded in several powerful but as yet unproven assumptions and beliefs about education in the United States, including: the belief that the future of this country's economic health depends on the improvement of student achievement, the belief that clearly stated and uniform standards will result in higher student achievement for all students in this country, and the belief that high-stakes measures will guarantee the implementation of the standards (McCaslin, 1996; Natriello, 1996).

As reported at the 2001 Education Summit, the states have already responded, and I discuss further details of this response in the chapters ahead. Every state with the exception of Iowa has standards, and most already have matching tests at benchmark grade levels. Fortunately, the states have shown respect for the creativity and commitment of the professional education community by involving them in some of the decision making of the development process. I will come back to the standards and their measures, but for now I go back a little more than two decades in history to search for the origins of this intensive effort to improve schools by raising standards.

THE ORIGINS OF THE CURRENT WAVE OF PUBLIC CONCERN

Although many writers have identified the Education Commission of the States (National Commission on Excellence in Education, 1983) *Nation at*

Risk report (often attributed to then Education Secretary Terrence Bell) as the beginning of this current wave of concern and reform, I suggest that we move back to the mid-1960s and recall that as part of the *Great Society* changes, Congress enacted the Elementary and Secondary Education Act (E.S.E.A.). This was the first major federal allocation of funds for the purpose of improving education. It encouraged innovation, the acquisition of new resources, and made special provisions for the disadvantaged with its Title 1 (later Chapter 1) part. Surprisingly, this infusion of federal dollars was not in reaction to any great public concern about the failures of schools. It was just the responsible effort of a government in relatively stable economic times to promote the educational process.[1]

In spite of this funding and many successful (and unsuccessful) programs,[2] the 1970s brought us the first evidence of declines in scores on tests, such as the Scholastic Aptitude Test (SAT; now called the Scholastic Assessment Test), and the beginning of public anxiety about education. The SAT and its accompanying achievement tests have been longtime performance standards for the American public. Because they are used by colleges as determining factors in selective admissions, they are examples of high-stakes tests, but private ones, and not derived from state or federal curriculum documents. Nevertheless, many local curriculum policies now reflect their content. This was not always true.

In 1976 I participated in a Teachers College (Columbia University) investigation of the possible causes for a decline in scores achieved by the students in two middle-class communities. We conjectured many reasons for this diminution of scores, including esoteric ones such as the birth order of the students in school at the time and clearly significant ones such as gender. My own additional hunches had to do with differences in the value placed on the test itself among the students and their teachers, parents, and peers. The results were quite interesting. Boys considered the test significantly more important than girls and their results were better. Parent and peer influence had some influence on the scores, but birth order and other contextual factors such as time spent in last-minute preparation or relaxing the night before did not have a significant effect. A major finding was that teachers made a difference. In the school district where teachers were newly motivated to place a greater emphasis on the test, there was an improvement in overall scores. There was no attempt to investigate the articulation between the school curriculums and the test; curriculum was assumed to be no different from that for the higher-scoring students of previous decades. Recent decisions by some universities to eliminate the SAT as a basis for college admissions have also been based on what some see as a disjunction between the skills tested and current high school curriculum.

The 1980s brought some new ingredients to the stew over declining SAT scores. Although there was some optimism in the scores for younger students on the National Assessment of Educational Progress (NAEP),[3] the scores for our older students were dismal. These were the students who were entering the work force at a time when competition from other countries became a threat. Several international test reports also showed that the United States was lagging behind many countries in the performance of its students in Mathematics and Science (see Chapter 2).

A Nation at Risk (National Commission on Excellence in Education, 1983) also recognized the possibility of disenfranchisement for those who could not compete within our society.

> Learning is the indispensable investment required for success in the "information age" we are entering. . . . The people of the United States need to know that individuals in our society who do not possess the levels of literacy and training essential to this new era will be effectively disenfranchised, not simply from the material rewards that accompany competent performance, but also from the chance to participate fully in our national life. (p. 7)

INITIAL RESPONSES OF THE EDUCATIONAL COMMUNITY

The educational community was not unresponsive to these reports. Supported by university researchers, several school districts experimented with "effective schools," "outcome-based education," and "site-based management." The effective schools movement, which began in the late 1970s,[4] was based on limited research that identified critical factors in schools that had achieved apparent success in spite of adversity in their environments. These factors apparently made them different and more successful than schools in comparable environments that were not as successful. The research attached school characteristics such as strong leadership; parent, teacher, and student involvement; clearly defined goals and curriculum; a safe and orderly environment; and high expectations to the likelihood of greater success for *all* students, including those identified as "disadvantaged." A number of schools then launched educational improvement plans using these characteristics as criteria for change.

Although the effective schools movement did not have a large-scale following, some of the criteria were adopted into other school improvement efforts. The idea of clearly articulated goals was at the heart of the outcomes-based education (OBE) reform model. The model quickly gained a strong following—including several statewide efforts—and was probably the source of the notion of national goals and standards. William Spady, who spearheaded many of the OBE efforts, writes that, "outcome based education was ushered into the 1990's with a resounding affirmation that this is the paradigm within which true improvement of student learning will occur for all students" (Spady & Marshall, 1990, p. 4).

The pervasiveness of the outcomes-based movement and its attention to a broad base of outcomes including attitudes and values may have heralded its demise. Critics, spurred by a small but vocal group of citizens, challenged the outcomes as "too vague, non-academic, or threatening to family values" (Vinovskis, 1996). The terminology of outcome-based education was quickly abandoned for the new terms related to standards and performance measures. By 1993, states that had written the outcome terminology into documents issued correctives and limited their new standards to the core curriculum areas cited in the National Goals (see below).

A similar demise was the fate of another aspect of some of the effective schools improvement programs: the concept of site-based management. The vision that decentralization of power would be helpful in bringing about school improvements has origins in the 1960s. In the cities poverty, crime, drugs, and family dissolution widened the gaps in an increasingly diverse population. Greater local control was a suggested solution. Large urban school districts such as New York City and Chicago, which had highly bureaucratized and appointed central boards of education, established locally elected school boards that assumed certain, but not all, decision-making authority from the central board.

The movement toward further decentralization, as a reform in school governance that would give more power to individual schools and their parents and teachers, emerged in the 1970s in a number of places including Florida, California, and New York. Some of these programs are still in operation. Ogawa (1994) identifies a network of a "policy actors" in the development of efforts to engage teachers in site-based decision making. He labels the actors working for organizations as *organizational entrepreneurs.* The organizations, which included the Carnegie Forum on Education and the Economy and the National Governor's Association, were supported in their efforts by teacher organizations, and particularly by Albert Shanker, then head of the American Federation of Teachers. As we shall see in Chapter 2, Shanker also supported the effort to develop and monitor standards. Although Ogawa does not identify the universities as instrumental in getting the movement going, he does say that it was their stamp of approval and documentation in articles that maintained the momentum.

The consequences of the original decentralization solution were so negative that local control in Chicago was effectively abandoned by the mid 1990s. In New York City, repeated incidents of local school board corruption caused the central board of education and its chancellor administrator to remain on constant guard. Ongoing disputes between a series of incumbent chancellors and the mayors created a highly volatile and unproductive atmosphere. The present mayor (Bloomberg) finally got state approval to abandon both the central board of education and its jurisdiction over the schools, as well as the community boards. Management of New York City schools is now directly in the hands of the mayor and his own appointed chancellor and advisory board.

The failure of decentralization to effect educational improvement in large cities has been mirrored by a similar lack of significant gains from the empowerment of single schools, teachers, and parents in local school governance. The large city efforts have been thwarted by corruption in both elections and management. The local school efforts have been hampered by the lack of expertise, resources, and time required for teachers engaged in the additional burden of managing schools, and by the unwillingness of those in power to give it to others (Solomon, 1995).

GOVERNMENT CALLS FOR REFORM

Perhaps because of the failure of grassroots efforts to reform education and continuing reports of declining student achievement, in 1989 the National Governors Association held its first National Summit on Education and outlined a major role for the states in educational reform—with a special emphasis on the creation of standards. A little over a year later, Education Secretary Lamar Alexander and President Bush (the father of the present president) announced the "America 2000: An Education Strategy" national education goals and reform strategy (U.S. Department of Education, 1991). The introduction to the announcement refers to *The Nation at Risk* report and notes that, "we haven't turned things around in education. Almost all our education trend lines are flat. Our country is idling its engines, not knowing enough nor being able to do enough to make America all that it should be" and that, "we're not coming close to our potential or what is needed" (p. 9).

The original goals state that by the year 2000,

1. All children in America will start school ready to learn.
2. The high school graduation rate will increase to at least 90%.
3. American students will leave Grades 4, 8, and 12 having demonstrated competency in challenging subject matter including English, mathematics, science, history, and geography, and every school in America will ensure that all students learn to use their minds well, so they may be prepared for responsible citizenship, further learning, and productive employment in our modern economy.
4. U.S. students will be the first in the world in science and mathematics achievement.

5. Every adult American will be literate and will possess the knowledge and skills necessary to compete in a global economy and exercise the rights and responsibilities of citizenship.
6. Every school in America will be free of drugs and violence and will offer a disciplined environment conducive to learning.

Two more goals were subsequently added:

7. The nation's teaching force will have access to programs for the continued improvement of their professional skills and the opportunity to acquire the knowledge and skills needed to instruct and prepare all American students for the next century.
8. Every school will promote partnerships that will increase parental involvement and participation in promoting the social, emotional, and academic growth of children. (U. S. Department of Education, 2001, online at http://www.ed.gov/pubs/G2Kreforming)

The goals were accompanied by suggested strategies for their accomplishment. These include "an accountability package based on 'World Class' standards for each of five core subjects" and a nationwide voluntary examination system in the core subjects. Other strategies include public reporting and reward systems such as presidential citations, merit school funding, academies for school leaders and teachers, and differential pay. The document also encourages creative experiments and major commitments by business and local communities.

The goals were obviously overly optimistic for realization by 2000. Some would believe that this is because they do not have the accountability bite of mandated tests. Several initiatives were enacted and funded by Congress. Programs for the improvement of math and science education that were previously funded by the Dwight D. Eisenhower Act received new allocations. Grants in specific response to Goals 2000 (in addition to other existing program grants) were also awarded for the State and Local Systemic Improvement program, the Goals 2000 program, the Technology Challenge program, and the Schools-to-Work transition program, but each year political wrangling threatened and undermined well-intentioned plans. Previously allocated money was rescinded and new allocations were subject to constant revisions.

INITIAL RESPONSES TO THE CALLS FOR REFORM

Following the Goals 2000 announcement, many state and local efforts were initiated for the purpose of developing new curriculum and assessment standards and corresponding reform programs. In addition to individual state and local efforts, coalitions were also formed. In 1991, The New Standards project, a coalition of six large cities, 14 states, the National Center on Education and the Economy, and the Learning Research and Development Center based at the University of Pittsburgh, embarked on a major effort to "set very high academic standards for all students, and create a system to measure their progress" (Borthwick & Nolan, 1996). With funding from private sources and the states and school districts that form its consortium, it operated under the premise that "what gets tested gets taught." The coalition partners believe that better performance measures will increase the possibility of accomplishing high standards, and they have focused their efforts primarily on the production of these measures in the areas of English language arts, mathematics, science, and applied learning. They may have set the stage for NCLB.

One of the most successful internal attempts by the educational community to reform education was initiated by the National Council of Teachers of Mathematics (NCTM) when it published its standards in 1989 (NCTM, 1989). The NCTM produced and disseminated the standards and several supporting materials that have been widely adopted. I discuss the influences of state policies, the NCTM, and other professional organizations in greater detail in Chapter 2.

STANDARDS IN OTHER COUNTRIES

In other countries, where the private rights democratic ideals are not as ingrained, the imposition of national constraints and rules is less likely to be counteracted by active and passive resistance. As an example, consider a law passed by the German government that officially changed the way certain words are spelled in order to ease the difficulties that children had in using correct spelling. The law didn't just make a recommendation; it provided for sanctions of teachers and officials who disobey. Although there was some debate on the issue (some felt it didn't go far enough), there were some very close and firm deadlines for implementation. Newspapers, publishers, and others are gearing up for the change. Contrast this with our nation's century-long debate over a switch to the metric system. We are now the only developed country not using it.

Borthwick and Nolan (1996) identify six qualities of national standards in countries that outperform us. Their standards are: specific, public, rigorous, high stakes, inclusive, and measurable. Japan identifies precisely what the core knowledge content is to be covered—but still leaves much of the detailed instructional decisions to teachers. In an interview for the 1996 National Summit (Lehmann & Spring, 1996), Diane Ravitch talked about the

Japanese national standards as a model of simplicity: "They are so much simpler and clearer and more challenging and more direct than anything I have seen from American standards writers," and Shanker agreed that, "Standards have to be doable." California's state superintendent of public instruction, Delaine Eastin, reported that plain language is a criterion for her state's standards: "very useful, usable and readable—they won't be written in Edu-speak" (Lehmann & Spring, 1996, p. 11).

Japan's standards may not be verbose, but the power of its government-prescribed spiral curriculum is further driven by the Japanese University Entrance Examinations that are given in three stages. There are also differences in the instructional components of curriculum. Japanese teachers emphasize problem solving in math whereas American teachers and their textbooks have been more concerned with facts and procedures. The Japanese teachers are also more likely to engage students in reflective discussion, include fewer but more real-world questions that require extended answers, and provide students with manipulatives (Stevenson & Stigler, 1992). I remember being awed by a particularly clever individual manipulative package that was given to every child to keep and use as long as it was needed. I even tried to buy them for my students.

Japanese textbooks also do a better job of what Mayer, Sims, and Tajika (1995) call *cognitive modeling* than do American textbooks (see below). They show students how to work out problems in detail instead of devoting space to unexplained exercises involving symbol manipulation. Most Japanese children do spend much more time on homework than children in other countries, and also go to private after-school coaching programs called *jukus,* which prepare them for the exams.

France's curriculum is published and widely available. Its yearly exams are followed by much public discussion of the questions and the results. Although Sweden has tests, they are not as rigorous as the high-stakes *baccalaureate* of France and the *arbitur* of Germany, both of which determine student access to further education. In contrast to the beliefs of many Americans, other nations have not only caught up with us in terms of secondary student retention, but have also insisted on uniform expectations with rigorous tests, even for those not planning higher education.

In 1988, Great Britain embarked on a major endeavor to develop specific standards in every subject area and by the mid-1990s matching tests. The original opposition to the restrictive nature of the system died down somewhat—perhaps because of the vast energies required in making necessary testing adjustments. In October 2002 (BBC, 2002) a pronouncement by exams chief Ken Boston, head of the *Qualifications and Curriculum Authority* (QCA), and the man now in charge of England's exams, says the testing system needs overhauling—with teachers being trusted to do more assessment themselves. Dr. Boston said the QCA would produce an easy-to-understand "new generic statement on standards" by the end of the month. It would work with all the exam boards on how statistics of performance from previous years should be used to set grade boundaries. These changes may generate teacher ownership and serve as an example for the United States. I address the possibilities of teacher-constructed standards-matching assessments in Chapters 5 and 6.

Surprisingly, with the exception of The Netherlands, where there is elaborate tracking of students and a free choice school voucher system, a study by Unks (1995) reveals that the standards in Japan and the European nations are the same for all students. Even in Germany, where at a relatively early age students are tracked into three different schools with varying emphases on the *pure,* the *practical,* or the *applied,* the curriculum is the same. Still, as Unks notes, the curriculum in the countries studied resembles that of the United States in that it is subject centered and "the evidence is weak, suspicious, or non-existent that the study of any particular school subject (as it is usually conceived and taught) promotes outcomes such as critical thinking, creativity, citizenship or many other desirable goals" (p. 425).

As elaborated below, we in this country do already have a variety of public and private standard-setting, inspection, and testing systems in place, but they are inconsistent. The growing public calls for consistency generated at the federal level have been responded to, but formal enforcement mandates are another matter. If history is our teacher, then we can predict that in this country these will not come easily.

A SUMMARY: SYSTEMIC CHANGE, RESTRUCTURING, AND REFORM

In an effort to distinguish the current attempts to change educational processes from previous educational innovations, which may have been superficial and often transitory, the terms *systemic change, restructuring,* and *reform* are most often used—sometimes interchangeably. Smith and O'Day may have been among the first to apply and define the term *systemic reform* (Vinovskis, 1996). They identified three major characteristics of systemic change:

1. Curriculum frameworks that establish what students should know and be able to do.
2. State policies that would provide a coherent structure to support schools in designing effective strategies for teaching the content of the frameworks to all their students.
3. Restructured school governance systems.

(Smith & O'Day, cited in Vinovskis, 1996, p. 59)

Certainly the first of the above actions has characterized the recent efforts to restructure or reform schools. Curriculum frameworks in the form of standards are omnipresent. As expected, the autonomy of the individual states has prevailed in the development of standards and in the development of matching performance measures. The resulting variations, however, have caused some confusion and difficulties in federal attempts to enforce the implementation of the standards with federally determined sanctions that provide authority. Experiments in restructured school governance systems have thus far not proven fruitful—although there are exceptions. Unfortunately, the energies and funds required for the first action, and for resolving the resulting difficulties, may have distracted us from the second action of providing a coherent structure of support for schools in their implementation.

Some of the actions taken have neglected to recognize the need for standards for opportunities to learn. There is still a lack of equity in the kind of educational environments that our students have available to them, and it seems unfair to hold everyone to the same standard if opportunities and the funds to create them are not equal. These are the issues that have been raised by educators, parents, and students. They are the issues we will have to deal with. I begin to address them in Chapter 2.

In any case, more than at any other time in this nation's history, attention has been brought to bear on American education. New controls threaten the very individual and personal system of classroom instruction that is our legacy from the one-room schoolhouse of the 1800s. These controls are formidable and in response to some widespread dissatisfaction with our accomplishments. The facts on which this dissatisfaction is based may be exaggerated and unfounded—ignorant of the many difficulties faced in a changing social and economic structure. But, nevertheless, we educators will have to respond to these by knowing and understanding what they imply, and by using our creative classroom decision-making power to do the most we can to help each child reach for the standards set. This is no easy task, but it is our investment in the future.

NOTES

1. Federal aid has come in the form of categorical and block grants. There is evidence that the categorical grants that are aimed at specific purposes are more effective in effecting school improvement (Kirst, 1995).

2. The Rand Corporation (Mann et al., 1975) study of the effects of these programs was one of the first to document the resistance of public schools to attempts to make serious changes.

3. The NAEP is a federally managed sampling test. It is designed to evaluate the national program and does not hold individual schools or students accountable. It is therefore not a high-stakes test. In the 1982 administration, the success rate of students on application questions in mathematics fell another 1.1% from an already low percentile of less than 50% in 1978 (Dossey, Mullis, Lindquist, & Chambers, 1988).

4. Ronald Edmonds (1983) and Lawrence Lezotte (e.g., 1981) spearheaded this effort to improve instruction by getting schools to meet the identified criteria.

2 Who Chooses the Curriculum:

Are Standards and Tests Necessary?

ABOUT THIS CHAPTER

Brad should have expected a few of his colleagues to respond this way, but the negative remarks still came as a surprise. They were nearing the close of a four-day summer workshop that was sponsored by the countywide professional development network. Many of the participants had been in previous network programs, but this was Brad's first time. More than 100 teachers of all grade levels from 12 different school districts and college faculty had come together to prepare for the writing of curriculum based on the state standards in math, science, and technology. The general mood was one of decided enthusiasm, tempered by some anxiety about the task ahead. Almost everyone had been inspired by the first part of the experience—especially by the opportunity for hands-on practice with some of the latest educational technology applications.

During the four-day interval, participants had rotated their venue among several county schools that had new computer labs, and their instructors were the teachers who ordinarily taught kids in the labs. They had worked on new interactive software at an IBM training facility and seen a demonstration of data-bank software by a research scientist. There were sessions in which the state standards and new vocabulary were shared. There would be four more days of interaction time during the summer and fall for writing and reflecting with each other in small groups.

Brad looked forward to sharing ideas with his grade level colleagues from other school districts who had joined him at this federal grant–funded workshop. Like everyone else, he had heard about the opportunity from his principal and had volunteered for the task, but he was pleased that the grant would provide some extra compensation for his effort. Their first charge was to write a sample curriculum unit based on the new standards that they could use and would try in their own classrooms. This would then be electronically shared among the whole group via a web page. Later, back at his own school, two other colleagues, Meg and April, would join him in the task of creating a whole curriculum for the grade.

The openly expressed complaints from teachers that surprised Brad reminded me of the difficulty in effecting change in schools with top-down policies. A comment that time outside of the four days would be required for typing the new curriculum at first seems to be just an example of a non-professional attitude and quite different from another anxious and honest comment from a high school teacher who remarked that there was no room in his course of study for an additional unit. There was just not enough time, he exclaimed. He had to use whatever time he had to prepare his students for the state test. I realized, however, that both protestors apparently saw the state standards and testing mandates not as ways to improve what they were doing, but as externally imposed, perhaps unnecessary "add-ons," and apart from their normal agendas and responsibilities. There was little "ownership," and they were consequently resistive.

This mixed reaction from teachers may be an illustration of what Richard Elmore (cited in Darling-Hammond, 1990, p. 235) calls "the power of the bottom over the top," but I believe that the manifestation of this power of active or passive resistance to change is in no small measure a result of the failure of policymakers to understand the many and often conflicting influences on teachers' autonomy and on the curriculum decisions that they make. This chapter examines some of these influences in an attempt to know them better and consequently to understand why some people believe that standards are necessary and others do not.

SOME CHARISMATIC DIFFERENCES OF OPINION

Teachers rarely see their rather private world in the classroom as a microcosm of the surrounding society. Nor do they clearly recognize the power of its influences. They are more likely to be concerned about the need to reach and control their students, the next administrator's observation, or uncooperative parents. Although teachers and their administrators may not have taken state-developed curriculum guidelines seriously in the past, new monitoring and enforcement measures attached to federally mandated tests may cause them to put these in proper context with the many other already existing traditional influences. Knowledge is power, and perhaps a greater understanding of the way in which external influences affect their day-to-day curriculum decisions would be useful to teachers like Brad, Meg, and April.

For example, it would be useful for them to know that their individual struggle for autonomy within their own setting is part of a larger conflict in which our public schools are currently engaged: the debate over control of local school curriculum. In some respects this debate mirrors our country's continuing conflict between two of its democratic ideals: the Jeffersonian ideal of political equality in which the majority controls and protects the public rights, and the realism of Alexander Hamilton who recommended an economy of free competition in which individual private rights take precedence and the powers of centralized government are strong.

In politics, the conservatives usually take the Hamiltonian position of unfettered competition in a free market and liberals the Jeffersonian ideals. In comparison to these positions, school conservatives seem to prefer the controls of national standards and cautious liberals are more likely to hold the line for local and teacher autonomy (Unks, 1995). Apple (2001) may have an explanation for this discrepancy from expected attitudes. He believes that tests and standards provide the comparative data consumers need to make choices in the free market preferred by conservatives.

Affirmation for this concept appears in the rising real estate prices within one of our local school districts, where the well-publicized state test results are better than those in neighboring districts. It also appears in a recent report that wealthier parents are seeking extra time dispensations for their offspring on the College Board SAT test, in addition to their already considerable outlay for preparatory tutoring. Previously, the College Board was permitted to notify colleges of the special conditions, such as extra time, allowed for some SAT test takers. Recent court rulings have disallowed this, and a California study established that private prep-school students won exceptions of an extra 90 minutes for the test at three to five times the national rate (Gross, 2002; National Center for Policy Analysis, 2000). Standardized certification tests for teachers have also paved the way in the marketplace for a number of nontraditional programs of teacher preparation.

The conundrum in the political tension is that free competition distributes wealth unequally and places too much power in the hands of the few—and this then undermines the public rights (Labaree, 1997). The market mentality of big business has influenced this new effort to reform education.

Can we turn it around and use the standards to protect the rights of everyone? Hopefully the added legislative components of disaggregated analysis of test results and support for individual tutoring will help.

THE PUBLIC RESPONDS

The general public is concerned about the apparent failure of children from our schools to compete favorably with children from Asian and European nations on international measures, but their acceptance of the mechanisms for change is less clear. The ideological struggle between those who wish more autonomy and less control and those who believe that the government must take responsibility increases in its depth and diversity as our society becomes more variegated and complex, and perhaps diverts attention from the real needs of schools and students. The teacher in her one-room schoolhouse had only slightly more autonomy than most teachers have today, but the pressures to infringe on that autonomy and reactive efforts to protect it are now much more intense. Before the tests arrived, much of the public reaction to the challenge of improving education by agreeing on uniform standards and high expectations was positive.

In 1998 Yash Aggarwal, who was born in Kenya and educated in India, France, and the United States, was our local candidate for Congress. An environmental scientist with a Ph.D., Aggarwal nurtured his part-time interests in my community's life into full-time alternatives as a spokesperson for our local branch of the American Association of Retired Persons.

Given his background, candidate Aggarwal's point of view in regard to education is predictable. He believes that we need national standards for education and cites their existence in other countries, the dissolution of American families, and the failure of American schools as the reasons for this. "If parents don't set the standards, then schools need to do it—school uniforms may not be such a bad idea." At a forum on the topic of education, which Aggarwal hosted, some of the participants saw the problem slightly differently. "Part of the problem is the manner in which society sees the education system," said a high school sophomore, and a retired teacher agreed. Another student saw apathy on the part of parents as the root of the problem: "If parents don't care, kids won't." Corey, a high school junior, seemed to agree with Dr. Aggarwal. He didn't believe that teachers were preparing students for the next level, but just making sure they "get by" (Guttwillig, 1996, p. 5).

A parent and teacher at that meeting lamented that, in contrast to the great changes elsewhere, there was little difference in schools from the way they were 100 years ago. She put the blame for this on the lack of funding to meet the lofty goals of the federal government. Practically everyone at the forum agreed that funding was a major problem for schools. Money is a limiting factor, but it is not the only one and it may not be the money itself that makes the difference. To most of us it represents the public and private interest and values. If education is important, it gets funded. If it is not funded, it can't be that important.

In the mid-1990s, Public Agenda, a nonprofit research organization, shared an analysis of Americans' attitudes about raising and enforcing higher academic standards in public schools at a previous education summit conference. Their findings were based on their own research as well as that of other opinion analysts such as the Gallup Organization and Louis Harris & Associates. The report declared that "support for academic standards . . . is at consensus level among the general public" and further concluded that,

> There is nearly universal support for the idea that public schools do not currently demand enough from students. Americans believe schools should set clear academic standards that significantly raise expectations of students from elementary through high school. (Immerwahr & Johnson, p. 1)

The authors contend that support for standards was shared by all demographic and ideological groups and "unbudgeable" even in the face of "trade-offs" such as the possibility that "some youngsters will be denied diplomas or kept back in school."

Their predictions of support from all groups for higher standards have been more or less accurate—but the accountability mechanism for assuring implementation via high-stakes tests has initiated some unexpected negative reactions. A test is high stakes if it is accompanied by consequences for the student, teacher, or school. These high-stakes standards-based (HSSB) tests have created climates of tension that to some are unwelcome.

A follow-up Public Agenda study, "Reality Check 2002," found little backtracking on the need for higher standards among students, parents, and teachers. The limited study sample of 600 middle and high school students reported that they take the tests without stress or worry. These students may not, however, have experienced a time when other educational values prevailed as motivation and measures of learning, and they accept preparation for tests as a necessary part of schooling. Parents and teachers also agreed that the tests may be helpful in identifying needy students. Nevertheless, 79% of the teachers and 66% of the parents expressed concern that "teachers will end up teaching to the test rather than making sure that real learning is taking place" (Public Agenda, 2002).

A California school district actually hired a private test preparation firm to provide workshops for teachers on how to teach test-taking strategies

(Ohanian, 2000). An Arizona special educator (Bornfield, 2000) notes that forcing disabled students to take a test in order to graduate is counterproductive to their needs. An unpredicted outcome of the testing requirement is that it has increased the numbers of referrals for special education placements because of the extra services provided for these students. A further consequence of the increase in referrals is a special education teacher shortage.

Public leaders who represent low-income populations, however, are generally in favor of the tests and standards because they believe that they will help force school improvement. On the surface and in some respects they have been right. There is evidence that scores on tests have been improved—even among minority students. The gap between minority and white students, however, still exists and long-term effects still need to be demonstrated. In stark and surprising contrast, protests have come from more affluent parents, who see a diminution of emphasis on innovative programs and love of learning, and an unhealthy emphasis on preparation for the tests. Parents from the affluent district of Scarsdale, in New York State, with support from some district faculty boycotted eighth grade exams by keeping their children home on test day, and accompanied their high school student picketers for the 150-mile journey to the state capital of Albany with signs that read, "I am not a test score." An investigation of the source of the protest was initiated by the commissioner, and a legal suit by parents is also in process (Bert, 2001; Hartocollis, 2001). A federal legal suit by Massachusetts parents also alleges that their high school graduation requirement exam is discriminatory against minorities and that school districts did not prepare students for the Massachusetts Comprehensive Assessment System (MCAS) tests (Vaishnav, 2002a).

TEACHERS AND TEACHER ORGANIZATIONS RESPOND

The Public Agenda report (Immerwahr & Johnson, 1996) cited earlier predicts a less vigorous endorsement from teachers for the proposals for raising standards. "Classroom teachers are receptive to higher standards, but it is questionable whether they will be the driving force behind them." The authors believe that American teachers are unresponsive to the "deep-seated public concerns and values" that are in addition to anxieties about the economy and moral decay. These concerns, they state, are manifested in complaints about the schools, which have "youngsters graduating without minimum basic skills, truants sporting diplomas alongside youngsters who worked hard" and "jargon-laden announcements of yet another educational 'fad.'" The solution they suggest for these concerns is that, "From the public point of view, raising standards guarantees that students will learn the value of working hard and the penalties of 'goofing off.' And unlike some other proposed educational reforms, raising standards appeals directly to people's common sense" (pp. 1–2).

Again their prediction has proved only partially correct. Individual teachers have responded because of their commitment to their students and parents. They have accepted the standards and tests not only as measures of their students' success, but also as measures of their own success and failure. Nevertheless, the underlying stresses created by the pressures of time, publicly shared results, and the inability to respond to individual needs and interests in creative ways may have resulted in as yet undocumented negative effects for their students.

Barksdale-Ladd and Thomas (2000) report the findings of interviews with teachers and parents in two states that searched for reactions to high-stakes tests. Among the significant results were the common feelings of stress for teachers, parents, and students created by the tests; a feeling by teachers that the tests were contradictory to everything they had learned about what was important for children; and, for some, the lack of acceptance of the appropriateness of the standards on which the tests were based. Teachers judged their teaching "worse instead of better" because of test preparation, and they expressed some concern that people would be turned away from the profession. Most parents also saw little value in the tests. The lack of involvement by teachers or teacher educators and researchers in test development by states was noted and may be a major reason for the lack of their acceptance.

Although the late AFT president, Shanker, was a strong and vocal advocate for high standards, my hunch is that he might not have been as receptive to the extensive mandated HSSB testing. At the 2001 education summit, the current AFT president, Sandra Feldman, reported that support for the standards had indeed taken a dive in response to extensive state testing programs. The AFT has, however, consistently maintained its support of state standards and promoted and evaluated them:

> States deserve recognition for their sustained commitment to developing common, challenging standards to serve as the basis for systemic education reform. And states are clearly serious about working to ensure that all their children are exposed to challenging curricula in English, math, science, and social studies. (AFT, 1999, Section II)

Teacher organizations are particularly concerned about having some flexibility in the process of meeting standards, and in the supply of needed back-up funding for externally imposed policies. In a commentary in response to the standards for New Jersey, a teachers' organization, the New Jersey Educators Association (1996), compliments their State Education Department for including the arts, health education, career education, and physical education in their standards and for "allowing flexibility in how local school districts, educators, and students will work to achieve these rigorous standards within the curriculum." Their editorial cautions us, however, that "these standards must be accompanied by an aggressive commitment to providing equal opportunities to enable all students to meet the academic criteria" and asserts that "that can only be done through a responsible state school funding program."

Some teacher groups and teacher educators have not been receptive from the very beginning of the standards movement. Keith Geiger, president of the National Education Association, agrees that teachers should be held to high standards, but only if they receive the proper funding support for their professional development and if they have the primary role in writing standards (Lehman & Spring, 1996). Other teacher organizations, on the other hand, have expressed their commitment to higher standards, but they have done little to get them implemented.

TEACHER EDUCATORS AND RESEARCHERS RESPOND

Teacher educators and researchers were originally optimistic, but concerned, especially about the performance measures. Discussants in a symposium at a 1997 conference of the American Educational Research Association suggested that we move toward the new standards with caution. They related the standards to opportunities for teachers as well as students to learn and predicted that "standards can be useful in proportion to opportunities for teachers to become learners." At the same time, they recommended that, "Visible indicators of school effectiveness be employed, but they should not be used to make negative decisions without evidence of validity." They were concerned about the difficulty of producing and administering performance measures that measure what they are supposed to measure.

When the reform emphasis moved quickly from clarification of curriculum, now in the form of content standards with some leeway for local adaptation, to inflexible standardization and accountability measures, the reactions of educational researchers have, in general, been negative. After a career spent in research on educational testing, Linn (2000) comes to the unfortunate conclusion that,

> In most cases the instrumentation and technology have not been up to the demands that have been placed on them by high-stakes accountability. Assessment systems that are useful monitors lose much of their dependability and credibility for that purpose when high stakes are attached to them. The unintended negative effects of the high-stakes accountability uses often outweigh the intended positive effects. (p. 14)

Linn's conclusions are based on a combination of factors, including the unreliability of single tests as determinants; the historical record, which demonstrates second-year improvements for new tests followed by smaller gains, if any; the selective exclusion of some students from tests; and the year-to-year fluctuations in the tested groups, which we have already discussed. On an international level, based on studies in the United Kingdom and the United States, Firestone, Fitz, and Broadfoot (1999) agree with Linn. They admit that assessment policy is useful for promoting easily observable changes and can influence what topics are taught, but conclude that the policy is less able to influence teachers' instructional approaches. Linn's further recommendation, that in order for standards to be useful they must be more specific and must serve as a guide for the constructs measured by the tests, is one that I will pursue in greater detail in the chapters ahead.

Others question the basis for the push toward standards. Berliner and Biddle (1995) believe that there is no real crisis in education and see the imposition of standards as a threat to local educators' autonomy. They wonder why we criticize ourselves in the press and contend that the crisis is a *manufactured one* and a *big lie.* Bracey (1996, 1997) challenges the authenticity and interpretations of international test results. He points out that there is greater variation within nations than there are differences between them and that although the United States is a little behind in mathematics, it is ahead in reading. And when the test results are confirmed and his objections are partially answered by researchers, he asks whether Americans want their children pressured like the Japanese children in order to achieve the same results.

Presenting the philosophical view of the debate, Kenneth Strike (1997) identifies one picture of national standards as an expression of a kind of nationalist communitarianism, a "view that believes that we need more of a shared culture" (No. 11). But he warns us that this picture of standards may put limits on the scope of the curriculum with his caution that, "Alternatively, we might claim that national standards assert only content that is objectively true or widely held and that is, therefore, neutral to our diverse cultures and moral and religious traditions." Strike also reflects on the work of Chubb and Moe (1990), who contend that schools work better when teachers are organized as teams and the climate is participatory, and that schools and teachers need higher levels of local autonomy.

In an earlier publication, Strike (1993) espoused a Habermasian view of democracy in which decision making is face-to-face and discursive. He fears that because the standards movement takes discussions about what is educationally worthwhile into national or state forums, that the educative community is left only with the charge to implement distally decided programs—which may or may not be relevant to their immediate needs. Strike (1997) conjectures that "in an educational system in which there is a stronger sense of community and ownership, efficiency will be easier to achieve." And that "perhaps we need to focus more on what makes schools good communities and less on what makes them efficient organizations." His final objection to the standards movement is that it views students as consumers of a service and as resources for national productivity wars who need to be motivated to comply with system expectations, but it does "nothing . . . to transform student interests or to reduce their level of alienation and disengagement" (No. 11).

Popkewitz (2000), commenting on school reform that is based on research and evaluation using existing "commonsense" schooling as a frame of reference, states that this "denies change in the process of change" (p. 18). He envisions the political use of power in controlling education as social administration—an attempt to control chance happenings and their risks: "The state was expected to shape a particular type of individual. . . . Policy was to police not only institutional development but also the construction of the 'self' who could function within the new political relations of liberal democracy and capitalism" (p. 19).

Perhaps as an example of social administration and its need to respond to the threats of worldwide terrorism, historian Diane Ravitch (2002) declares that we must teach students to appreciate and defend our democratic institutions. She suggests education standards to help prepare the American population for this purpose. To me, they represent not only "what students need to know" but also "how students need to feel" about life in this country. Ravitch thinks it is important that students know or feel that

I. It's OK to be patriotic.

II. Not all cultures share our regard for equality and human rights.

III. We must now recognize the presence of evil in the world.

IV. Pluralism and divergence of opinion are valuable.

V. American history is important.

VI. World history and geography are important.

In spite of the reservations of the liberal view, efforts to identify and monitor educational standards are well on their way; the ball is rolling, and with a momentum that may be difficult to stop. Will standards and tests achieve greater equity? Does it make sense to strive for uniformity and acceptance of diversity at the same time? That depends on what kinds of skills we want equity for and how we accommodate diversity. Will national standards make a difference? That depends on the opposing influences, on the effectiveness of their new authority or enforcement method, HSSB tests. Most of all, it depends on the ability of educators like Brad to translate the standards into local curriculum policy, accept ownership, and make the standards work for them every day and in every classroom. While doing this task educators must understand and remain aware of the many and diverse influences that may affect its accomplishment.

CONTROL OF CURRICULUM

Federal and State Government

Following the 1994 and 1996 National Summits on Education, which were essentially governors' conferences, many states leaped onto the standards bandwagon. At the time of the 1996 conference only three states did not have new standards and matching assessments in place or in progress, and by the time of the 2001 conference, all states except Iowa had them. These actions are in line with tradition and the constitutional allocation of control of education to the states. In contrast to government subdivisions in many other countries, the United States Constitution gave individual states the right to manage education, and they have taken up the cause for standards with vigor.[1]

As I described in the previous chapter, if the federal government had any influence on what happened in individual states prior to the NCLB legislation, it was by virtue of its allocation of funds. For example, much of the funding for improvements in math and science education and for the development of new state standards has come from federal funds appropriated as part of the Goals 2000: Educate America Act.

In 1997, when President Clinton proposed a plan to provide federally developed tests to states on a voluntary basis, there were mixed reactions to the plan. Governor Roy Romer of Colorado, the general chairman of the Democratic National Committee, defended the concept. He said that the program would not create the federal intrusion that many critics said they feared and that what the president was saying was, "In order to make this work, you need to have a test, and what he asked for was not federal government standards, but national standards." Romer noted that the proposal "preserves for the states . . . the kind of education policy that people want to keep at the local level" (Hoff, 1997).

Within a short time following the 1997 suggestion, state leaders in Maryland, Michigan, West Virginia, Kentucky, and North Carolina promised to offer the assessments, and other cities and states soon joined them. Some states, such as Nebraska, take great pride in their independence and were not immediately ready to offer Mr. Clinton's tests. Nevertheless, Nebraska now has state standards and in 2001–2002 gave its first statewide test in writing.

A comment from Republican representative Robert L. Livingston of Louisiana strangely echoed the original position of liberal education leaders: "The federal school board is not what we need to be," he said. "We need to give the resources to the teachers in the classroom." Another representative presciently concurred: "What we don't want to have are national standards that are mandated and national tests that are mandated" (Hoff, 1997).

Nevertheless, George W. Bush, the succeeding Republican president, pushed for state-developed tests and the federal sanctions that gave them authority. The new NCLB legislation has also called for one additional measure besides the state tests, and the National Assessment of Educational Progress (NAEP), a federally developed test that has been given in the past on a controlled sample and volunteer basis to assess the progress of our nation's schools is strongly recommended. Most states and professional organizations have already embarked on ambitious assessment plans for their own standards. Whereas previously, state officials in Nebraska and other states in the Midwest and West didn't have the constitutional authority or the political inclination to issue a testing mandate, they now have federal legislation to force the issue or back them up.

New York State has a long history of Regents examinations that were required for endorsement on respected, but optional, Regents diplomas. Commissioner of Education Richard Mills is a staunch advocate of higher state standards and is leading the effort to add new forms of mandated Regents exams for all students while eliminating its minimum competency testing alternatives. New York State also has a concurrent plan for changing its high school graduation requirements. The greatest value in the whole standards movement may be that we all look more carefully at what our expectations for our students are.

In its introduction to its new standards, Wisconsin provides a position statement with a rationale and clearly set direction for implementation and enforcement. The statement is representative of the many state documents that have been produced or are in process and appears in Table 2.1. All of the state documents imply the need for accountability and appropriate measures. Several openly recognize that some of their substance was derived from the work of professional organizations such as the NCTM and university-based

Table 2.1 Position Statement of the Wisconsin State Standards

The public cares deeply about education.

For parents, business, and taxpayers, the bottom line is what graduates know and can do.

The public wants, and their elected representatives demand, educational accountability. Accountability requires clear statements about what students are to learn.

If educators don't write clear, explicit and rigorous standards, someone else will.

To have credibility, educators must provide evidence of effective academic performance by public school students.

There will be statewide assessments. If educators are to have a meaningful role in these assessments, they must communicate with the public and elected officials.

Effective education requires standards—clear statements of what is to be learned.

The general citizenry should determine those targets of education with advice from educators.

Educators are best equipped to determine how those targets are to be met.

Judgments about the effectiveness of education should be based on student knowledge and performance.

The primary purposes of assessment are to improve learning and to provide accountability.

What is assessed is what gets taught (and learned).

Assessment should cover the full range of learning described by academic standards.

Effective assessment systems measure complex thinking and applications as well as basic knowledge and skills.

Assessments must be credible and technically defensible.

Public disclosure of assessment results should focus attention on learning that will lead to its improvement.

Schools and districts should be evaluated on results rather than on inputs. The need for various inputs can be determined only when assessments have established a base line against which attempts to improve learning can be tested.

SOURCE: Wisconsin Department of Public Instruction (1996).

groups such as the New Standards Project, which I discuss ahead. Many also recognize the need to involve teachers and parents at the local level. But where do the local school boards stand in this apparent show of state authority over education?

How Governments Manifest Their Power

In an analysis of evidence for a shift of control of curriculum from local school districts and teachers to state (and now federal) governments, Tyree (1993) describes the ways in which state governments manifest their authority. He identifies these ways as law, expertise, norms, tradition, or the charisma of politicians. For example, the states of Florida and Texas have passed legislation that stamps their curriculum documents as law. But Florida's curriculum documents are not very specific and therefore leave much to local districts and teachers to decide. It has little in the way of sanctions to enforce the law and does not imply the credibility of experts in the production of its documents. Nor does Florida have a tradition of state control like that of New York with its explicit and extensive curriculum guides, Regents exams, and graduation requirements.

Texas, on the other hand, has laws and sanctions. It also has some normative authority in the long-term consistency of some of its curriculum. California has no law, tradition, or norms to give it authority. It does have much expertise and a pioneering spirit to try new things. This may, as in the example of whole language curriculum dispute that I describe ahead, create problems. Authority without law has been invoked in New York, New Jersey, Ohio, Illinois, and Maryland, where states took over the management of the deficient city school districts. In these cases it may be demonstrated that, in the long run, money has power. The withdrawal of state funds for local administration allows this to happen. The withdrawal of federal funds (a growing though still smaller part of the education budget) and the newly enforced mandates for how money must be spent (see Chapter 1) in turn forces both the states and the local administration to conform.

Presidents such as Bush and Clinton, as well as many local politicians, who made education a significant component of their political platforms, may be the best examples of attempts to use charisma to gain authority. Tyree's conclusion, however, is that although there is a potential for states to channel or reduce local curriculum options, much decision-making power still remains at the local level.

Local Government Control

The next question is: Where at the local level? In an interview for the *Kappan* journal, Anne Bryant, the executive Director of the National School Boards Association, and Paul Houston, the Executive Director of the American Association of School Administrators, discussed their definitions of the relative roles of school administrators and the political entities that engage them (Bryant & Houston, 1997). Ms. Bryant saw the school board role as "establishing a vision" and "taking the conversation to the community" (p. 757). In reference to state standards, she felt that they should be asking how they could "go beyond the standards." Mr. Houston said that the relationship between the board and its administrators should not be adversarial, and that it was the administrator's function to deal with the public.

In a document published in 1990, before the current emphasis on standards, the New York State School Boards Association (NYSSBA) expressed a similar role for Boards to "set the tone and direction for the district's curriculum by developing a curricular philosophy, policy and goals" (p. iii). They recommended that the board should hire and evaluate administrative personnel "based on their ability to provide leadership for curriculum planning, development, implementation and staff development" (p. iii). The NYSSBA document also suggested that state curriculum guides should be consulted, but that the state should allow more flexibility to local districts. The tone of this may have changed within the past seven years, but careful examination of recently completed New York Standards documents and messages from the commissioner reveal that there is still much to be decided at the local level in terms of specifics.

As I discussed in Chapter 1 and will address in the chapters ahead, the stated standards in most cases are in the form of general performance indicators. In response to this vagueness, some school districts are so concerned about the tests and the market impact on their reputations that they have developed highly structured curricula, often based on texts, that prescribe exactly what a teacher must do from day to day. Others are more sensitive to individual student and teacher interests and have more open-ended curriculum guides. Some have not made any effort to prepare teachers to address the standards in any specific way.

Teachers will have to pay careful attention to how any of these specifics (or lack of them) of the local curriculum are related to the challenge of assuring improved performance on HSSB tests. The sanctions for lack of adequate yearly progress (AYP) and yearly state report cards that expose their students' performance and theirs to public view may push them into the task. The task is formidable in the context of prescribed visions, leveled and publicly measured expectations, the many other nongovernmental influences, and the challenge of individual differences among their subject students.

NONGOVERNMENT INFLUENCES ON CURRICULUM

Professional Organizations

The charge of writing new state standards-based curriculum was a rather new one for Brad and his colleagues. They were more accustomed to writing individual lesson plans—often derived from the text they were using, a favorite grade level theme, or some professionally developed curriculum package. Like Sara Mosle, the New York City teacher who wrote a pro-standards cover article in the *New York Times Magazine,* they recognized that original curriculum writing required "time, energy and devotion." While recognizing that teachers did not necessarily implement the City's prescribed experience and theme-based curriculum the way it was intended, Mosle discounted its value and yearned for the textbooks of her childhood (1996a).

This had been typical of distally produced curriculum documents. In practice, they were rarely used as intended. Teachers tended to adapt them in fragments for their personal use. The previous state documents that Brad, Meg, and April had been handed when they first were hired or when new ones were published had uninteresting and unclear formats and didn't seem to relate to what their students needed, and they were given few supporting materials and/or implementation ideas. They certainly didn't compare to the textbooks, with all of their extra activity workbooks and teachers' guides.

There had been a districtwide emphasis on the standards of the National Council of Teachers of Mathematics (NCTM, 1989, 2000), but these seemed to be a more general thrust that encouraged a greater focus on mathematical reasoning, problem solving, and using manipulatives.

The teachers in Brad's district did not view the NCTM standards as a curriculum (it was not intended to be one) or even as the basis for writing one of their own. The district had arranged for several staff-development workshops in which they were given suggestions for use of a variety of math manipulatives. Their new texts had many more problems and pictures in them and the questions were more challenging. However, they still needed to get the students prepared for the computations on the standardized tests and therefore supplemented the texts with worksheets.

For many years, professional organizations such as NCTM have had a palpable and growing impact on curriculum. Much of that influence has been indirect, working principally through its publications and conferences. Many teachers and schools subscribe to the organizations' periodicals, which contain brightly illustrated and well-presented ideas for lessons and units at all levels. They try the suggestions of their colleague writers, and sometimes they contribute suggestions and articles of their own. Teachers also look forward to and enjoy conference experiences. It makes them feel like professionals and gives them the opportunity to communicate on an adult level with new people in different settings. They often come back refreshed and enthusiastic to try the new ideas to which they have been exposed.

The NCTM standards document was an exception both in its premise and in its wide acceptance by the educational community. I think there are several reasons for its success. To begin with there was immediate support from the business community, which was concerned about reports of the failure of U.S. students to compete on an international basis with students in other countries, as well as with their own frustration with mathematically unprepared employees. The Second and Third International Mathematics and Science Study (SIMSS & TIMSS) reports revealed that performance on international tests by U.S. students was about average when it was compared with other countries involved in the test. It was well below countries such as Japan, Korea, Hungary, and even our neighboring Canada (see McNight et al., 1987; Schmidt, McNight, & Raizen, 1996). The studies also revealed that mathematics curriculum in this country was less focused, emphasized arithmetic rather than more challenging topics such as algebra and geometry, and that our schools devoted less time to mathematics, had lower expectations, and in contrast to 85% of the other countries evaluated, no uniform standards.[2] Our own National Assessments of Educational Progress showed similarly disappointing performances, especially among the older students (Dossey, Mullis, Lindquist, & Chambers, 1988).

The timing of the NCTM document was most propitious in its issue immediately following the first of the reports, but there were other reasons for the success of its standards.

- They were developed by a teachers' organization and therefore got the immediate support of teachers and school administrators.
- It was a set of recommendations by teachers for teachers.
- The standards stated in a very clear and forceful manner what was right for math education.
- Mathematics is a "value or issue free" content area that is little subject to local variation or cultural difference.
- NCTM has, in contrast to other organizations, a broad spectrum of membership that includes college mathematicians and teacher educators as well as primary and high school teachers.
- Its statement of standards was not a prescribed curriculum monitored by mandated measures.

Many school districts initiated professional development programs in response to the NCTM standards. Colleges used them as a basis for the preparation of preservice teachers, and even textbook publishers responded. There is some evidence of overall progress for all groups from scores on the TIMSS and NAEP tests, but the overall proficiency level is still not adequate and the achievement gap between white and minority and higher- and lower-income groups remains. A long-term effect on student achievement or on teaching practice is still undetermined. Part of that lag may, in effect, be due to a lag in the local assessment forms (see Chapter 6), but it may also be due to missing elements of professional development (see Chapter 7).

In contrast to the success of the mathematics standards, similar national efforts in science and social studies have thus far had less success with wide dissemination and adoption. "Project 2061: Science for All Americans" was published in 1989 by the American Association for the Advancement of Science (AAAS), which is generally an association of professional scientists and university professors. It had support from private organizations such as the Carnegie Foundation and several states for the purpose of developing standards in science. The original Project 2061 document was supplemented by its "Benchmarks for Science Literacy" in 1994. It was a comprehensive, content-focused curriculum intended to "identify a minimal core of critical understandings and skills" that constituted science literacy.

It never gained widespread recognition or acceptance. It may have been the missing involvement of K–12 teachers that slowed down acceptance. Science teachers' organizations, which do not have much representation from higher education, did not take ownership of the benchmarks. Science teachers also tend to be fragmented into the different science areas and present a less cohesive force for change.

Another prestigious organization of scientists, The National Academy of Sciences' National Research Council (NRC), issued its standards document in 1996. With an emphasis on scientific inquiry and a call to teach science the way science itself is done, these standards were closer to the agenda of science educators. There was also attention to assessments and a better organization than that of the AAAS documents.

Perhaps the coldest reception and greatest reactive furor followed the 1994 publication of the "Curriculum Standards for the Social Studies: Expectations of Excellence" by the National Commission for the Social Studies (NCSS). These were certainly not "value or issue free." Commissioner Richard Mills explained his preference for traditional subject area organization thusly: "You can easily get lost in this, and it has caused some people to get very touchy-feely-fuzzy about what they expect. And that has opened the standards movement to charges from more conservative folks who worry about government and school intruding into issues of values" (Lehman & Spring, p. 8). In its attempt to be politically correct, the NCSS document precipitated the first vehement protest against standards. In spite of the furor created by some of the inclusions and lack of them, several states used much of their work in developing their own standards but carefully explained that new inclusions did not exclude other important items.

Most of the publications of standards by professional organizations have been used as the basis for the state and city standards documents. In a survey of the status of arts education, Peeno (1995) discovered that 49 states used the standards issued by the National Art Education Association (1994) as a guide and resource for their own curriculum documents. States have also learned lessons from the efforts of the organizations. The introduction to the Colorado history standards explains why it includes world history:

> The Colorado Model Content Standards for History address both world and United States history, including the history of the Americas, and may very well necessitate reorganization of the social studies. The inclusion of content from world history and the history of the Americas suggests that all students should participate in instruction in these areas. The inclusion of areas of the world that have often been neglected in the study of history is in no way intended to exclude the continued study of Western Civilization and its significant place in the history of the United States. Because of the increasing interactions among all nations of the world and the effects of these interactions on our daily lives, it is imperative that students have knowledge of the history of both our nation and that of other nations. (www/stst/colorado.html)

Several professional organizations and state standards documents also recognize that standards are not enough; that schools must also do some reeducation and reorganization. A world languages study group considering the inclusion of special education students in language classes realizes that it will require extensive training for language teachers. The Massachusetts State standards clearly recognize the need for reorganization.

> Both the Common Core of Learning and the Curriculum Frameworks state that change in the classroom is directly related to how schools are organized for learning. The Common Core of Learning and Chapter Two of this framework advocate an instructional focus based on inquiry, problem solving, and learner-centered classrooms, all of which have implications for how schools schedule instructional time. The expectation that each and every student should achieve high standards has implications for how schools group students. Similarly, teachers cannot integrate the strands of Social Studies unless there are longer classroom periods to accommodate extended discussions, Socratic dialogue, and primary source research. (www.stst/massachusetts.html)

The University

Leadership for the initial standards movement has also come from a traditional source of influence on the curriculum, professors in teachers colleges and universities. Aside from their major role as teacher educators, universities have had an important influence on the substance of what is taught in schools as well as on instructional methods. Unfortunately, even though it usually has good intentions, that influence has been inconsistent, uncoordinated, at times obscure or incoherent, and always tenuous, subject to the charisma of its guru and vacillating interest in the latest fad. Many good educational researchers separate themselves from practitioners, and practitioners are often intimidated by the special language and quantitative parameters of their research. A few individual faculty members who have a better understanding of the nature of the classroom successfully pitch their ideas with good marketing techniques. And a profession hungry for ways to deal with the ever more challenging task of educating a diverse population buys their ideas.

Neither the teachers nor the professor innovators are to be blamed or held blameless. Sometimes what seems like a good, intellectually sound idea is just not effective in the hands of an unskilled or resistant practitioner. Follow-through and follow-up classroom support to help the teacher struggling with a new technique or curriculum are rarely provided. Inadequately implemented new ideas are quickly pitched for the next interesting innovation.[3] Some notable exceptions include the long-standing impact of science curriculums produced by the federally funded Biological Sciences Curriculum Study (BSCS), which originated at the University of Colorado, and the Science Curriculum Improvement Study (SCIS), which originated at the University of California at Berkeley.

Several universities produced and piloted math programs that meet the NCTM standards. There has also been widespread support from professors for local school programs that employ the whole language approach to reading and writing. Efforts in both subject areas have been subjected to a backlash of pressure from parents, local politicians, and some teachers. A few conservative educators who pushed to restore phonics as the major emphasis in learning how to read caused the rollback of California's 10-year-old whole language program. A recent heated discussion on the controversy among the "university authorities" at a conference of the International Reading Association can serve only to undermine teachers' confidence and fuel undercurrents of mistrust for the approach among parents, who have had different learning experiences. Among the whole language detractors at the conference was a publisher of phonics books, and among the questioning parents were some who had been subjected to radio commercials for "Hooked on Phonics." Phonics never were eliminated from the whole language concept, but their place in the program was never clearly delineated or understood by some teachers and many parents.

Just as NCTM was releasing its newly revised document, "Principles and Standards for School Mathematics" (NCTM, 2000), the "math wars" erupted. Lack of clear understanding of the intent of math reform by teachers and the frustration of helping their children deal with the requirements of new kinds of mathematical knowledge nurtured the wars. Teacher educators and researchers may have contributed to these reactions as they debated the specifics of the nature of learning among themselves and failed to engage the practitioners in the discussion. They may have failed to recognize the need for clear connections of their new knowledge to the daily task of dealing with many kinds of learners and learning environments (Cobb & Bowers, 1999; Kirshner, 2002). It is this lack of shared vision, comprehensive knowledge, and communication that makes us subject to the competing lure of the marketplace. I address the differences more specifically in Chapter 3 and present a proposal for developing a shared vision in Chapter 7.

A mechanism for exerting influence on curriculum used by teacher-education institutions is through their role as facilitators and instructors for inservice education. Although as I described above much of this has been haphazard and subject to the varying demands of a competitive marketplace, networks of teachers and schools that include higher education institutions offer a better solution. The summer workshop that Brad attended was planned and organized by the Marie Curie Math and Science Center, a network of local schools and a local college. The college took a leadership role in consolidating the separate efforts across districts and got some needed outside funding to form the network. The agendas of the college and the schools were synchronized, and teachers had an opportunity to learn in a new, comfortable, and nonthreatening environment (see Chapter 7).

On a much larger scale that involves a large university, whole states, and urban cities, major groundwork for the standards movement has come from the New Standards consortium, mentioned in Chapter 1. The consortium has focused not only on the standards themselves but also on the development of coordinated assessments that combine conventional and alternative forms (see Chapter 6). They have done extensive field testing of their products, and their standards and terms have become a model for much of the work at state and local levels.

Commercial Materials

Commercially published curriculum materials include books and their supplements, kits of hands-on materials, and now software for computer-assisted instruction. They may appear in more holistic, organized form or in small fragments that teachers incorporate in many different ways. These materials dominate teaching practice in this country; they are the stuff of lessons and units (Ball & Cohen, 1996). When teachers choose or are assigned texts, they often accept the text as their curriculum. The text then constrains and controls knowledge and teaching.

The quality of modern texts is questionable. In a scathing criticism, Tyson-Bernstein (1988, p. 194) called them superficial, with unexplained facts and missing contexts: "The prose is dumbed down to accommodate the poorer reading skill; faddist and special interest group messages, however meritorious appear as bulges or snippets of content; flashy graphics and white space further compress . . . text." I have on my bookshelf an early 1940s science text written by the renowned science educator, Morris Meister. It has little white space and black and white pictures. But it has superb and interesting narrative and well-developed ideas. Its form and content are worth considering for a new and better generation of texts.

The power of texts as an influence on curriculum is particularly evident in states that have textbook adoption policies, which limit teachers' choices. These large states then have an influence on what is published and on what is available in other places. Publishers are not totally to blame; they publish what sells. If educators made different choices, the market would respond.

Teachers cling to these commercial materials because they help them maintain control and relieve them of the burden of creating original materials all of the time—but they still take great pride in the original materials they do create and resist attempts to deprive them of that freedom to create. Reformers sometimes use commercial materials in their attempts to change what teachers do. In actual practice, confronted with great variation in their students and personal skills and their imperative to maintain autonomy, teachers tend to adapt rather than adopt the reformer's materials.

Technological items, including satellite interactive video, graphing calculators, and computer software, will probably be the major form of instructional material in the near future. Preparatory hardware in the form of classroom computers has been a major investment for the nation's K–12 schools in the late 1990s. They spent an unprecedented $4.34 billion on computers in 1996, an amount that grew in the next few years.

Some of the new educational software is a decided improvement over the previous generation's drill and practice on screen. I have recently viewed programs that use real science databases being developed by Lamont Doherty Earth Observatory geologists, observed students take original measures in a wind tunnel in a smart technology lab, watched second graders do PowerPoint presentations and fifth graders embellish them with video clips. I have put students in touch with research scientists over the Internet, and had them read the e-mailed poetry of a class in Africa. Educational software and Internet sources may replace much of the traditional materials of the classroom of the near future, but they may, for a while at least, face the same problems as previous materials: lack of quality, insufficient teacher skill in their use, and over-dependent and uncreative engagement with them by the teachers and the students. To be effective they will have to be connected: to the achievement of standards that are desired, to what we know about how learning happens, and to the real lives of the students they serve. I address technology in its tremendous potential, but as yet unproven promise, for the future of curriculum in Chapters 3 and 7.

Ball and Cohen (1996) identify five intersecting domains that define the influence of materials on teachers as they enact their curriculum. They include (but not in the same order):

1. The political context in which teachers function, as it was discussed above.
2. Teachers' knowledge of individual students.
3. The social environment of the group. (This is addressed when we come back to the more specific role of materials in constructing classroom environments in Chapter 5.)

Two of the domains are related to teachers' autonomy.

4. Teachers' own understanding of the materials they use, and the way they fashion them for students.
5. Individual teacher autonomy (a major influence on school curriculum, which is addressed below).

Ball and Cohen omit two important influence domains: knowledge of how learning happens and assessment; I address these in Chapters 3 and 6.

The Teacher's Right to Choose

My friend Diane teaches in a special-education program in an urban area. She often complains of the unbending bureaucracy with which she has to deal in order to get things done. One day she mentioned that her program card had to be posted on her door. "What is a program card?" I asked. She quickly replied, "Well, you know, it says that you are going to be teaching thirty minutes of reading and thirty minutes of math and that you will have two periods of art for the week and so on—but it's all nonsense for these kids, I just try to keep them busy and motivated." Diane is a conscientious and effective teacher. Her honest belief is that control structures like the program card are just for show; something to justify the administrative role. In spite of the structures, she has no compunctions about doing the right things, the things she believes her kids like and need. In spite of the structures that may put limits on the environment in which she acts, she has autonomy over the real stuff of learning because there are no real measures of her compliance and her effectiveness, or sanctions for not being effective.

Diane's experience is not an aberration—although there are exceptions, and a strong push toward standards and accompanying measures may change this. It was confirmed as illustrative of the existing status in a recent study by Glass (1997) and in studies by Darling-Hammond (1990) and Sedlak, Wheeler, Pullin, and Cusick (1986). Darling-Hammond, reflecting on previous studies, notes that they revealed that "regulations were imprecisely and differentially followed from place to place" (p. 234). In reviewing an analysis of implementation of mathematics changes in California she notes that teachers viewed the new curriculum framework as a policy statement handed to them by administrators with new locally approved textbooks. "As a consequence . . . teachers were unsure of what the policy really consisted of, and what it meant for their teaching. . . . They had too little information . . . and too little opportunity to discuss their ideas with others" (p. 236).

Most of the teachers in the large group that attended the professional development program with Brad had not even seen the new standards for which they were supposed to write curriculum. Others had seen them, but had difficulty understanding their organization and had no clear ideas about how they were supposed to respond to them. Their plans before this workshop were to do what they had done in previous years—generally, their own thing.

Comparing the status of teachers' control of curriculum to previous times, Glass (1997) cites from Sedlak et al., who found that teachers today enjoy more freedom and autonomy than their predecessors (p. 115). The professional codes of conduct of the 19th and early 20th centuries, which were much more controlling and enforced by administrators, are no longer the standard. As a beginning teacher in 1949, I was told to wear a hat and gloves to school, and my weekly plan book was turned in on Monday morning. My principal had it in front of her when she came to observe.

In retrospect, however, I remember that I didn't always follow my plan or feel that compelled to do it when she wasn't sitting there. The experiences reported by teachers in the Sedlak et al. (1986) study support the popular belief that once they close their classroom doors, teachers are "able to exercise enormous discretion" (p. 121). Despite what might be construed as constraints imposed by the larger bureaucracy of state departments of education on public schools or large district-level administrations, public school teachers frequently maintain autonomy. Like Diane, they take control and experience freedom in a bureaucracy by ignoring or working around supposed constraints, or using "passive circumvention" (Sedlak et al., 1986, p. 120). They use their ingenuity and skill to circumvent mandates.

Even if new state standards and district curriculum documents attempt to set limits to the range of possibilities available to teachers, it is doubtful that they will remain within them. In the Glass (1997) study, one teacher responded to a question in reference to state mandated curriculum standards thusly:

> You have the standard things you go by . . . but for the most part, it is pretty much that you do your own thing. . . . You shouldn't impose (curriculum) upon teachers, but let teachers be more creative. On the district level we have curriculum that we must follow . . . but the core curriculum is only meant to be about 60% of the curriculum. Forty per cent of the curriculum we can decide on. (No. 1)

Glass (1997) also questioned teachers in reference to their relationship to school administrators:

> One time school administrators imposed an in-service program on us. We behaved so badly they have, since then, let us determine what goes into them. So I would say currently we have a great deal of control. I resist bitterly and strongly changing my teaching style . . . I resist and I do it either overtly by speaking out—expressing it; or, if that fails, one can very simply do it covertly in the classroom. Simply not do it. Chairs still exist, but we are more of a local autonomy school now. We have a committee that meets and decides things with the principal. The state has a list that they give out to districts. The department discusses the different kinds of textbook . . . but individual teachers make their own choices. (No. 1)

This seems to minimize the power of school administrators and contradict the findings of the effective schools literature, which found that effective schools had strong principals. However, strength does not always come from using power; it can come when power is given through support and opportunities for responsible decision making and capacity building. Many of the participants at the curriculum workshop that Brad attended had been encouraged to attend by their principals, and in follow-up assessments indicated that their principals' support was critical in being able to implement the new curriculum. In the Glass (1997) study, principals concurred with the impressions of the teachers.

> Everything that I do is a collection of information and input from teachers in this building, the department chairpeople in this building . . . They give me an awful lot of input. I'm constantly asking them for direction. While the public school expects teachers to follow the district curriculum guides, they are just that—guides. An established curriculum does not mean there is no room for innovation. The presence of a curriculum does not deny creativity. (No.1)

Glass (1997) did not indicate whether or not the autonomy the teachers in his study had was as a result of formal involvement in site-based management. In my own personal experience with a structured engagement of teachers in the decision-making process, there were decided benefits of diminution of teacher isolation and a growing sense of professionalism for teachers so engaged (Solomon, 1995). As Chubb and Moe (1990) also discovered, teachers in my experience made some excellent and productive curriculum decisions for their students. Among the problems that I identified were the lack of willingness of those in power to share it, the reluctance of teachers to accept responsibility for their decisions, and the failure of schools to provide teachers with necessary resources such as new skills in consensus building and time needed for their engagement in the management process. There have been mixed reports of success with ventures into formal structures of site-based management. Perhaps the reason why teachers and their organizations have not pushed so hard for this is that they already have autonomy—and without all the work.

Parents

Parents have an uneven effect on curriculum and teacher autonomy depending upon the socioeconomic structure of the community. For example, parents wishing that their children gain admission to prestigious colleges may exert influence on schools to offer advanced placement (AP) courses and produce National Merit Scholars—or they may insist on special services. Surprisingly, these parents may also be apprehensive of innovations that stray from the traditional core curriculum, especially if they are nontested subjects or concepts. They want their children's school to be a copy of the one that brought them success. In an attempt to implement a new standards-based math program, I experienced resistance from parents whose children already were doing well with rote computation. They distrusted manipulatives and wanted more worksheets to come home (Solomon, 1995).

Parents who are consumed with the expectation of high achievement will be more likely to serve on district committees and pressure administrators to make changes. Many of these changes, however, will be related to their individual child, rather than to the school program as a whole. They will pressure principals to place their children with teachers whose classes achieve high scores or in honors classes. In school districts with upper socioeconomic populations, some teachers feel more intimidated by parents than by their administrators. The parents are their day-to-day monitors. Teachers will consequently make curriculum decisions that will appeal to parents. A teacher in the Glass (1997) study described how pressure from parents to prepare students for an Advanced Placement exam undermined her right to select her own curriculum and in effect diminished the value of her professionalism, expertise, and training.

As reported in Chapter 1, parents from the affluent district of Scarsdale, in New York state, protested the new HSSB graduation tests because they did not see them as appropriate for their district's own innovative and challenging curriculum (Bert, 2001; Hartocollis, 2001). In their case, they also had the support of the teachers.

GETTING READY TO DESIGN CURRICULUM

As Brad, Meg, and April embark on their task of writing curriculum that articulates with new state standards, they bring with them a history and habits of practice that have been framed by the many influences that I have described above. To help them understand those influences, they may wish to seek answers to the following questions.

What exactly are the federal, state, and district mandates that exist?

How are they enforced?

What tests are based on them?

What concepts are specifically measured by the tests?

What do the experts say about the curriculum I need to address?

Do I agree with them?

How will parents view this curriculum?

Do I know how to use the materials I need and will they be suitable and available?

What kind of support will I get from my administrators?

How much autonomy do I have to decide on the day-to-day specifics of implementing this curriculum?

In response to this chapter's title question: "Are standards necessary?" I trust professionals like Brad, April, Meg, and my readers to come up with their own answers. But with all of those influences pulling in different directions, some consistency in knowing where we have to go might be the light that we all search for at the end of a dim tunnel with many branches. Just as long as they can make some of their own choices along the way. I know that the place where I want to go has to do with learning, and before I made any decisions about curriculum I would want to know how learning takes place. We come to this next.

NOTES

1. The State of California, which got a head start on establishing the NCTM standards and on changes to whole language approaches, has had to deal with some repercussions to these and this slowed implementation of statewide standards in all subjects. Other places such as Alberta, Canada, have openly dealt with protests to their new mandates.

2. The Third International Mathematics and Science Study revealed some improvements, especially in science, but still found the United States trailing other countries in student achievement and much less focused in its curriculum.

3. For further thoughts on innovation and change, see the works of Michael Fullan (1990), Seymour Sarason (1983, 1990, 1993), or Pearl Solomon (1995).

3 What We *Now* Know About How Learning Happens

ABOUT THIS CHAPTER

Serendipity is not to be taken lightly. Just as I am considering the necessary updates on this chapter, confusion reigns about one component of the NCLB legislation, a focusing of educational dollars for proven, research-based approaches that will most help children to learn. Scientifically proven methods of reading instruction are specifically mentioned in the legislation. Several states have also legislated the required recertification of teachers every three years, and the reason given for this legislation is that *teachers need to be updated on educational theory*. In the previous chapter, I addressed the many influences on teachers' curriculum decisions. Although some of these influences often begin as distal or indirect, they are quickly transferred to the more direct effects of local power, school organization, and leadership. But what about the science of teaching, the theory and the practices, that researchers have proven as effective—do they influence us? Are those as easily transferred?

This chapter shares a sample of the emerging ideas of educational philosophy and the findings of cognitive research that could have a powerful and proximal influence on instructional decisions. Unfortunately, history has shown us that this influence often has a limited and transitory impact.

Although university-based researchers are constantly engaged in exploring how learning takes place and evaluating the effectiveness of various educational strategies and contexts, their findings are only rarely transferred broadly to educational practice. The roadblocks that make the transfer of a few new ideas easy and many others difficult are elusive and unpredictable. They may be a factor of the nature of the competition within the research community and perhaps its relative isolation from and lack of respect for practitioners. Within the university setting itself, the scholarship and research agendas of teacher-educators are often disparaged and consequently sparsely funded.

Hiebert, Gallimore, and Stigler (2002) suggest that teachers have their own knowledge base. This knowledge base differs from the scientific in that it is less generalizable and less independent of the context. On the other hand, the teachers' knowledge base is more concrete and rich in context. The authors suggest that given the many successes of teachers acting apart from scientific knowledge and practicing the "craft" of teaching, it might be worthwhile to accumulate, verify, and share practitioner knowledge so that it is less personal and gains in its credibility to others. My hunch regarding this suggestion is that ultimately the findings of successful practices of "craft" will be readily explained by the scientific findings. The difference is that successful practices of craft are often learned by trial and error or mimicking others—frequently the copied practice is the one through which the teacher learned. In my practice of professional development for teachers I have found modeling effective instructional strategies with children to be the most effective mechanism for change.

Occasionally some findings are translated into "craft" language and techniques and there is a spate of enthusiasm for the new cure-all. My own rationale for the disparity in how scientific research findings get translated into practice is that it has less to do with the quality of the findings and more to do with the charisma of the researcher-salesperson. Nevertheless, a coherent scientific and craft-connected research base would spare a generation of teachers from the disappointments and wasted energy of trial-and-error approaches. Somehow we must make the scientific findings more concrete and the craft more transferable to a variety of contexts. I discuss a process for achieving this in Chapter 7.

Human resistance to change in institutions we cherish and trust in their original form also makes the transfer of such new knowledge difficult. The great variations and fluctuations in the culture, politics, and philosophy of schools, and the need to respond to the individual differences in human beings and their social interactions add further complications. These situational variables are not ignored in the research; along with the other variables of the learning process they are treated in a less than holistic fashion, and not always clearly connected to each other. This is, perhaps, an example of the modernist focus on the specialization of knowledge (Doll, 1993). Such specialization not only accounts for the lack of connections within the research base itself, but, more important, a consequent loss of value to the teacher, who must deal simultaneously with all of the variables.

An example of the difficulty in making holistic connections between research and practice is witnessed in the fall 1993 edition of *The Review of Educational Research.* An attempt by Wang, Haertel, and Walberg (1993) to organize the disparate elements of educational research into a comprehensive knowledge base is followed by several articles that either refute the suggested organization or declare the endeavor impossible to achieve. Similar (perhaps semantic) philosophical dialogues about the existence of knowledge and reality and about whether or not the acquisition of new knowledge is situated (confined to a particular context and not readily transferred to new situations) periodically appear in editions of *Educational Researcher (*Anderson, Reder, & Simon, 1996, 1997; Cobb & Bowers, 1999; Greeno, 1997).

Such discourse may be stimulating to the research community and in the long run produce a more tested theory, but it has not helped those who are immediately accountable for practice and has weakened the prospect of incorporation of the findings of research. Teachers are already resistant to change and wary of new ideas derived from research as panaceas for their problems because many of these have proven unrealistic in their real school applications. They don't know who to believe!

Nevertheless, many of the findings are valid and should be considered valuable contributions to our understanding of how learning happens; and because I believe that it is possible to transfer this generalized knowledge to the new situations each teacher confronts, some of these ideas are presented here. This is not meant to be an inclusive survey; there is much that is omitted. Instead, I have selected some of the more holistic and seminal findings that can be woven into a simple framework that can help guide teachers in making curriculum decisions.

To help focus directly on connections to practice, I extract a series of *knowledge construction curriculum applications* from these finding in this chapter, and in the following two chapters refer back to them as I address the mechanisms of constructing curriculum.

I begin with some of the current epistemology or thinking about the nature of knowledge. A review of recent cognitive science theory on the general nature of intelligence and brain function and some more specific findings on motivation, control, and interest follow. The role of human goals as controllers of the process of constructing new knowledge is identified as a significant and unifying connection between the cognitive science and the philosophy. Finally, there is a summary of the theory and its connections to the curriculum.

An Exciting Conference

Meg and April talked animatedly with colleagues from other schools at the conference luncheon. Dr. Gardner's[1] ideas on multiple intelligence seemed to make so much sense. They had fun doing the morning activities that allowed them to explore their own intelligences. Meg commented, "I always knew I was better at the spatial things. It was easy for me to come up with the picture . . . but forget about mathematical logic." April responded, "Remember the conference we attended on right and left brain research? I wonder which intelligence is where? Does this mean that my kids who are good at art can't think logically? How about Leonardo DaVinci?" Meg retorted, "I do not think Dr. Gardner meant to say that at all, but it would be so hard to change our lessons to meet every kid's needs. And think about the standardized tests; they are so verbal or mathematical. Can you imagine giving kids an alternative of drawing a picture?"

Meg and April walked away from that conference alerted to something that may have made an impression, but probably resulted in little long-term change in what they were doing in their classrooms. Although progress has been made because based on theories of multiple intelligence some teachers are adding variety to their activities and forms of assessment, the recent emphasis on standards and their measurement poses a threat to innovative and difficult-to-measure departures from tradition. Unless the standards call for them! There is much to warrant such a call. The nature and scope of knowledge and its accessibility have changed dynamically; so must our educational enterprise.

EDUCATIONAL PHILOSOPHY: PIAGET AND CONSTRUCTIVISM

Although they are usually treated separately, educational philosophy and cognitive development theory often overlap, and better integration would be most useful. The branch of philosophy that explores the nature of knowledge and knowing is *epistemology.* The notion that knowledge is self-constructed had early origins in the ideas of Locke (see Longstreet & Shane, 1993; Orton, 1995), but is most frequently connected to the work of Jean Piaget (1926, 1977). Piaget considered himself a child psychologist (Piaget, 1926, p. xx), and much of his early work was based on clinical observations. His later work tries to integrate what he learned into a more generalized explication of *knowing,* and therefore many would classify him as an epistemological philosopher.

Piaget's (1926, 1977) work is frequently misinterpreted. He is most readily identified with sequential stages of cognitive and moral development, and these stages have often been (justifiably) refuted as more flexible or mutable than some of us originally believed. Less emphasis has been placed on Piaget's later ideas on the construction of knowledge; recently these, too, have been misinterpreted. Piaget believed that knowledge is self-constructed. "Real comprehension of a concept . . . implies its reinvention by the child. . . . It is important first that the child should have been able to find, by himself, the reasons for the truth that he is expected to understand" (Piaget quoted in Ginsburg, 1989, p. 96). Such statements have been interpreted to mean that knowledge construction is a highly individualized process, not a social one.

Piaget may not have meant this at all. Although he believed that these reinventions, or "schemes," are at first based on actions with objects, he carefully observed children in their discourse with others in the environment and attributed the construction of schemes to their interactions. He concluded that at early ages most new schemes are internalized but not really shared in conversations with peers. Early language is monologic or a collective monologue. The child with a companion at her side is essentially talking to herself but uses the language expression to help internalize the scheme. As time makes the child less egocentric, language becomes adaptive—it is listened to and responded to—and then the child and the construction of new knowledge become more responsive to social interactions (Piaget, 1926). Piaget never discounted the role of the teacher or parent. Reinvention "does not mean that the teacher (or parent) is useless, but that his role should consist less of giving lessons than in organizing situations provoking investigation" (Piaget, quoted in Ginsburg, 1989, p. 97).

A guiding knowledge construction principle that we can extract from the research and thoughts of Piaget follows.

Knowledge Construction
Curriculum Application Number One

The curriculum should provide experience-rich environments that promote opportunities for students to learn with understanding as active participants, rather than environments that rely on passive students and teacher telling. Dialogue among peers should be encouraged even if it is at first monologic. Technology and manipulatives should be employed to provide the richest possible active environment.

Recent Interpretations of Constructivism: Radical Constructivism

Recent interpretations of constructivism build both upon the individual and social elements. A more individualistic and *radical* interpretation is that each of us constructs his or her own schemata: bits of knowledge, explanations, or pictures of reality according to their fit with our individual goals, previously existing concepts, and new perceptions (von Glasersfeld, 1990). This definition also builds on the work of Ausubel (1963, 1968), who recognized that before new knowledge could be absorbed or reinvented it would have to fit with what was already there and be chosen by the learner.[2] Learning, from that perspective, is much more under the control of the learner and less likely to occur when information is fed in an unconnected way into a passive learner. The learner must take ownership.

Knowledge Construction
Curriculum Application Number Two

The curriculum should pay attention to and address students' prior knowledge and their goals. New perceptions are needed to create new knowledge. You cannot just feed information and expect it to be absorbed, because the learner has to "fit it in" to what is already there.

Radical constructivists would argue further that there is no one real "truth" or reality. They contend that knowledge is different in each of us, because it has been situated in a highly individualistic learning experience, subject to the variations of prior knowledge, genetics, and perception. From this perspective, Meg and April would have walked away with completely different concepts of Gardner's talk and their own conversation.

This radical constructivist or "situated learning" interpretation has created a conundrum for some cognitive researchers and practitioners who depend on empirical measures of learning as the basis for their findings and practice. How does one measure learning that is different in every individual? If reality is so individualized, what is the role of the adult, the parent or teacher as a communicator of culture? Does this perspective also deny the validity of well-grounded research that demonstrates the effects of social intervention on student achievement?

Social Constructivism

The ideas of Vygotsky (1978), the Russian psychologist, present a more socially interactive picture of the construction of knowledge. He places a stronger emphasis on the sociocultural context and the role of mediators. In his theory of cognitive development Vygotsky distinguishes two types of learning experiences: those that occur from the "bottom up," giving rise to "spontaneous concepts" that are undirected and unimpinged on by adults, and those that result from adult generated, or "top down," activities that produce "scientific concepts." He suggests that these two types of learning inform each other and that learning takes place when the child's knowledge and adult structures approach each other in a "zone of proximal development." The adult or other mediator sets a learning environment of objects and spoken dialogue that stretches the child above his present knowledge level toward a higher level. Eventually the stretching becomes internalized and the child reaches higher-order thinking levels.

Other researchers (e.g., Wertsch, 1979) have expanded on Vygotsky's ideas with demonstrations of an interactive process that connects the bottom-up experiences of the child and the top-down dialogue of the adult in what they term a "scaffolding" process. Resnick (1983, 1989) uses the alternate term "instructional mapping" to describe how teachers might use dialogue and manipulatives to help students make the connections between their informal experiences and formal schooling. In a recent application of this to the teacher's role in setting the stage (or planning) for the construction of new knowledge by children learning mathematics, Steffe and D'Ambrosio (1995) suggest that teachers create a "zone of potential construction." This is a kind of prediction of the "zone of proximal development" that is based on the teachers' knowledge of what the child already knows and their experience with how other children learned. Planning for such a "zone" would require teachers to make better use of their assessments. It would engage them in the research-based instruction I describe in Chapter 7.

The cooperative learning environment, which has been proven effective by many researchers, incorporates the social contexts needed for learning that are implied by Vygotsky, and it supports or supplants the direct role of adult mediators with peer mediators. In the cooperative learning setting, peers can construct mutual zones of proximal development in a context of interactive discourse where social goals of affiliation (being part of the group) and personal goals of efficacy (feeling that you can do something) may enhance the chances of new knowledge construction (Johnson & Johnson 1989; Johnson, Johnson, & Holubec, 1987; Sharan et al., 1984; Slavin, 1987, 1990).

Knowledge Construction
Curriculum Application Number Three

Learning environments should provide a multitude of social interactions such as those provided in cooperative learning or artifacts such as interactive computer programs. Teachers need to plan to stretch their students' knowledge across the "zone of proximal development or construction," carefully matching environments, prior knowledge, and planned outcomes or standards.

Figure 3.1 A Philosophical View of Knowing

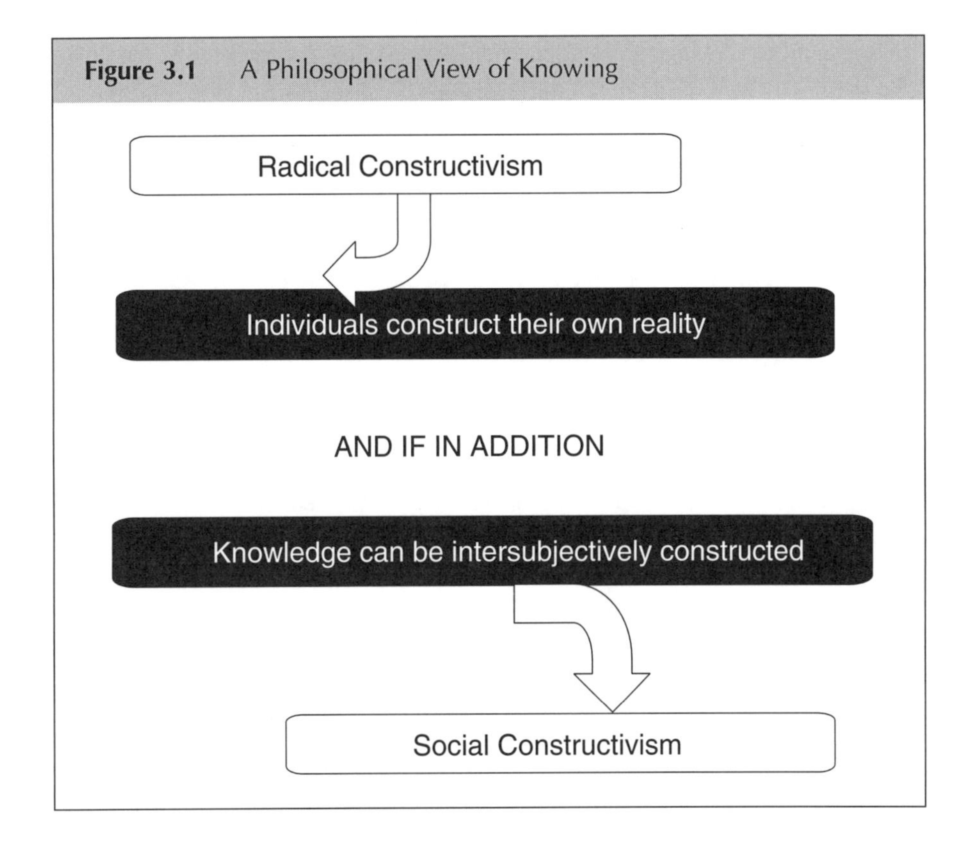

A Compromise

Some constructivists have attempted a compromise (see Figure 3.1) between the radical and social constructivist philosophies with the recognition that social processes mitigate the individual construction of knowledge. This was, of course, suggested by Piaget. Children learn when their thoughts are listened to and they receive a response. Cooperative groups may be doing more than transferring what each knows to the other, however; they may be learning new things together. Schemes that are newly constructed for each interactor in a shared process have been defined as intersubjective. Lerman (1996) argues firmly for intersubjectivity in the actual acquisition of knowledge. He quotes Vygotsky's argument that "the true direction of the development of thinking is not from the individual to the socialized, but from the social to the individual" (p. 136). Lerman, in his own words, continues, "When an action gains significance for a child, becoming bound up with goals, aims, and needs and associated with a purpose it is a social event" (p. 136). In this respect, learning also becomes "situated" in the social context.

Meg and April then would collectively construct new knowledge based on their experience and their conversation; knowledge that might not have been constructed had they not had a social interaction, and this knowledge would be new to both of them and to Dr. Gardner, whose reality in regard to intelligence may also be quite different from that of several other cognitive scientists. Cobb (1990) ascribes the realities that we hold in common and use to communicate with each other to the "consensual domain." When Meg and April discuss the eight intelligences suggested by Gardner in school the next day, they know what each other means when the term *logical/mathematical knowledge* is used; it is in their consensual domain. The standards we choose as we collectively construct curriculum for our students come from our consensual domain.

Even when they are formed in social interaction, however, individual pictures of reality may or may not be correct as judged by comparison with what most other human beings see as reality. The instructional process then becomes a matter of bringing the learner's reality closer to the reality of the teacher—a social process of helping the individual develop, confirm, or correct his own schemata or reality pictures so that they approach the realities of the consensual domain. I address the applications of the social construction of knowledge more specifically in following chapters but a guiding principle follows.

Knowledge Construction
Curriculum Application Number Four

In addition to the knowledge transferred from individual to individual so that it may be shared and in a consensual domain, knowledge new to each may be constructed in their interactions. Curriculum content standards should consist of the knowledge of the consensual domain that educators judge as appropriate for the individual and learning situation; and the enabling standards and enactment activities of the instructional process should be considered a way of building and correcting individual realities.

Constructivism provides an overall way to look at knowledge and knowing; it tells us that prior knowledge, new perceptions, and human goals are factors in creating new and individual knowledge. It does not tell us how to construct the specifics of our curriculum or deal with the differences in our students, but it sets the stage for further study and understanding. And it raises further questions. For example, if new knowledge is constantly being constructed, how does the construct of in-place intelligence fit into the paradigm?

THE CHANGING NATURE OF THE CONCEPT OF INTELLIGENCE

Back at school, Meg and April continued their discussion about Dr. Gardner's talk. Meg wants to know how to measure the eight different forms of spatial, logical-mathematical, bodily-kinesthetic, linguistic, musical, interpersonal, intrapersonal, and naturalistic knowledge and asked, "Do you then average them? How will I know what to expect of my students? How will I know if I have made some progress with them?" April responded, "I always thought that intelligence was something you were born with and couldn't change; but didn't he say something about nurturing the different forms?"

Early debate among cognitive scientists was similar to the discussion above. It contemplated the origin of intelligence in the individual and its nature. Debate centered on whether intelligence is innate and inherited, or acquired in an acculturation process; whether it should be accepted as a psychological entity or merely a mathematical abstraction that can be used to measure individual differences (Lohman, 1989). The present consensus concerning intelligence is a compromise that accepts the presence of some genetically determined psychological or physiological components, but also recognizes the powerful influences of the environment. Current debate focuses more on the various typologies, such as Gardner's, that propose multiple subsets of the construct of intelligence, and on the hierarchy of skill levels and their developmental sequence.

Multiple Intelligence Theories

This dialogue, as yet unresolved, has led to several theories or, as some would prefer to call them, models of intelligence. They are all modular, seeing the brain as having multiple intelligence forms and/or levels. They also introduce such variable factors as what is considered as intelligent behavior in the particular culture and the influence of previous experience with similar situations. In contrast to the wide recognition and effects of Gardner's ideas of multiple intelligence (Figure 3.2), other theorists' ideas are less well

Figure 3.2 Multiple Intelligence: Gardner's Eight Areas

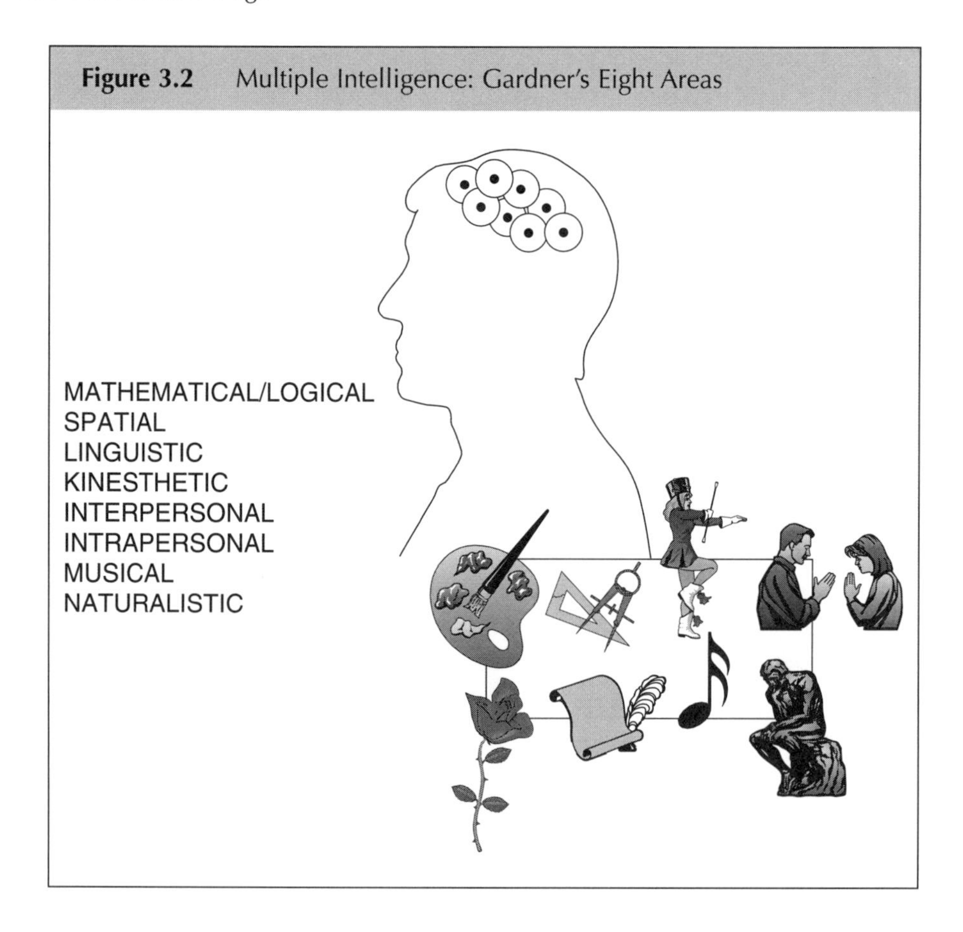

recognized by practitioners. They are, however, highly respected by researchers and have helped change some of our notions about intelligence.

In an early compromise between the concept of intelligence as an innate construct and its acceptance as an acquired one, Cattell (1963) hypothesized intelligence to be comprised of a *fluid* ability that is "physiologically determined" or innate and a *crystallized* ability that is the result of the fluid ability interacting with experiences in the environment. Crystallized ability, then, is measurable intelligence. Cattell's dichotomy of fluid and crystallized intelligence (Figure 3.3) is widely accepted and incorporated into other theories. It essentially moves from the notion of a passive and immutable or in situ image of intelligence to a more active process of cognitive development and one that fits well with constructivist ideas.

A rationale for funding of early intervention programs was the discovery that the extent and nature of human interactions in the first year of life had a profound effect on future ability to learn. This would seem to confirm the Cattell theory—with one exception. There is evidence that there are physiological reasons for this. Apparently, brain cell growth is incomplete in the

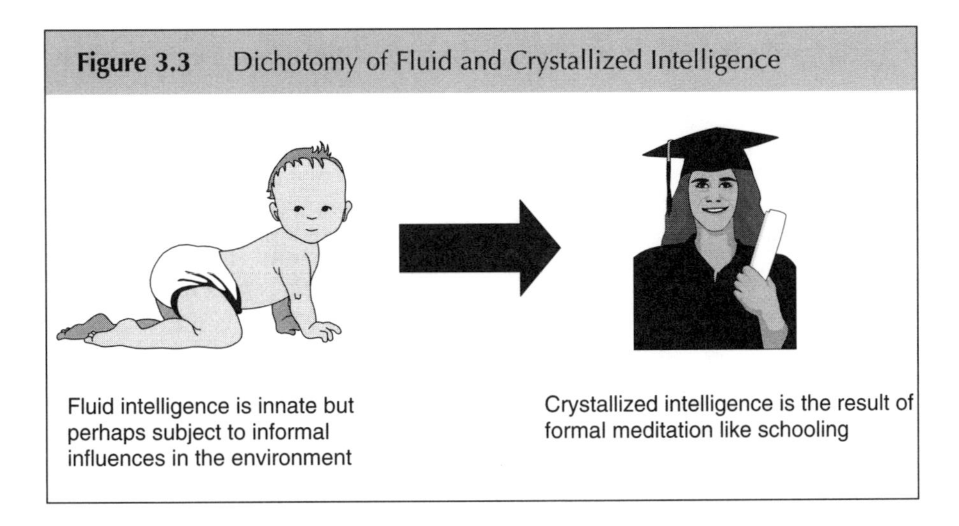

Figure 3.3 Dichotomy of Fluid and Crystallized Intelligence

newborn and stimulated by human interaction in the first year of life. Is this then fluid or crystallized ability?

Horn (1985) also questions the innateness of fluid ability. He believes that differences in fluid ability reflect differences in "casual learning" or "independent thinking" (perhaps the spontaneous knowledge described by Vygotsky), whereas crystallized ability differences reflect differences in acculturation learning—the differences in the child's experience (Vygotsky's scientific knowledge). Promoting the idea that intelligence is a multiple or modular construct, Horn describes other factors of intelligence, such as perception, retrieval, speed, and processing, but places fluid and crystallized ability at the top.

Sternberg (1985, 1988) defines intelligence as the mind's ability to govern itself and presents a triarchic modular theory that has three subtheories (see Figure 3.4). His *contextual* subtheory connects the assessment of skills as intelligence indicators to their recognition in the culture as desirable. An implication of this concept relates to our presently used intelligence tests. They are based on Western culture and emphasize linguistic and logical-mathematical skills. Other cultures may value the interpersonal (social) or intrapersonal (knowledge of self) skills identified by Gardner more highly. Middle-class suburban parents may view skill in mathematics as an important indication of intelligence. The parents of urban ghetto children may see their children's interpersonal street survival skills as evidence of their intelligence. Recognition of the role of cultural values as criteria for judging intelligence has had growing acceptance, and to some this makes our present testing systems seem invalid.

Sternberg also describes a *componential* subtheory. He sees intelligence as composed of varying levels or components of cognitive function and

Figure 3.4 Sternberg's Triarchic or Three-Part Theory

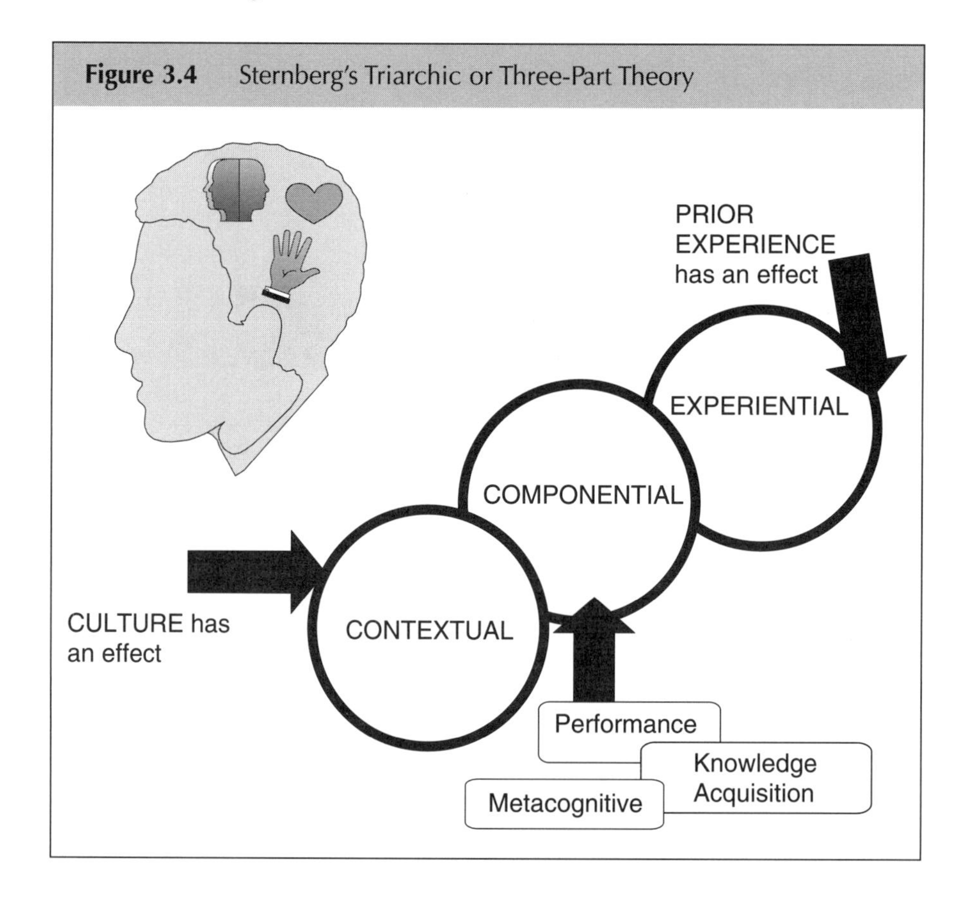

identifies these as metacognitive, performance, and knowledge acquisition components. The metacognitive component controls the other two, which produce actions and acquire information. Performance components carry out the plans and strategies of the metacomponents. They use inference, application, and comparisons to respond to information and relate it to concepts in prior knowledge. The performance components also work interactively with knowledge-acquisition components, which perform a kind of sorting process to evaluate and categorize new information. Together these lower-order components send information back to the metacomponents.

In his third *experiential* subtheory, Sternberg (1985) gives weight to experience with a situation. Repeated experience moves a situation from one of novelty to automatization, and coping with novelty is an integral part of intelligence. Whereas novel situations require attention, automatized responses allow diversions to other concurrent inputs or tasks. Meg, who is an experienced teacher, has automatized her patterns of classroom dialogue. She can concentrate on the responses her students are making and analyze the problems metacognitively. April, less experienced, must still struggle with what she is going to say next. She gropes for a quick solution to problems (Rosko, 1996).

Neither Sternberg's (1985) nor Gardner's (1983, 1993, 1995) model focuses on innate individual differences as distinguished from acculturated or acquired differences. Nevertheless, although it may be politically discomfiting, genetic research gives us growing evidence of some predetermined personality and physiological tendencies that may affect crystallized intelligence.

In addition, neither theory suggests a hierarchical sequence of skill development levels that preclude parallel development of lower-order skills and relatively complex or higher-order thinking. This supports our previous questions about some of the interpretations of Piaget's early work. Research in mathematics education has also demonstrated that it is not necessary to learn algorithmic procedures in order to solve complex problems, and that it may be better to learn or reinvent the procedures (if necessary) after confronting and understanding the problems (Fuson et al., 1997; Heid, 1988). Concrete experiences may be needed at various ages for some new constructions, but even toddlers can reason abstractly. I remember my grandson at age two, when cautioned about the danger of the swimming pool in my back yard, saying, "Is that like the hot stove?" He made an abstract connection between two very different situations and generalized the concept of danger. Taken as a whole, modular intelligence theories have several important implications for curriculum.

Knowledge Construction
Curriculum Application Number Five

Intelligence is a complex characteristic that is influenced by some inherited traits but also profoundly subject to the influence of environmental experience. It is not one limited set of abilities, but a variety of them. These abilities may exist and vary in different areas such as linguistic and kinesthetic or in different phases of processing such as metacognitive controls or sorting and organizing information. The sequence in which these abilities develop in different areas or phases is not hard and fast. Individuals may vary in their power among the contents and the processing phases. Curriculum should reflect this variation among individuals in its support of already existing ability and in the further development of all abilities.

Memory

Intelligence has often been studied in terms of one of its components, memory, or the ability of the brain to take in information, process it, and store it. Most cognitive psychologists agree on the distinction between long- and short-term or working memory. PET (Positron Emission Tomography) and MRI (Magnetic Resonance Imaging) scans of brain function and observations of the results of brain damage have identified the hippocampus of the brain as the center for working memory and the thalamus as the receiver and initial processor of information from the senses. The working memory has a limited capacity, but is essential in processing information it receives and preparing it for storage in the longer-term memory of the cerebrum. It is also where connections to previously stored memories are connected to new inputs. A variety of factors can affect the efficiency of working memory. Its capacity can be helped by purposeful repetition or rehearsal and by organizing little bits of information into larger chunks, such as thinking of the whole number 1,054 rather than the four individual symbols: 1, 0, 5, and 4. Working memory may also be affected by emotions—positively or negatively—by connecting the new information to previous experiences. The working memory requires attention and is easily interrupted by distractions. It is transitory, disappearing quickly if not transferred to long-term memory. The interactive scaffolding process of constructivist teaching helps maintain attention and make the connections that produce the schemata of long-term memory frames (Sousa, 2000).

Long-term memory has been divided into episodic, semantic, and procedural categories. Episodic memory is memory of events and experiences. Semantic (or declarative) memory is the memory of concepts or ideas, and procedural memory is the memory of how to do something or perform a task (Slavin, 2000). Although these are distinguishing characteristics, I believe that they work in harmony and support each other. Procedures are best remembered when strengthened by concepts and experience. Concept development is facilitated by experience and procedural practice. Learning the procedure of making a left turn in traffic is supported by understanding the concept that you must judge the speed of opposing traffic in order to be sure that you will be able to clear it in time. Repeated practice with the procedure strengthens the concept.

Different parts of the cerebrum also seem to house different categories of stored memory, and for some areas of knowledge there is a limited window of opportunity for new knowledge to be stored. Young children learn new languages with less difficulty than adults, and the skills of spatial relationships and positioning are best learned at about the age of nine.

Measuring Cognitive Ability

Reflecting on the preceding, educators can assume that there is a potential for schools to provide an environment in which all kinds of abilities can develop, but we also must recognize that we are not the total culture or experience and that therefore there will be differences in the rate at which children

Knowledge Construction
Curriculum Application Number Six

There are two distinguishable actions of memory. Short- (or working) and long-term memory work together and in sequence to effect the transfer of information received by the senses into two categories of long-term memory frames or schemata (semantic and procedural). Short-term memory is affected by emotions and attention distractions. Curriculum activities should strive to maintain attention and other organizational elements for the working memory. Activities need to combine memory categories and stimulate connections to prior knowledge for improved transfer to long-term memory. Curriculum planning needs to consider the age-bound windows of optimum memory storage capability.

learn and a measurable difference between them at the end of schooling. Preoccupation with highly constrained performance tests that measure these differences may, however, be wasteful—perhaps even dysfunctional.

If intelligence is subject to cultural values and previous experience, and the brain is a multiple organ structure with independently operating units and performance levels, the use of specific performance tasks, with measurements such as response time to predict overall intelligence, is dead-ended by the narrowness of the tasks. Initially promising correlations of these tests with broader measurements of ability proved to be nonreplicable (Lohman, 1989). This is even acknowledged by Anderson (1990), who for many years employed such tasks in his intensive research on the mechanisms of cognition. After much soul searching, he has ascribed the fruitlessness of some of this work to the fact that a variety of inputs can achieve the same output—hence the behaviors measured by these tests cannot be associated with particular cognitive mechanisms in the brain.

From the practical viewpoint, speed of response may be helpful on timed tests and also of value in some life situations that require such skill, but may be valueless in determining how good the brain is at synthesizing new and previous perceptions and memory frames (pieces of knowledge or schema stored in the brain) to help form new situation-adapted ones. Anderson (1990) posits that an elaborate memory fan (store of related or categorized declarative knowledge) may even require a longer time to process and retrieve. And if the brain's activity is rational and the human brain optimizes behavior, given different goals and environments, the speed of human response may also vary.

Modular theories of intelligence also finally recognize that the "common sense" that some individuals with high measures of IQ lack may be an independently functioning set of skills; and that, somewhat correspondingly, just because students cannot remember the rotely memorized steps in long division does not mean that they cannot reason logically.

Based on experimental evidence, several theories recognize that there is a difference between the ability to solve problems that have been experienced and the ability to solve novel problems. Experience with a problem type decreases solution time. Therefore, traditional measures of innate intelligence or fluid ability have attempted to use novel problems to separate it from crystallized ability. Comparative and valid measures of fluid intelligence, then, require us to design tasks that are equally novel to every tested individual. Can a test with such equity be constructed? Every child's experience is unique. April and Meg may use different experiences to teach the same skill. If the test question is similar to experiences that Meg has provided, it may skew the results on the test her class takes.

Anderson et al. (1996, 1997) believe that it is possible to generalize from one previously learned situation to another novel one. They posit that skill with novel problems is perhaps related to the ability to encode memory and convert it to a production or procedural rule (algorithm) that helps one find a solution. The creation of such procedural rules may be highly specific and generated only when needed because it is costly to the brain's energies (Anderson, 1990).

The difficulty in constructing generalizations may be related to the current dialogue on situated learning: a growing emphasis on the value of presenting real-life environments in schools that suggests that it is difficult to transfer knowledge gained in the traditional nonrealistic environments of schools to new life situations. I agree with Anderson et al. (1996, 1997) that although this is difficult, it is possible. The true value of real-life situations may be in their ability to motivate learning or control it through the social and rational bands. Teachers can structure experiences that facilitate the production of generalizations and motivate learning.

Tying the study of human intelligence to the existing tests that differentiate individuals may have been part of our difficulties in understanding it. Recent studies of general intelligence have consequently placed a greater emphasis on how connections between parallel systems or hierarchical levels take place. These studies also recognize the importance of a knowledge base upon which to build connections and have therefore shifted from tests of in-place knowledge to analyses of how the brain processes information and consequently how achievement occurs, especially in such areas as mathematics and reading. The findings of these studies and those that investigate the effect of various learning environments will do much more for the schooling process than the tests that decided way ahead of time, in a vacuum, who would or would not succeed. A preliminary discussion that relates the role of goals to information processing theory follows. Studies of the metacognitive and affective factors have already led to instructional approaches that consider the influence of thinking about learning, social goals, control, and attitude on the learning process. I address other goal-related influences further in Chapter 5 as they apply to the creation of learning environments, but another guiding principle is implied here.

Knowledge Construction
Curriculum Application Number Seven

Traditional tests of intelligence depend upon timed solutions to novel problems and evaluate only part of an individual's abilities and potential to learn. Time for task completion may not be a valid criterion, and it may be impossible to find problems novel to every tested individual. Teacher expectations of students and consequent student self-expectations should not depend upon current forms of intelligence tests. It is more important to know how learning happens and about the factors that affect it. Learning experiences can be connected to realistic situations and facilitate the creation of transferable generalizations.

The Information Processors

Intelligence and memory are concepts we usually think about in the passive sense, but their value is in their ability to act and can be measured only by virtue of their actions. It makes sense, therefore, that intelligence theory should have the same patterns that learning theories have. Sternberg's componential subtheory reflects the work of those who study information processing: cognitive psychologists who study the brain's processing functions and use computer analogues to explain how learning happens. A great deal of this research is connected to the computer scientist's desire to achieve artificial intelligence (AI)—or the ability to simulate the human brain with advanced computer technology. In support of these efforts there is also basic research on how the brain functions physiologically.

Like Sternberg (1985), the cognitive scientists propose several different mechanistic functional levels of brain function that correspond generally to the architecture of the computer. There are different parameters and nomenclatures for the levels but they agree on their presence. A better understanding by Meg and April of how these levels function may be as helpful as knowing that there are different kinds of intelligence, and may be critical to the potential improvement of the whole schooling process. For example, as we discuss below, the metacognitive controls of learning have been studied in several research contexts, but these findings have had little influence on classroom environments (Chapter 5).

Surprisingly, the information processing ideas may even present a resolution for the philosophical debate between radical and social constructivism: whether reality exists only as an individual construction or as the shared reality of the consensual domain. The outcome of the debate may, as Orton (1995) suggests, be of little consequence to educational practice because the new knowledge offers a compromise between the constructivist philosophies. It provides a supportive empirical base for each philosophy. The work of John Anderson and the "Adaptive Character of Thought" (ACT) theorists is one example of this base.

In support of Piagetian ideas, Anderson's (1983, 1990, 2002) *adaptive character of thought* theory, in its latest version identified as ACT-R, unifies previous research on modular brain processes by positing that they are all part of the same system; individual subsystems, bands, or levels that code information from the senses to form representations, frames, or chunks in the memory (see Figure 3.5, page 70). Relatively fragile short-term chunks are reconstructed for storage in the long-term memory. As we have previously discussed, short-term memory function is very brief and easily disrupted by distractions. It can, however, be enhanced by rehearsal (saying a new phone number over and over to yourself) or by connecting chunks with familiar forms.

Anderson notes the adaptability of memory to revise or recode stored representations in response to new situations and calls the revised representations *adaptations*. These may correspond to Piaget's (1977) notion of *accommodations* as new constructions of knowledge. Current physiological research on brain function suggests that these adaptations or accommodations probably occur as a result of synchronous timing of brain actions in which previous memory frames are retrieved at the same moment in time as new messages from the senses (Blakesley, 1995).

Like von Glasersfeld (1990) and the radical constructivists, Anderson (1990) believes that several levels of cognitive processes are governed by human goals. Building on an architecture of cognition suggested by Newell (cited in Anderson 1990, 2002), Anderson places two rather iconoclastic (in cognitive science) bands at the top of brain function—distinctly human and therefore not analogous to present computers—the social and rational levels recognize the social and physical environment and goals. These levels cause cognition or learning to operate "at all times to optimize the adaptation of the behavior of the organism" (1990, p. 28). In other words, the human brain adapts its behavior so that it can best accomplish its goals in each given environmental situation. He describes human goals as controls of the selective retrieval of previously stored adaptations and suggests that it may even be unnecessary to really know how the brain does its lower workhorse functions if one can predict on the basis of its rationality how it will respond in a given environment.

Explanations of how different environments influence what the human brain sees as optimal need to be explored, but we have some ideas from previous research and practical craft experience. If Meg knows that her students are more likely to be motivated by a problem that concerns computer games than they would be by a problem that concerns books on a shelf, she will write computer game problems. It is also not much of a stretch to realize that the social and physical environment of the social band can create and modify the goals that constitute the rational band. Most children will have goals that lead them to prefer social interactions and goals that make them compete or comply with their social group. Knowledge of what a student sees as optimal may be of the greatest significance for teachers as they create the learning environment of their classrooms.

Anderson's (1990) hypothesized bottom or biological band of brain function is analogous to the computer's machine language and corresponds to the neural function of the brain. It is the workhorse of production—carrying out the instructions provided by higher bands. Managing this bottom band are three upper ones, the algorithmic, the rational, and the social bands. The algorithmic band contains the brain's programming directions. This would be where prior knowledge is accessed from long-term memory and new perceptions are categorized, connected, perhaps to previously formed or newly constructed generalizations. This is where adaptations happen.

The rational band is where the controlling goals operate. Recent ACT-R learning experiments and theory analyze the specific role of goals in the problem-solving process. There is an indication that goals actually operate in the selective retrieval of stored chunks or frames from memory. They evaluate and choose what the brain attends to, and may in turn be quickly changed by what is retrieved. Goals respond with rapidity to environmental stimuli and may also be stored (Anderson & Douglas, 2002).

Recent ACT-R theory updates, based on experiments by Anderson (2002), describe interaction between the rational and algorithmic bands. In response to a rational goal, a procedural rule is selected from long-term memory and this calls for retrieval of declarative chunks. In an attempt to synthesize ACT-R theory and other explanations of how we categorize objects, Anderson and Betz (2002) offer several suggestions. A goal to categorize an object may initiate the retrieval of stored memory chunks that represent similar objects as well as chunks of procedural rules for placing that object in a category. Immediate guessing may be a first step, or purposeful matching and elimination may occur. Several sample objects and rules may be retrieved at once, and placement of the new object in a category may

Figure 3.5 Architecture of Cognition: ACT-R Theory

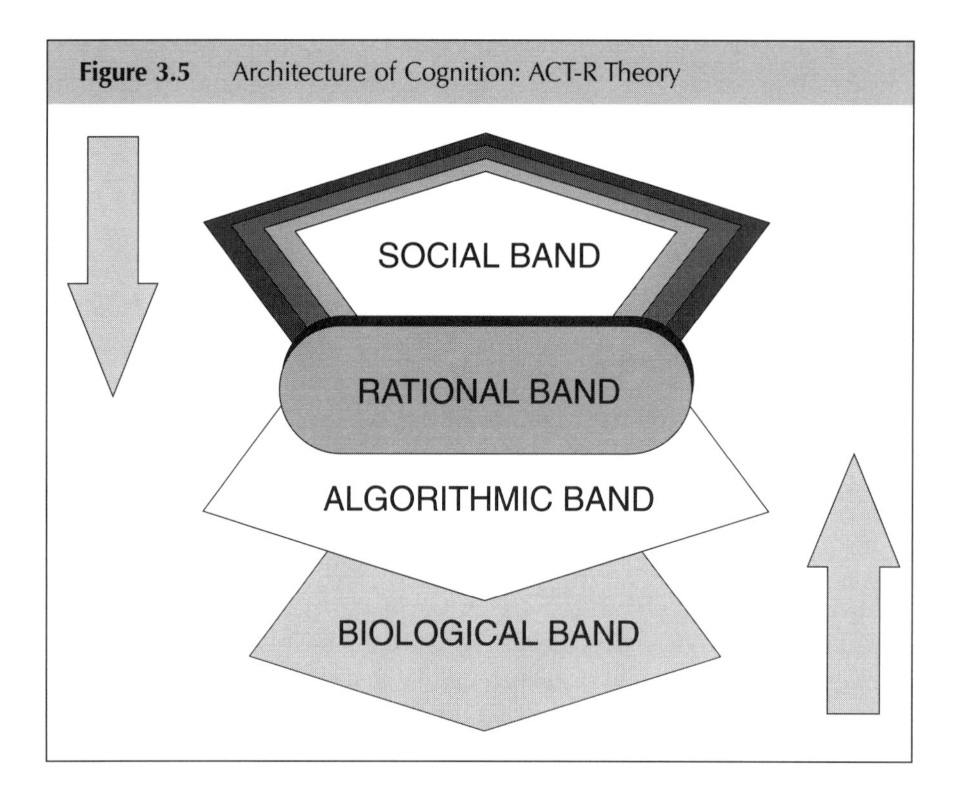

depend upon its closeness to the one already stored and to the quantity of previous practice with placing objects in a particular category (Anderson, 2002). One of the first categories my own children (and others) were able to learn and name was "car"—an easy sound to repeat and plenty of practice with very similar objects.

Anderson does not think that the biological band will be of ultimate significance in the explanation of human cognition, and because of difficulties in identifying the nature of this band's processes in the human brain, he does not think the energy needed to investigate the biological band to be worth the effort. Experiments in the timing of band action and visual perception are, however, under way (see Anderson & Douglass, 2002; Anderson, Matessa, & Lebiere, 1997). Empirical physiological evidence of the nature of regions of the brain certainly does not make a comprehensive theory based on understanding of the biological band easy to come by. If, as reported by scientists studying minor stroke victims, the verb form of the word "march" is stored in a different place than the noun form of the word, and one may lose one form without losing the other, it is unlikely that knowledge must be developed in a sequentially fixed pattern. The brain also seems to be adaptable, with damaged areas being replaced in completely different places.[3]

Anderson has great hopes, however, for the algorithmic band,[4] which outlines the steps that must be taken and helps form the goals. His focus on the rational band also coincides with von Glasersfeld's emphasis on control by human goals as significant in the construction of new knowledge. I begin our discussion of the rational band of human goals below and then come back to them as we address the classroom environment in detail in Chapter 5. Meanwhile, there are some general implications for practice that can be abstracted from the work of the information processors.

Knowledge Construction
Curriculum Application Number Eight:
An Information Processing Approach

The senses perceive and transfer information (Biological Band) to short-term memory. Short-term memory has a very limited capacity, but it can form memory frames or chunks that connect the new perceptions with previously stored long-term memory chunks (Algorithmic Band). It may cause a change or adaptation in these. Short-term memory is enhanced by:

- Rehearsal or repetition
- Attention
- Chunking very small pieces into familiar units

Transfer of short-term memory chunks to long-term memory is controlled by specific but transitory processing goals (Rational Band). **Goals** may be affected by the social and physical environment (Social Band).

Transfer is enhanced by:

- Affective goal factors such as motivation, interest, and self-efficacy
- Connections to other familiar chunks
- Decomposition of very large units into smaller units

Transfer into long-term memory is impeded by:

- Distractions
- Negative goals
- Large-sized new chunks unconnected to familiar ones

Long-term memory consists of chunks of knowledge. Knowledge chunks may be grouped into:

- Procedures (steps for doing something)
- Semantic or declarative ideas or concepts

Declarative chunks include recognition of words, pictures, and categories. Procedural and declarative chunks support each other and work together.

COGNITION, METACOGNITION, AND GOALS: CONNECTIONS TO PRACTICE

The concept of a systematic connection between cognitive brain processes and controlling goals that serve to optimize behavior sheds new light on something we educators have long been aware of—the influence of students' goals on their ability to learn. This recognition adds organization and continuity to previous research on the effects of goals on achievement. It also serves to connect what we have previously considered separately as cognitive and metacognitive processes. Metacognition has been defined as being aware of our thinking as we perform specific tasks, and then using this awareness to control what we are doing. The degree to which we are aware of our thinking and knowledge as we learn or work on problems has been demonstrated to have an effect on our ability to learn and find solutions. Sternberg's (1985) metacomponents are the conscious directors or executives of other brain processes. Generalized problem-solving skills (strategies) are examples of these.

There may be cultural differences in our metacognitive strategies, in the way goals control how we learn and remember. For example, Japanese students will consciously try to memorize more often than Australian students (Purdie & Hattie, 1996). Nevertheless, McInerny, Roche, McInerny, and Marsh (1997) discovered that differences among learners within the same cultural group were no less than differences between learners of different cultures. Metacognition, however, also presupposes control of self, and previous definitions of metacognition by some have included such affective factors as motivation, efficacy, attitude, confidence, interest, expectation, commitment, and attention (Marzano et al., 1988). These factors have been demonstrated by considerable research to be controls of the learning process.

The affective factors can be logically defined in terms of both the human goals addressed by the constructivist philosophers and the controlling role of goals in the brain actions of the rational band explored by cognitive researchers. The understanding that goals govern the cognitive process adds structure to previously demonstrated relationships between effective instruction and the affective factors. It connects scientific knowledge with accumulations of "craft" knowledge and offers generalizations for practice. As an example let us consider motivation. Motivating reluctant students to want to learn is in effect changing the goals that helped govern the construction of previous realities or schemata. The athletic coach knows well the motivational power of achievement and social goals in improving performance—although some of the improvement may be physiological, much of it may be cognitive. Although human goals may sometimes be subliminal, even reflexive (such as eating without noticeable hunger), they can quickly be retrieved into consciousness and used to govern the cognitive process. A hungry hunter learns quickly how to stalk his prey.

Another example in support of the concept of goals as controls of cognitive function is the evidence that self-efficacy (see, e.g., Pintrich, Marx, & Boyle, 1993) is connected to knowledge acquisition. Human goals for learning are mediated by our beliefs in our ability to succeed, and ultimate success by expectations thereof (e.g., Cohen & Lotan, 1995; Weinstein, Madison, & Kuklinsky, 1995). Attitudes that recognize the relationship between effort expended in the learning process and pay-off have also been correlated to performance efficiency (e.g., Rogers & Saklofske, 1985). From a negative view, it can be a human goal not to care to learn or not to pay attention—especially if previous experiences have been unsuccessful or socially uncomfortable.

William Glasser (1986) defines a control theory axiom with a trenchant metaphor in this description: "What students (and all of us) do in school (and out) is completely determined by the pictures in their heads." He believes that all children come to school with a picture that school is a satisfying place and are willing to work to achieve satisfaction. Lack of success changes the pictures in their heads—and their sense of power, which he declares is a strong human need *(and goal)*. Teachers, mothers, and the peer culture help put these pictures *(and goals)* in children's heads. Can we be successful in changing the goals of students and get them to feel more power, and to achieve more?

Connecting to the notion of social construction of knowledge and to the ACT-R social band, Urdan and Maehr (1995) define goals as "the perceptions and beliefs about the purposes of academic achievement" (p. 215). They identify social goals such as "the values of whom one is affiliated with or from whom one seeks approval" (p. 221) as having possible negative or positive effects on educational outcomes. This has special bearing on the potential success of female students in science and mathematics; their present affiliations, cultural history, and traditional school settings may not promote the goals required for success in these areas. Competitive environments that place a greater emphasis on speed and grades than on cooperative and realistic endeavors may be the least desirable for women, but in the long run be less productive for both male and female students (Bailey, 1996).

INTEREST

Interest, as another goal framer in the acquisition of new knowledge, has been studied in some depth. In a review of the research literature, Tobias (1994) relates interest and prior knowledge to each other and to the acquisition of new knowledge. Knowing something about a topic increases interest and encourages the acquisition of further knowledge. Tobias cites several studies that provide evidence for these relationships between interest and knowledge, and usefully explains the difference between situational, topic, and domain interest. He posits that situational interest can lead to broader and more sustained domain interest. Having fun with the experience of building a robot can lead to further interest in science.

In an aside related to his previous research, Tobias also notes that students with low interest probably acquire much knowledge in school only because of other goals, such as high grades. Such prior knowledge rarely leads to long-term retention or increased receptivity to related domain knowledge.

Knowledge Construction
Curriculum Application Number Nine

The construction of new knowledge is an overall rational process that hinges on human goals and on previously learned metacognitive strategies. It involves complex processing of new perceptions, which are interpreted in terms of prior constructions that are selectively retrieved from memory. These interpretations may include sorting processes and connections to prior or brand new generalizations or algorithms. Prior constructions or schema may or may not be accommodated or adapted to form new ones. Educational experiences need to be responsive to these processes and educators need to understand them.

Interest is a goal framer: Increased interest results in more effective knowledge construction. Real problem situations and educational technology may heighten interest and other goals.

Curriculum and learning environments must consider the effects of goals on the learning process. In order to be effective, teachers may need to manage student goals.

REAL EXPERIENCES AND TECHNOLOGY IN THE INSTRUCTIONAL PROCESS

Related to the situational interest developed as one builds a useful robot is another part of Sternberg's (1985) theory, which refers to the element of intelligence that is demonstrated in practical (relevant to life) applications (Sternberg, Okagaki, & Jackson, 1990). In addition to adding domain interest, experiences such as these may strengthen the pictures, goals, and power of students who naturally possess practical or contextual intelligence. As a result, interest in further learning may be heightened. Girls, in particular, may be positively affected by relevant-to-life applications, but as Bailey (1996) notes, "Although girls may be most enthusiastic about pursuing science when they see it as relevant to daily life, boys will surely not be less interested when presented with more relevance!" (p. 78).

The reality and relevance for all of our children today, regardless of gender, is the preponderant influence of technology. In an e-mail message to me Belinda Hill defines the Internet as an unexplored region and a border between countries, an "electronic frontier." She quotes Barlow's (1991) definition of it as,

> A place where trespassers leave no footprints, where goods can be stolen an infinite number of times and yet remain in possession of their original owners, where businesses you never heard of can own the home, where the physics is that of thought rather than things, and where everyone is as virtual as the shadows in Plato's cave. (p. 19)

This definition can serve to remind us of the great possibilities of technology as a tool and a component of curriculum. It also warns us of possible dangers.

Let us begin with the notion of technology as a place for the physics of thought. This does not describe the first generation of school software applications. This software was a mere replication of print materials. It did, however, have an advantage over print materials in its immediate feedback and student control components. It fed students' needs for interest, self-efficacy, and their intrinsic goals. It was that kind of motivation that produced the current generation of technology users. Although this software has been in use in schools for more than a decade, it has never really been integrated into the curriculum. Like dittos from an extra workbook, the software programs were "add ons" that the kids seemed to like.

The advent of CD-ROMs with their multi-media potential for interactive engagement of the learner not only heightened the previous motivational advantages for students, but also introduced some of the physics that Barlow talks about. If students have to make choices about how to design an airship that they can then race, they face a different and more constructive challenge. The Internet has expanded this potential exponentially. If students can use their programs to directly access scientific data banks to help them make predictions about earthquakes or sunspots, they are beyond a level that any traditional classroom with the best possible teacher can provide. If they use their programs to communicate visually and individually with the scientists who collected this data, they are reaching beyond the still necessary human interactions of their own cooperative groups. If they use computer interfaced environmental probes, wind tunnels, and bridge constructions to gather environmental data and make original designs, not only have they used technology as a tool to learn something that is already in the consensual domain, they have used it to create completely new knowledge.

This potential extends beyond the science classroom. If second graders can write their book reports and design their PowerPoint presentations so that others will want to read the books, they have reached a new level of communication skill. If social studies classes can maintain ongoing communications with students from all over the world, get original geographic and economic data from data banks in the countries they are studying or original transcripts of congressional discussions, and then use these communications and information to simulate new situations and make decisions, they are doing something my teachers never dreamed of.

Technological applications in the classroom greatly enlarge the possibilities for situational interest and practical applications. Even when the child interacts alone with the computer program, there is a simulation of social activity and relevant-to-life experience; there is ongoing assessment and immediate feedback to confirm efficacy; the child is in control and nurturing or building upon a variety of intelligences. A well-done piece of software provides multiple stimuli at a learner-managed pace. It can also decompose larger goals into smaller manageable ones while keeping track of progress. I watched my four-year-old grandson, Edward, manipulate his mouse with "Gizmos and Gadgets," an interactive science-technology CD-Rom,[5] and listened as he planned his strategy for building a better car. He was only on the brink of reading, but managed to identify the key words. At 10, his computer knowledge and interests have turned to intricate and sophisticated games that require complex strategies, which ultimately may be transferred to other problems outside the world of technology. Although he will become engaged

Knowledge Construction
Curriculum Application Number Ten

Technology can create situational interest in an active and interactive environment.

It provides opportunities for multiple stimuli. These may respond at first to individual variations in existing areas of intelligence strength, but can also serve to enlarge other less-developed forms of intelligence.

Technology provides opportunities for immediate and unthreatening feedback that makes self-assessment safe and has the potential for building self-efficacy.

and learn alone, he prefers to have an adult or another child by his side. And as I have noted above, I have little doubt that what he learns will be generalized and transferred to new situations; I have already seen that happen!

CONNECTING RESEARCH TO PRACTICE: SUMMARY HYPOTHESES

It may be helpful, before we summarize our hypotheses in Table 3.1 and then suggest specific applications to the instructional process in the following chapters, to clarify the different meanings that the terms *connection* and *adaptation* and *schemata* have assumed for us. Schemata or memory chunks are the previously connected units that are stored in the brain. Connections apply to the first active phase of learning, both to the conscious adult-induced analogies and to the dynamic, multilevel and time-ordered processing that takes place as the brain retrieves previous knowledge, matches it with goals, aligns it with newly coded input, and fits it into generalized algorithms. The adaptations of previously stored schemata would be the result—the ah-ha!—of new insight and correspond to the new picture of reality described by the constructivists. The new schemata would then be stored as retrievable units.

An understanding of learning as a dynamic goal-controlled social process of forming new constructions by making connections between prior knowledge and new *top-down* formal learning experiences, presents a challenge to education practitioners. Some of the prior knowledge may have been *bottom-up* or informally acquired outside of structured learning experiences, and it will vary with the individual child. The constructivist process suggests a method of instruction that is grounded in interest-high "doing" endeavors; accepts and considers the student's present knowledge, fluid and crystallized intelligence, culture, and goals, but plans for the stretching or correction of this knowledge toward what is in the social mediator's consensual domain.

In conclusion, we suggest that teachers like Meg, Brad, and April not limit their understanding to one theory, but know and consider the breadth of hypotheses and premises that have a possible impact on the construction of curriculum, and then view each situation to see how it fits. With experience they will generalize and automatize. The suggestions in Table 3.1 are a summary and a beginning based on a constructivist philosophy, which is supported by the empirically derived learning theories of cognitive psychology that also recognize the controlling influence of human goals on cognitive processes. In the chapters ahead, I refer to these hypotheses as I discuss some of the decisions teachers must make in terms of the written contracts, the enactments, and the measures of their curriculum.

Table 3.1 Research on Learning, Curriculum Inferences, and the Technology Advantage

Theory or Finding	***Inference for Curriculum***	***Technology Advantage***
Each individual must construct his or her own new reality or knowledge based on connections between previous knowledge and new experiences. Individuals construct new adaptations of knowledge as a result of actions on the environment or interactions with others.	The curriculum should provide experience-rich environments that promote opportunities for students to learn with understanding as active participants, rather than environments that rely on passive students and teacher telling.	Technology facilitates inquiry and invention, discovery and exploration of relationships and patterns, higher order cognitive tasks such as the critical assessment of data, compare and contrast activities, and transformation of information into something new.
The construction of new knowledge is enhanced in active or "doing" situations, particularly those that present high-interest novel situations.	Learning environments should provide for active participation in real-life situations, problem solving, and self-assessment.	Technology can provide the richest possible active environment.
The construction of new or ever-changing adaptations of knowledge is governed by human goals.	The curriculum should pay attention to and address student goals such as affiliation, control, interest, and efficacy.	Technology allows for control and choice. It can provide immediate positive assessment feedback in small increments that impart self-efficacy.
Human goals can be interpreted in terms of the affective factors such as motivation, self-efficacy, attitude, and interest that have previously demonstrated and recognized effects on learning. The building of self-efficacy is	Students need to be interactive and in more control—even engaged in self-assessment. The curriculum should consider the differences in individual and cultural goals, and provide an environment that enlists or modifies those goals toward the purpose of learning.	Technology allows time for reflection. Its impersonal and private nature decreases the risk of making, admitting, and trying to correct a mistake. It changes the classroom from a teacher-centered one to a student- and activity-centered one.

Theory or Finding	Inference for Curriculum	Technology Advantage
managed by the assessment process.	Activities need to be realistic, interesting, and allow students to achieve at ever more challenging levels, without dependence on extrinsic rewards.	*Classrooms need to be student centered.*
New knowledge and goals are frequently framed and modified on a social plane. New knowledge is constructed as a mediator stretches the child from previously internalized knowledge to new knowledge.	Teachers need to plan for this stretching by carefully matching environments and planned outcomes or standards. These standards are the knowledge of the *consensual domain*.	Technology increases the opportunity for the teacher to structure authentic learning environments and discovery of the standards or knowledge of the *consensual domain*.
The knowledge that they then share and that others may share is in the *consensual domain*. The social plane may involve social artifacts such as texts and computer programs but is most powerful when it involves interaction.	Learning environments should provide a multitude of social artifacts and interactions such as those provided in interactive computer programs and cooperative learning.	The Web allows for expanded interactions on a social plane, for children to use the same tools as are used by experts (e-mail exchange w/experts, Web publishing, etc.). It also expands the opportunity for interpersonal exchange, as well as intrapersonal exchange through feedback that promotes self-assessment.
Intelligence is a multiple construct. It may include tactual, spatial, logical-mathematical,	The curriculum should respond to diagnosed differences in students' learning strategies, experience, and goals.	Technology offers the teacher an opportunity to provide and assess a varying level of

(Continued)

Table 3.1 (Continued)

Theory or Finding	*Inference for Curriculum*	*Technology Advantage*
and other differences. The individual's ability to construct new knowledge and solve problems may be a factor of the function of each of these levels or areas of brain function, as well as a factor of the previous experience and goals.	Curriculum should provide opportunities for students to achieve satisfaction and a sense of power in their high-skill areas, but it should also stretch their lower performance areas.	experiences and easily accessed alternatives that address them. Technology allows for careful assessments to measure progress toward meeting standards.

NOTES

1. Howard Gardner's work has been widely disseminated both in the literature and in workshops for teachers. This scenario is based on an actual conversation I overheard at one of these workshops. Gardner's list of eight areas of intelligence include: Spatial Intelligence, Musical Intelligence, Linguistic (Verbal) Intelligence, Logical/Mathematical Intelligence, Interpersonal Intelligence, Intrapersonal Intelligence, Bodily Kinesthetic Intelligence, and Naturalistic Intelligence. See Gardner (1983, 1993, 1996). See also Checkley (1997).

2. Although Ausubel addressed the notion that the child had to choose to learn, most of his application suggestions concerned the fit into prior knowledge. He believed that the teacher needed to program that fit and recommended the use of advance organizers, which may be a more direct form of teaching that is in contrast to the more open ended and inductive approach suggested by constructivists.

3. A possible example of growing congruence between physiologists and psychologists may be the recent finding of evidence that the hippocampus of the brain functions as a connective region at the same time that psychologists using computer models suggest that new connections and adaptations of previous cognitions are the basis for new cognitive storage.

4. This algorithmic band has a significant carryover to the construction of Artificial Intelligence—or the ability of computers to imitate human intelligence. Some recent research in this area can easily be accessed on the Internet.

5. The Learning Company ©1993, 1994.

4 Choosing Standards and "Designing Them Down"

ABOUT THIS CHAPTER

Educators must function within the spheres of many influences: the ambient society, predetermined externally imposed standards and assessments, the parameters of their immediate school cultures, and the realities and variations of the teaching-learning process. Nevertheless, even in countries that follow uniform national standards, much is still left for the school and the teacher to design. The national standards for all schooling in Japan are found in three slim volumes—hardly the scope of what goes on in a child's educational experience in that country (Japan Society of Mathematical Education, 1900).

Given the power of creating instructional events, therefore, teachers must make responsible and situation-bound decisions regarding these events on a daily basis, with little time for analyzing them in terms of their source, influences, and appropriateness. In preparation for this, they need to develop designs and patterns of thinking and decision making that will facilitate their task. These designs and patterns are the process of curriculum development.

This chapter brings us directly into the "how to" stage of curriculum development. In response to these influences and knowledge, how do we translate existing content fragments and state standards into clearly articulated designs that are meaningful and useful to the teacher and of value to the student? Whether we are directed by national, state, professional organization, or local standards, we will need to know how to map the smaller trips on our journey toward their accomplishment, and we will want these to be on productive and rewarding paths. To do this, we need a common language for giving and reading directions, and we need to understand the way the roads feed into each other: from small individual paths for special excursions to large highways carrying us all toward the same places. How else will we know we are on the right road and how else will we know when we get there?

Consensus about the need to change and transitions from previous forms may need to come first. I therefore begin with a brief scenario of teachers engaged in the curriculum writing process that may help the reader understand the setting for this task. Then, because new constructions must be connected to prior knowledge, I review the form of the most commonly used curriculum design in schools over the past four decades and compare that to the new forms and standards-based language.

Even for experienced teachers, some of the new terminology related to standards may be strange and cumbersome. What do we mean when we use the terms *outcome, commencement standard, benchmark, content standard, performance indicator,* and *enactment activities?* How do we use these terms to tell us and others what we want our students to know, understand, and be able to do? What is needed to provide students with "opportunities to learn"? In constructing learning environments, how do we group students for instruction? How do we use the resources of time, space, materials, and human energy? What kinds of skills do students need to become better problem solvers? How can our expanding knowledge of how the brain processes and stores information guide us in the choice of experiences and interactive dialogues to help build those skills? Creating the horizontal and vertical articulations of the design is a challenge and therefore the suggested patterns will be accompanied by step-by-step templates and some criteria for evaluating the products.

THE CURRICULUM COMMITTEE MEETS

Meg was not that pleased to be in the science planning group. She had not been able to attend the summer professional development workshop, but along with the others had been charged with revising the school science curriculum so that it complied with the new state standards. She began their first third-grade group meeting with this comment: "Why don't they just tell us what else to teach—or get us a new text series that follows the standards to use with our kits?" She was perfectly happy with the science kit she was using. The kids loved playing with the magnets, the light bulbs, and the batteries. It was her own enthusiasm with these materials that got her on this committee, and the thought of abandoning the kit activities made her uncomfortable. April, on the other hand, was gung-ho for change. Her kits were rarely used because she found them cumbersome to implement. The kids messed them up and were noisy when they did the activities. She thought higher standards might put a greater emphasis on the content that was so difficult to extract from the activities. It always seemed to her that the activities were little more than play and accomplished only minimal science. April's own background in science was not too strong, and she always felt more comfortable with a science textbook that covered the material.

Brad was enthusiastic and anxious to share what he had learned and accomplished in the summer workshop. But he was still concerned that his group of ESL students would be unfairly challenged by the rigor of the new standards and once again put down by the tests. He was apprehensive that most of the new science standards would require an emphasis on definitions, which were so difficult for his students. He had always enjoyed his own science classes and often used a science activity to generate interest and discussion with his students. At the workshop, he had seen some new CD-ROMs with animations that were especially good for his students, who were limited in their use of the English language. Maybe this was an opportunity to meet some of their needs in a different way. "Where do we begin—these standards are so general," he asked to initiate the discussion.

April saw an easy solution.

"The advertisement for these new textbooks says that they meet the new state standards; why don't we just take a look at them and write a curriculum around the content in the text?"

"The workbooks that supplement them are full of good stuff for the kids to do," she added.

"What about our kit activities?" Meg protested. "My students get so much out of them and science is supposed to be a process."

Brad knew that reaching consensus was not going to be easy. Educational reform is not easy.

In an interesting proposal for evaluating recent educational reforms, House (1996, pp. 6, 7) recommends that we examine reform suggestions in terms of three factors taken from *transaction cost* economic analysis; he suggests that these factors may affect the reform adoption and success rate. The first factor is "bounded rationality" or the reality that not everyone understands everything in a rational manner. April demonstrates this in her conclusion that the new standards mean new content, easily accomplished with a new book. The second factor is "opportunism" or the reality that people choose courses of action based on the promise of personal gain. Brad's motives may have been less selfish than this factor implies, but there is no doubt he thought this might be a good opportunity to meet his personal needs. Meg, who was not so willing to give up her successful and satisfying investment in her present science program, illustrates House's third factor. It is not easy to implement change in educational settings because teachers' already acquired skills are "asset specific" and they have already sunk time and energy into them. Meg needs to see ways to redeploy her already useful skills or be tempted by a greater reward for learning new ones.

The above scenario is a common one, often repeated in just the same tone in our country's schools as teachers try to come to a consensus and comply with the call for greater uniformity in the written school curriculum. Perhaps, as a manifestation of bounded rationality, teachers who do not seem to be challenged by the task of planning day-to-day activities for their students and can also state desired goals or standards in a general way have difficulty translating the generalities into more specific expectations. Aligned activities that lead toward the accomplishment of the goals are also more difficult. Choices of activities are usually loosely connected to the content standards, but are frequently based on other criteria such as accessibility, student control and interest factors, and public relations appeal. For example, worksheets are easy to obtain and use; they control the children and document and advertise the curriculum to a parent and supervisory audience. This makes them asset specific (and comfortable) investments. By design, they mimic the standardized tests that are used as measures of our own performance as well as the children's, and are, therefore, opportunistic.

A BIT OF HISTORY

In consideration of House's principles, before we suggest a different way to organize curriculum it may be useful to avoid some bounded rationality by examining our already comfortable asset specific investment: the history and substance of our current curriculum forms. We then may be able to illustrate how making the required changes in forms and substance may prove "opportunistic" in its potential benefit to teachers and learners.

Many of us attribute traditional organization of the curriculum and usage of the terms *goals* and *objectives* to curriculum theorist Ralph Tyler (1949). For most of the latter half of this century written school curriculums using these terms were organized into related and hierarchical units that described the scope of what children were expected to learn. They not only described the breadth of this knowledge and suggested experiences, but also were often explicit about what was to be covered at each grade level. Broader goals and their related, more specific objectives could be stated in terms of either the *giver* or the *receiver.* A giver objective or aim might be, "Students will be required to read one Shakespearean play in the tenth grade." If the objective described what the student or receiver would be able to do, it was a behavioral objective such as, "Students will be able to discuss Hamlet's state of mind."

In their most expanded form behavioral objectives that were designed to lead to the accomplishment of the goals also had specific levels of performance attached to them. These behavioral objectives were sometimes so isolated and focused on a specific behavior, such as, "Students will correctly identify the forms of the verb 'to be' with 80% accuracy" that teachers found them cumbersome, confining, and detached from the original broader goals. In addition, attempts in the 1960s and 1970s to attach behavioral objectives to extensive designs for individualization of instruction dampened teachers' and students' enthusiasm as classroom activities deteriorated into the tons of ditto sheets that comprised the "learning activity packages." Teachers soon were bogged down in paper grading and in the management of many students doing many different things. The social interactions and group processes that motivated both teachers and students were missing from this scheme; their human, adaptive interventions were undermined by this process. As a consequence of the resulting diminution of interest in individualized instruction and a countercurrent of cooperative learning in the nineties there was less focus on behavioral objectives, but much of our curriculum and assessments still bear this organization. The recent use of computers to manage independent activity has kept this approach alive.

American individualism and the prevailing spirit of local control of education worked to prevent the organizational form of written curriculum as goals and objectives from providing much in the way of consistency from school to school or state to state. The design was never meant to be a prescription for a nationwide curriculum. Instead, there were many adaptations and variations. These official written curriculums of individual schools were also frequently unaligned with the actual curriculum as it was enacted in the classroom. Any degree of consistency was more likely to be attained by commercial textbooks and standardized tests.

In an attempt to place more emphasis on broader, more meaningful, but measurable "outcomes"—always focused on the receiver—the "outcomes-based" movement of the late 1980s gained rapid interest and favor. The curriculums of several communities and whole states were reorganized around exit or commencement outcomes that were then "designed down" or articulated with benchmarks at critical grade levels and finally with grade level or unit outcomes. Common to all well-structured examples of units of curriculum design is a design-down element that articulates the general with the more specific so that the smaller curriculum fragments will lead toward the accomplishment of the broader desired ends. Outcomes were to be carefully matched to assessments, with a focus on the more "authentic" performances (Spady & Marshall, 1990).

Unfortunately, as reported in Chapter 1, just as the outcomes-based education effort was gaining national momentum in the early 1990s, it suddenly was met by grassroots opposition from conservative groups that objected to some of the values-oriented outcomes and the concept that everyone be held accountable for the same goals. Quickly, the term *standard* replaced *outcome* in the educational literature and governmental plans. The change was accelerated by the new term's more politically palatable connotation of traditional excellence. The concept of an articulated "designed down" curriculum, however, transfers easily to the new terminology.

DEFINING STANDARDS IN NEW TERMS

Evidence for the remarkable political power of the concept of higher standards is clearly embedded in current national calls for action on raising education standards at both the state and federal levels, which I have already described in Chapter 2. As they have been developed by states and professional organizations such as the National Council of Teachers of Mathematics, standards are essentially outcomes or receiver-based objectives that may or may not have attached performance measures. They retain the "design-down" potential of outcome-based instruction but differ in their intent from goals and objectives in that they are prescriptions designed for the purpose of higher expectations and uniformity.

As outlined in Table 4.1, in many respects the standards parallel traditional goals and objectives as well as outcomes. But they have been more specifically organized (by the McREL Institute, 1993, and others) into "content standards," "performance standards," and variably into "curriculum" or "opportunity to learn standards." For the National Summit Conference in the spring of 1996, Borthwick and Nolan (1996, p. 1) defined the terms as follows: Content standards "provide guidance for the design of instructional programs" and "a tool for checking the quality . . . in terms of coverage of expected knowledge and skills. Content standards tell us what we want our students to know and what we want them to be able to do" (p. 1). But they are "limited in their ability to improve student achievement because they do not tackle the crucial question of performance" (p. 1). Aligned performance measures are therefore necessary.

The original response to this need was to design separate, but matching or reflective "*performance standards.*" These, which contain specific performance indicators and performance tasks, more clearly describe "how good is good enough" (Council for Basic Education, 1996; McREL Institute, 1993). The statement of a "performance standard" is intended as a clearly discriminated "level of the bar" or model of acceptable performance. When properly

Table 4.1 Comparing Traditional Goals and Objectives with Standards

Goals and Objectives	*Standards*
☞ **Overall Goals** are general statements of the broader intents of the educational process. They may be stated for large groups of students at varying levels or for smaller groups at specific levels. They usually are neither specific nor suggest any action or measures.	☞ **Commencement level standards** resemble goals in their generality but describe the individual's capability at a specific terminal education point such as high school graduation. They may or may not have attached performance measures.
☞ **Objectives** are designed down from **goals.** Objectives may focus on the giver or the receiver: On the giver: *To prepare students to be good citizens.* On the receiver (behavioral objective): *Students will be able to make decisions that are good for society.*	☞ **Benchmark-level standards** are designed down from **exit or commencement level standards. Grade-level or course standards or outcomes** are designed down from benchmark standards. Standards focus on the receiver—although the receiver may be a group such as a school. *Students will become good citizens. Students will be able to make decisions that are good for society. The school will prepare students for the technological future.*
☞ Goals and objectives may be described in terms of a description of self, or in terms of conceptual or procedural knowledge. **Conceptual knowledge** objectives answer the question: "What should students know?" For example: *Students will know that selective burning is an effective measure for controlling forest fires.* **Procedural knowledge** objectives answer the question: "What should students be able to do?" *Students will be able to prevent forest fires.*	☞ Standards may be described in terms of a description of self, or in terms of conceptual or procedural knowledge. **Conceptual knowledge** standards answer the question: "What should students know?" For example: *Students will know that selective burning is an effective measure for controlling forest fires.* **Procedural knowledge** standards answer the question: "What should students be able to do?" *Students will be able to prevent forest fires.* Procedural knowledge standards that do not have specific performance measures (see Table 4.2) are **performance indicators.**

(Continued)

Table 4.1 (Continued)

Goals and Objectives	*Standards*
☞ **Behavioral objectives** may or may not have a level of performance stated; if they do, they are performance-based. *Students will be able to choose environmentally sound actions from a list with 80% accuracy.*	☞ If standards have specific performance indicators and performance tasks, they are **performance standards**. *Given a written problem situation, students will be able to describe three measures that prevent forest fires*. Performance standards are embedded in specific rubrics and more generally in state proficiency standards
☞ **Goals and Objectives are planning guides.**	☞ **Standards are prescriptions for creating uniformity.**

constructed, performance standards are translations of content standards that additionally provide specific measures or levels of attainment. An analogy that might help is to compare them to the two sides of your hand. The back of your hand defines its form and its potential, but the palm is the implement and measure of what it does. To help summarize the above definitions, Table 4.1 compares the current terminology content and performance standards to the historic usage of goals and objectives.

Some confusion about the application of the two related terms *content standard* and *performance standard* developed because of the overlap of skill-defining terms found in performance standard statements and similar statements that respond to the skill-defining second part of the content standard definition (what students should be able to do). Many standards documents therefore use the term *performance indicator*. These usually are the skill-defining parts of content standards and do not have embedded measures or levels of attainment. The widely adopted standards of the National Council of Teachers of Mathematics (1989, 2000) and many state documents are more representative of skill-defining content standards. To supplement the content standards and performance indicators, curriculum writers have resorted to assessment rubrics as a substitute for specific levels of performance. At the assessment policy level, *proficiency standards* have attempted to fulfill the need for measures. These are simply quantitative summaries of performance on an assessment. Unfortunately, as discussed in previous chapters, there is a critical need for better clarity and connections between the proficiency standards and the curriculum. I demonstrate how a rubric can incorporate a content-matching performance standard or proficiency standard in Chapter 6.

CURRICULUM ENACTMENT

Curriculum, in its current interpretation, implies the total school experience. Content standards represent a kind of planned vision for the desired results of the curriculum, and performance standards a design for measuring these results. Neither of these addresses the many other variables that affect what happens in schools: the day-to-day variations in students, teachers, and the classroom environment that more closely frame the "enacted curriculum" (Ball & Cohen, 1996). They are a destination without a road map. And in Weinstein's (1996) words, "Simply willing higher expectations without attention to effective teaching practices will not result in higher achievement" (p. 16).

The enacted curriculum is what ultimately affects student achievement, and it requires the equal attention of standards. Although standards attached to the variables of the enacted curriculum have been defined as "curriculum standards" or "opportunity to learn standards" (Council for Basic Education, 1996; McREL Institute, 1993), this may be confusing terminology. The term *curriculum* in its modern interpretation is broad and includes all of the facets of instructional delivery. "Opportunity to learn" has socially positive implications but encompasses such a broad scale of variables that I believe that it may be useful to group and separate the variables. I borrow from the historical term *enabling objectives,* which referred to the activities that supported the desired goals and objectives, and apply the term *enabling standards* to those often overlooked aspects of the school environment such as time, place, materials, and the training of teachers—or as I refer to it in Chapter 5, the setting. Although there may be some alternatives here, there are basic requirements that need to be stated as standards. I need my manipulatives to teach math! I need a place where my students can work in small groups. I need some uninterrupted time!

Reflecting on the traditional meaning of curriculum enactment as the actual experience in which the student is the engaged, the specific discourse and actions with materials, I hesitate to use the term *standard.* My hesitation is because of convincing evidence that these experiences need to be alternative, innovative, and child responsive. There is often more than one way to solve a problem and more than one way to reach a standard. The various classroom experiences and dialogues used to help students achieve standards are the "*enactment activities.*"

Table 4.2 illustrates the very important "design-down" or vertical articulation process, and Table 4.3 the horizontal articulation of content standards, performance indicators, and enabling standards. A general standard such as, "Students will be good problem solvers" can be met at many different levels and in the context of different content areas. Comparison samples of some

Figure 4.1 Curriculum Planning

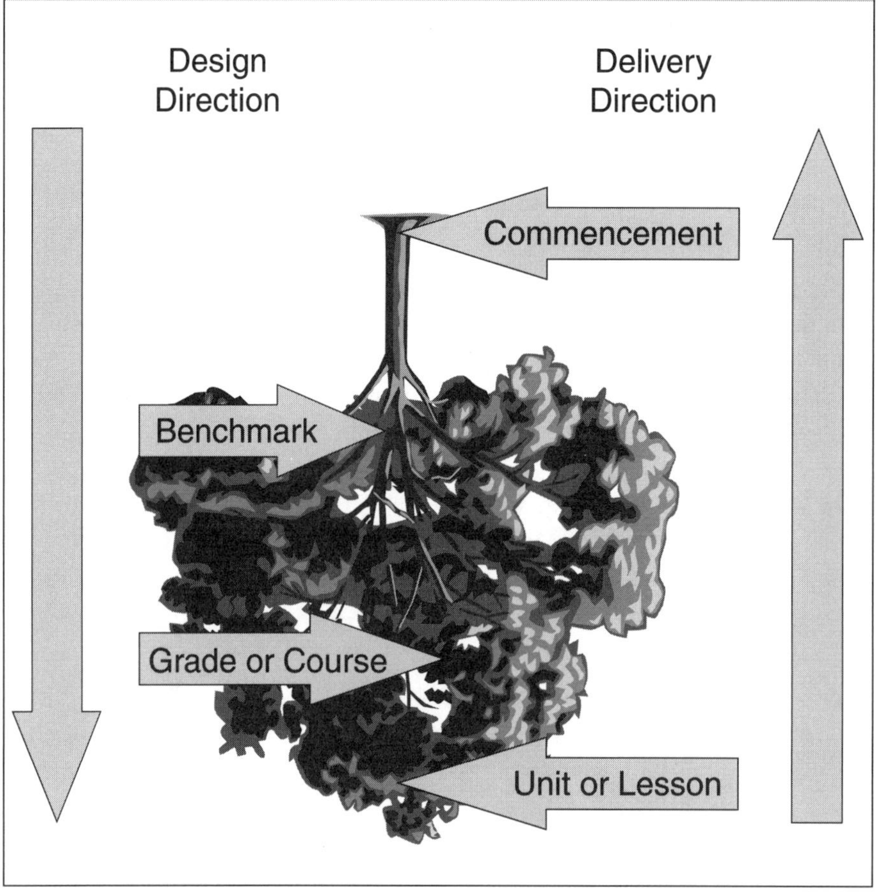

very specific and matched standards of each type appear in Tables 4.2 and 4.3, but the listed standards are not meant to be all-inclusive. It is in the enactment activities that there should be the greatest flexibility and choice. With consistency in the content and performance standards as the objective, teachers can be creative, responsive, and timely with the activities they use to achieve the standards.

The upside down tree in Figure 4.1 illustrates the design-down and delivery process. Like the trunk of a tree, the general standards support a widely reaching set of branches and leaves. Curriculum is designed down from the more general commencement or exit level to the more specific benchmark level and then to the even more specific level of the course, grade, and unit. But just as the leaves in turn must manufacture food and nurture the trunk, the more specific "designed-down" content standards must feed the general ones—they make the general ones happen. None of this works if the connections of internal flow are impeded. The junctures where twigs meet branches and branches meet a trunk are particularly important. The outcome of each lesson of the leaves is fed through a twig to the branch that is the unit and then into a larger one that is the grade level. Several grade levels may feed into a larger branch at a benchmark juncture and this, in turn, finally meets the main trunk. The tree is shown upside down because the design is the beginning and we think of the processes as "design down" and "deliver up."

At the same time, there must be horizontal articulation. As the leaves turn toward the sun, the carbon dioxide must enter them. The performance indicators must match the content standards and become part of the achievement measures. The enabling standards and enactment activities must be specifically designed to help students reach the stated standards. If the teachers' knowledge, materials, and allocation of time and space of the enabling standards are in place, and the enactment activity dialogues, experiences, and interactions in the social contexts of peers and adults are based on the teachers' carefully reviewed previous experience, students have a reasonable probability for achieving success.

Attention to a comprehensive design process can bring some needed coherence and clarity to planned school curriculums. However, the achievement of greater equity in the enacted curriculum for all students is a far greater challenge. The preplanned design is only the first step.

Tables 4.1, 4.2, and 4.3 are merely illustrations of possible articulations. I address the specifics of performance and enabling standards in greater detail in following chapters.

Getting Started on Planning Curriculum

As I have explained and illustrated in previous chapters, most of the standards that are being produced by the states and by national professional groups are very general. This gives the local school and individual teacher both the freedom and the responsibility to provide the specifics. This is as it should be, because unless teachers are directly involved in writing or choosing standards, their ownership in them will be diminished and implementation encumbered (Solomon, 1995). Meg, April, and Brad (from our scenarios) need to understand the above and then approach their task from a pragmatic point of view. Instead of feeling threatened by the charge to plan curriculum that addresses the new standards, they might seize this opportunity to carefully revisit what they are already doing and see how it does or doesn't fit.

There are a number of criteria to consider to determine the goodness of fit of the present program. Does it work to accomplish any mandated standards? Does it work to meet the social and motivational goals of their students, such as personal self-efficacy? Does it work for the teachers, giving them a sense of accomplishment and intrinsic reward? Does recent research on how learning takes place and constructivist theory, which states that each individual must construct his or her own knowledge, explain why it may or may not be effective?

In considering the enabling standards and enactment activities of their curriculum, teachers may also consider some new alternatives that have already been tried elsewhere. Current technology allows us unprecedented access to the work of others. The Internet is an astounding resource, but each situation is different; each population of students and the expectations of the community from which they come are different; the parameters of time and space are different. New alternatives must be carefully approached with the same and additional questions. What kind of additional outside help will we need to implement this new program? Will we be discarding something that is *asset specific* to us (House, 1996); something we do not wish to discard? Too often, we educators blindly buy into a new cleverly packaged program that we do not truly understand or that has little application for our present situation and needs.

Teachers now engaged in curriculum construction have to confront the general standards that have already been decided at a state, city, or district level. Powerful high-stakes assessments are based on them. An often neglected but critical component of this task is to examine each general standard and try to identify the more specific chunks of knowledge it encompasses. I call these *embedded concepts*. The general standards will require careful interpretation and the specificity of embedded concepts if they are to be of any value as a guide for teaching and learning. Examples of embedded concepts may be found in the designed-down content standards of Tables 4.2 and 4.6. A more complete set of designed-down elementary and middle school math concepts may be found in *The Math We Need to Know and Do* (Solomon, 2000).

A Template for Action

A good way for April, Meg, and Brad to get started on planning their new curriculum is to begin, as I did, with a first stage review of current knowledge of how learning takes place. An analysis of mandated standards and student results on previous assessments tests comes next or perhaps concurrently. They must ask themselves some simple questions that will further diminish their bounded rationality and help them bring clarity to the task.

- What specific embedded concepts do these standards and tests require **our students** to know?
- What specific procedures do they require **our students** to be able to do?

- How are the standards measured by the mandated tests?
- What will be the consequences of poor performance on these measures?

Next they might consider the feasibility of the task and the circumstances with which they will have to deal. These questions need to be answered:

- What is our students' present level of development? What are they ready for?
- What is our students' present level of knowledge? What do they already know?
- What are the missing chunks of knowledge?
- How can we help them achieve these standards (and what others)?
- How will their cultural differences, goals, and interests affect their ability to achieve the standards? How can we deal with these differences?
- What are our own resources of time (schedules, etc.), space, human energies, and materials? How much allotted time and space can we use for this purpose and how can we make some necessary adjustments? What other new resources will be available to us, such as new technology, books, manipulative materials, and teacher assistant time?

April, Meg, and Brad may need help from experts and colleagues who have already tackled the task. I address the potential for this in Chapter 7. Nevertheless, they should not forget the support they can give each other.

- How can we share the effort, the acquisition of resources and knowledge, the risks?

The answers to these questions and the decisions made in response to them form the framework for decisions about curriculum. The consequences that can be attached to lack of student achievement on the required measures of high-stakes standards-based (HSSB) tests may leave teachers with little choice or opportunity to be creative with the content standards and performance indicators. But as educators review these and simultaneously structure their enabling standards and enactment activities, greater clarity may surface and ways to adapt may be uncovered. If team teaching is a necessary time or space parameter to accomplish the new content standard, then that becomes an enabling standard. If Meg, April, and Brad believe that an outdoor experience is necessary to accomplish the new content standard of knowing how organisms interact with each other, and the ability to identify three different animal habitats in an outdoor setting is a performance indicator,

Table 4.2 "Designing Down" from Commencement Standards to Benchmarks and Courses

SOME VERTICAL ARTICULATION EXAMPLES

COMMENCEMENT-LEVEL CONTENT STANDARD: *Students Will Be Good Problem Solvers*

Benchmark Level I (sixth grade)

Content standard: *Students will understand and apply skills related to gathering, evaluating, interpreting, and presenting information.*

< Fourth-grade content standard: *Students will know that the length of the bar on a bar graph represents a measure and each bar represents a separate measure of data.*

< Matching fourth-grade performance indicator: *Students will be able to record sets of data and translate them into a bar graph.*

< Fourth-grade performance standard: Student records three different sets of data and makes graphic translation accurately.

Benchmark Level II (tenth grade)

Content standard: *Students will use formal and informal reasoning processes in applying problem solving, decision making, and negotiating techniques.*

< Algebra course content standard: *Students will know that and explain why subtraction of a negative integer results in an increase in value.*

< Matching algebra course performance indicator: *Students will be able to translate problem statements with negative integer values into symbolic subtraction equations and solve the equations.*

< Performance standard: *Student performs translations of subtraction problem statements with negative integers and solves the problems with 85% accuracy.*

COMMENCEMENT STANDARD: *Students Will Be Good Communicators*

Benchmark Level I (sixth grade)

Content standard: *Students will be able to communicate their thoughts and ideas in written form.*

< Fourth-grade content standard: *Students will know that a good topic sentence provides focus for a paragraph.*

< Matching fourth-grade performance indicator: *Students will be able to write paragraphs with focusing topic sentences.*

< Performance standard: *Students will write a book report that has topic sentences that provide four paragraphs with good focus.*

Benchmark Level II (tenth grade)

Content standard: *Students will understand the forms, techniques, and stylistic requirements of a variety of written communications.*

< Ninth-grade content standard: *Students will know the form and vocabulary for a persuasive essay.*

< Matching ninth-grade performance indicator: *Students will be able to write a persuasive essay.*

< Matching ninth-grade performance standard: *Students will write a persuasive essay that clearly delineates a point of view with at least four reasons that support it.*

Table 4.3 Horizontal Articulation Examples of Standards

Content Standards	***Performance Standards***	***Enabling Standards***
At Grade 1, students will know that: addition is an increase on the number line, subtraction is a decrease in the number line, and that there are also symbols (+ and –) for the operations.	*At Grade 1,* students will be able to provide the correct new number by counting on a number line when solving change/result unknown addition problems that simulate their own prior or present experience.	Grade 1 teachers will understand the sequence of the way research has told us students learn to add and subtract: from the changes on a number line to counting on and down from the first number to the more complex choices and interpretations of noncanonical problems. Classrooms will be provided with interactive technology and manipulative materials such as unifix cubes and bead frames.
At Grade 2, students will know that: addition (+) is a combining of parts to form a whole, and that subtraction (–) is a separation from the whole; that the parts and whole can be represented by number symbols representing the real amounts (referents). Students will have achieved the cardinal principle (see quantities as units) and not	*At Grade 2,* students will compute the correct new number by counting on (adding) from the first number or counting down (subtracting) from the first number, in change/result unknown problems, combine problems, and part unknown problems based on their own present or prior experience. Students will correctly identify the unit parts and whole in canonical and noncanonical problem forms.	Grade 2 teachers will structure appropriate problems and dialogue, diagnose student misconceptions, and use the necessary materials. Each Grade 2 student will have at least one uninterrupted hour for math each day, including some early morning time. Group problem solving with peer interaction will be integrated into every math lesson and supersede time spent on computation practice. Classrooms will be provided with interactive technology and manipulative materials such as color tiles and

then the outdoor experience becomes an enabling standard. Teachers in an inner-city system may have some difficulty with that enabling standard, but if it is understood as necessary, adjustments will have to be made—hopefully not in the content standard.

In the **second stage**, they can design their own matched performance measures for each standard and carefully evaluate their articulation with those that are mandated. These measures should answer the following questions: How will we know when students get there? And, How good is good enough? They also need to address such subquestions as the following:

- How reliable and valid are the measures?
- Are the assessments equitable in terms of the variations among my students?
- How easy are the assessments to administer?
- How meaningful are the interpretations to the parents and the students?
- What is the value to the child of the assessment experience?

The answers to these questions are the beginning framework for measures of **performance standards or assessment.** As previously noted, the specifics of the planning for enabling standards and activities that constitute **stage three** and the forms of teacher-constructed assessment will be further addressed in the following chapters, but the process of specifically clarifying expectations and measures ahead of time is in itself a worthwhile endeavor. For example, a traditional statement of a science objective or standard might be that, "Students will know the parts of a cell and their functions," but the parts that you may wish sixth graders to know are probably very different from the parts and functions that you wish a tenth grader to know. The measure of how well they know these parts will be different. A well-stated content standard will be more explicit about what parts and a well-constructed performance standard will describe exactly how to tell whether students know them. This may bring much greater clarity to some of the present curriculum fuzziness that sometimes exists.

If the task of adding explicit clarity to the standards is shared among teachers with common responsibilities, there is the greater advantage of social construction of new knowledge and the sharing of risks. Reaching consensus on everything may, however, be difficult, and absolute equity of resources may be unattainable. Individual alternatives for enabling activities may need to be considered. If they do not compromise the equity of expectation of all students in reference to the content standards, they should not be discouraged. Teachers need to meet their own needs for creativity and individuality, and the disparities of students, cultures, and learning environments require flexibility.

Figure 4.2 organizes the steps listed above in graphic form. As work for each content standard progresses, it will be useful to stop and reflect on some more specific criteria for assessing the quality of the proposed standards.

Figure 4.2 Building a Standards-Based Curriculum

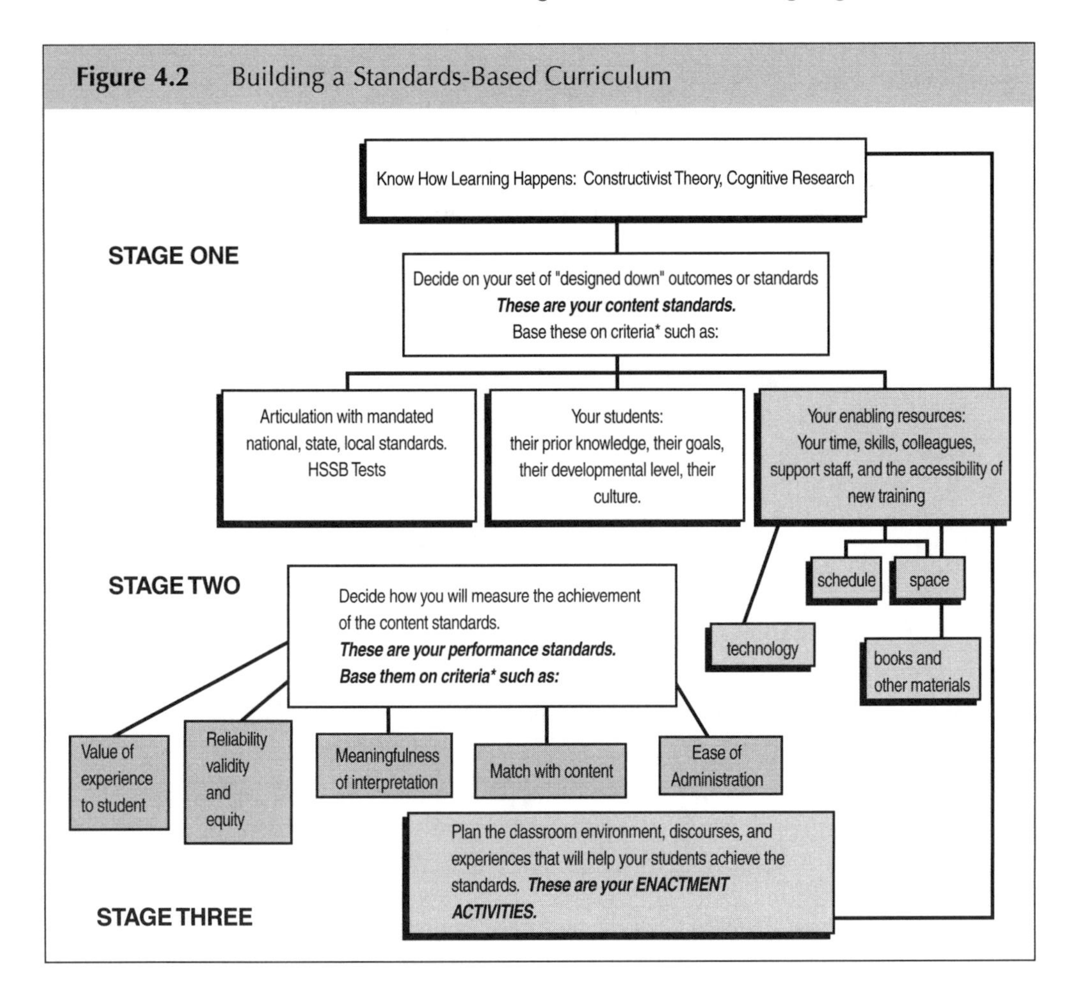

At the end of this chapter, Table 4.4 suggests criteria for evaluating locally chosen content standards and Table 4.5 provides a rubric for assessing a curriculum unit as a whole. Table 4.6 offers an example of the standards for a single unit. The assessment components for this unit and additional specific criteria and examples for enactment activities and assessments will be found in Chapters 5 and 6. These, again, are by no means all inclusive. **Individual teams and individual teachers should add their own criteria**. Students themselves can offer good suggestions for what they may need and what will work for them.

Once curriculum is documented it becomes a contract, an agreement to try to achieve what has been decided on. Although this contract requires respect and compliance, it should never be cast in stone. The curriculum has to be able to respond to the many variables of human interactions in a classroom. Most of this flexibility should be in the enactment activities. Teachers need to be free to try new approaches to reaching the common content standards. The timeliness of curriculum is also a factor that requires flexibility. Two years ago, I made entreaties to my students to learn to use the

Table 4.4 Sample Criteria for Evaluating the Content Standards of a Grade-Level Curriculum

The Content Standards: (Check all that apply and comply)
Meet mandated state, district, and local standards or nonmandated professional standards
Articulate with the commencement and benchmark standards or outcomes
Are realistic in terms of available resources of time
Are realistic in terms of available resources of space
Are realistic in terms of available resources of human energy
Are realistic in terms of available resources of materials
Are developmentally appropriate for the student
Respond to evidence from recent research on how learning happens
Challenge all students to reason with higher-order thinking skills
Are comprehensive and comprehensible
Pay attention to the potential for cross-disciplinary connections
Prepare children for life in a world of cultural and political differences
Are measurable by a matching performance standard
Meet the child's needs to succeed in the present and future societal context

searching capabilities of library computer networks. This year I cautioned them to be careful and critical of the unjuried publications on the Internet. Ten years ago my favorite suggested math problems for fourth graders involved the Power Rangers; they would turn kids off today. Owning or trading Nintendo computer games would be a better bet!

It also takes time for change to happen. In spite of the greater availability of ever-changing technology, some teachers are not yet comfortable with it. They may need time and other professional development resources to develop their own skills, and adjustments in the enabling standards may have to be made. Meg, April, and Brad may feel imposed upon by the external pressures of power and control that have energized this latest (and perhaps misinformed) public effort to improve our schools by setting common standards. They can, however, seize this timely opportunity to make the new standards work for them. The process of analyzing what they are now doing in reference to the more organized and ultimate purposes called for in the standards may help them focus together on a new and better way—or convince them that what they are already doing will be just fine. But the task should never really end. It requires constant reflection and adjustment, and support from all who care.

Table 4.5 A Rubric for Evaluating a Standards-Based Curriculum

Level 4: (Above Standard)
State standards clearly defined as content standards and performance standards
Designed-down unit standards articulated with state commencement standards and show clear and appropriate developmental levels toward reaching them
Unit enactment activities articulated to accomplish standards and inspire students to go beyond the standards
Performance measures designed to diagnose deficiencies in standards achievement and direct students and teachers toward remediation measures
Activities clearly outlined; creative and inspiring for others to follow
Technology creatively employed
Level 3: (At Standard)
State standards clearly defined as content standards and performance standards
Designed-down unit standards articulated with state commencement and benchmark standards
Unit enactment activities articulated to accomplish standards
Performance measures adequately measure standards
Activities clearly outlined for others to follow. Activities are original or appropriate adaptations.
Technology employed
Level 2: (Approaching Standard)
State standards clearly defined as content standards and performance standards
Some designed-down unit standards not appropriately articulated with state commencement and benchmark standards
Some unit enactment activities not articulated well enough to accomplish standards
Performance measures not articulated well enough to adequately measure standards
Some activities not outlined clearly enough for others to follow. Some originality.
Technology not adequately employed
Level 1: (Below Standard)
State standards not clearly defined as content standards and performance standards

(Continued)

Table 4.5 (Continued)

Designed-down unit standards not articulated with state commencement and benchmark standards
Unit enactment activities not articulated well enough to accomplish standards
Performance measures not articulated well enough to adequately measure standards
Enactment activities not outlined clearly enough for others to follow. Little originality.
Technology not applied

Table 4.6 Sample Curriculum Standards Design

The subject and grade level that this unit aims for. Mathematics Grade 2
The in-school time total for this unit. Two weeks
The theme or topic of this unit. Addition, operations and patterns

Commencement content standard: *What students should know and be able to do when they graduate*

New York State Standard 3: Mathematics, Science, and Technology.

Students will understand mathematics and become mathematically confident by communicating and reasoning mathematically, by applying mathematics to real-world settings, and by solving problems through the integrated study of number systems, geometry, algebra, data analysis, probability, and trigonometry.

- **Benchmark content standards:** Elementary

Number and Numeration: Students use number sense and numeration to develop an understanding of multiple uses of numbers in the real world, use of numbers to communicate mathematically, and use of numbers in the development of mathematical ideas.

Table 4.6: This curriculum standards design is based on the "design-down" process depicted in Figure 4.1. It is not the complete unit, only an adapted sample of the standards stated. The entire unit is accessible with permission from teacher writer Andrea Holland, on the Internet at www.stac.edu/mcc/indexrev.htm.

Operations: Students use mathematical operations and relationships among them to understand mathematics.

Patterns: Students use patterns and functions to develop mathematical power, appreciate the true beauty of mathematics, and construct generalizations that describe patterns simply and efficiently.

- **Unit embedded concepts and performance indicators**

The children will know that:

- The addition process is the combining of parts to make a whole.
- The symbol (+) represents the combination of parts to make a whole.
- The symbol (–) represents a separation of a part from the whole.
- Like parts must be combined separately (ones and ones) (tens and tens)
- The total sum is the combination of the sum of the ones and tens.

The children will be able to:

- Use the symbols (+) and (–) in written representations of word problems
- Create, extend, and identify 2-part patterns using a variety of materials.
- Use manipulatives to explore number sentences, operations and their relationship, and the cumulative property of addition.
- Successfully add and subtract using 2-digit numbers without trading.

5 Constructing Creative Classrooms

Striving for Equity

ABOUT THIS CHAPTER

Meg was determined to find some justification for adding the science kit activities she had previously enjoyed to the new curriculum. She searched her closet for the state curriculum guide she remembered storing but had rarely referred to. It was never mandated and there was no test in science at her grade. She had always more or less followed the directions in the kits she had ordered from a commercial supply company. There were some sections in a science textbook that she had students read from time to time, but these seemed unrelated to the kits. The students also produced some interesting things for the annual school science fair, but Meg always felt that the competition was unfair to students whose parents couldn't help.

In the past, the basic curriculum has not traditionally been prescribed in most states, merely recommended.[1] In New York, for example, long before the new standards were generated, recommended state and local curriculum documents were written, disseminated, and updated from time to time by state employees working with teacher committees. Nevertheless, with the exception of high school Regents courses, where the assessments were specifically based on the content of the written documents, the formal objectives of written curriculums were often ignored by classroom teachers (Ball & Cohen, 1996). New HSSB assessments at the elementary and middle school levels, in their effect, mandate curriculum.

The disparity between the written and enacted curriculum has been attributed to several factors, including the lack of preparation of teachers to teach in new ways, their own individualistic need to be creative, and their imperative to respond to the individual needs of students (Sarason, 1983, 1990; Solomon, 1995). Even when curriculums are developed and contracted by teams of user teachers, they are often not consulted and left to collect dust on closet shelves—unless they are rich in the details of suggested student experience activities and materials. Meg and her colleagues tended to focus more on the activities and less on specific desired ends. Good activities and materials were what Meg needed to make her day successful. She assumed that if these worked with her students, in the long run and over time the outcomes or objectives in the written curriculum would come automatically. And, based on previous records of success, this often did happen; but not all the time.

Activities and materials are the stuff of classroom environments, the everyday plans and teacher choices. Unfortunately, these choices are sometimes based on factors such as habits of practice, student control, teacher interest and comfort, and on the availability of the materials and other resources, instead of on how well they will accomplish a particular desired standard. The choices teachers make may also be constrained by forces outside their control, such as school schedules and grouping or tracking policies.

The ultimate expectation of the educational reformers who insist on higher standards for the students of this nation is that written and agreed-on standards will have a positive effect on educational outcomes. This belief is based on the assumption that the problems of some groups of students were caused by a lack of equity in expectations. But these expectations in their written standard form will again collect dust on a closet shelf if the environment that is created for every child does not enable them to happen. It is the possibility of equity in the enabling standards that offers the educational community the greatest promise for improvement in its endeavors. In this chapter I address these standards of the environment and the enactment activities that energize them.

ORGANIZING THE ENVIRONMENT

Teaching has frequently been described as performance. Perhaps it may be useful to take the students out of the audience, place them into the action as performers, and then continue the metaphor by adding the other elements of effective drama. The ultimate theater of the school environment revolves around three pivots: the setting and its props, the actors (including the student-performers and the teacher-director), and the dialogue and movements of the script. If everything works, when the classroom curtain is raised, we may have an educational hit!

Included in the instructional setting are factors that research has related to the rate of learning, such as student group formations (including those of tracking and cooperative learning), the use of time and space, the props of materials and technology, and other classroom management elements. The effectiveness of the setting on the performance of the actors hinges on many other components. The student-performers must be engaged, alerted to new perceptions, connected to prior experience, and driven by personal and social goals that enhance rather than deter the knowledge construction process. The teacher-director must have outcomes in mind, but be open to and ready to seize upon the unexpected ones. Expectations and directions need to be communicated with clarity. The varying talents, personalities, skills, and prior experiences of the actors must be considered and incorporated into both group and individual plans for new growth, adaptations, or corrections.

The dialogue and physical interactions of the script are critical. Not just the words count, but who speaks to whom and in what form and with what emphasis. The positions and nonverbal signals of the performers and director are significant. The script elements also include scaffolding the stretch across the zone of proximal development or, as Steffe and D'Ambrosio (1991) have redefined it, the *zone of potential construction;* directing and creating new perceptions; assessing and stimulating prior knowledge; nurturing and adapting goals; and suggesting metacognitive strategies.

Each of these pivots of the theater of school learning is discussed below with reference to how they connect to our knowledge of how learning takes place, and is accompanied by specific suggestions for creating productive environments.

The Setting: Organizing Groups of Students

Among the attempts made to deal with the achievement gap in urban areas has been the creation of smaller school units, sometimes based solely on student interests and other times based on a combination of interest and prior achievement. There is gathering evidence that the smaller school environment creates a more controllable and nurturing setting for learning. Closer relationships with parents and community; more frequent and closer interactions among teachers, administrators, and students; goal focusing; intensive professional development; and a shared and individual culture are among possible reasons for the success of smaller schools (Wasley & Lear, 2001). The anonymity of individual students and the possibility of overlooking their needed adult attention is certainly diminished. Teachers sharing the same smaller groups have greater ability to communicate about students with colleagues and create coordinated plans and activities for them. The question of the benefits of separation into smaller groups based on ability has, on the other hand, been the subject of much debate among educators and the public. Special programs for higher achievers or "gifted" students are highly subject to the influences of parents, often with the support of other political entities and the entrenched beliefs of school personnel (Wells, Hirschberg, Lipton, & Oakes, 1995). Similar influences are exerted by some groups of parents of students who have been identified as having minor learning disabilities and in need of special education.

Homogeneous grouping of students based on ability or achievement can be accomplished in several different forms. In addition to the formation of whole special schools, there is a continuing practice of within-school grouping. The major dichotomy within schools is inter-class grouping, in which large groups of students are tracked into special classes, and within-class grouping, in which there are small groups formed within a class that are based on differential abilities. Traditional reading groups are an example of the latter. There are also variations, such as regrouping of students among teams of classes for different subjects. Within-class homogeneous grouping is much less politically volatile, and is suggested as the inclusion alternative for the spiraling growth of special education classes.

Another less political but much more difficult approach to implement is differentiated instruction. Differentiated instruction considers the very varied needs and interests of the individual student as the basis for choosing appropriate curriculum enactment activities. Tomlinson (2000) sees no conflict between standards and differentiation—as long as the standards determine "what to teach" not "how" (p. 8). The problems inherent in individually differentiated instruction are similar to those related to the individualized instruction of the 1970s and 1980s. The potential loss of interaction among students and the tendency to rely on independently completed worksheets, when coupled with the strain on teacher energies, diminish its chances for success. Perhaps a compromise is ongoing individual analyses of student needs coupled with differentiated activities for small within-class groups.

The research evidence on the effectiveness of grouping is mixed. In multianalytic studies Slavin (1987, 1990) found little academic gain but no detriment for students placed for the full day into homogeneous whole (inter-class) groups, but he does not recommend such grouping. Instead, he suggests various homogeneous within-class groups. Kulik (cited in Allan, 1991) found, in contrast, that there was an advantage for high ability students in whole-class homogeneous settings, somewhat less of an advantage for middle ability students, and none for low ability students.

In a more recent review of the effects of within-class groupings, Lou et al. (1996) studied 145 research reports and discovered that while middle-level students gained the most from homogeneous groupings, lower-level students benefited most from heterogeneous groups, and higher-level students showed no significant difference between their performances in the two group forms. In addition to their important overall discovery that achievement was significantly greater in classes organized into small groups than it was in classes that were instructed in whole class groups, Lou et al. found other interesting and affecting group factors. The level of teacher training, the size of the groups, and the subject matter made a difference. As would be expected, better teacher preparation increased the positive effects of organizing students into small groups, and smaller size groups of three or four students were more effective than larger groups. Math and science benefited more from small-group work than reading and language arts—perhaps because they had the added component of problem solving. And in an unsurprising and much supported finding, they concluded that small groups accompanied by the cooperative learning element of structured interdependence between group members were the most effective (e.g., Johnson & Johnson, 1989; Qin, Johnson, & Johnson, 1995).

Connections to our understanding of how learning takes place explain these findings. From the goal and control perspective, the small-group setting nurtures the human need for control of the learning process; interactive dialogue and time and movement adjustments are easier and more frequent. Small groups proffer satisfaction of the social goal of peer affinity (the group needs to learn this and I belong to it). They provide more opportunities for achieving a sense of self-efficacy (there are more chances for venturing an answer and there is less risk for a wrong answer). They have the advantage of sharing metacognitive strategies and receiving reminders and corrections from peers as the group proceeds—especially if the context is one of problem solving.

From the cognitive perspective, there are increases in perceptions from the interactive dialogue and greater opportunities for students to experience disequilibrium, discrepant events, or dissatisfaction with currently held constructs that will prepare them to revise, enlarge, or correct these constructs. There are mediating peers to scaffold the stretch across the *zone of potential construction,* and freedom for students to think out loud as they construct new knowledge.

For students grouped in lower-level homogeneous groups these advantages may be diminished. They lose the advantage of scaffolding by more capable students, especially if these students are responsible for this—and there is evidence that higher ability students ask more complex questions. Certainly, the label of being in the lower group may decrease their feelings of self-esteem. Higher-level students in heterogeneous groups may lose some of the advantage of having the more challenging and complex questions of additional high-level students, but this may be overridden by the greater feeling of efficacy and the cognitive advantage of having to communicate constructs to others (the best way to learn something is to teach it).

I distinctly remember that my own children had less than accurate self-concepts when they were placed in highly competitive homogeneous groups of high achievers and did not end up at the top of the class. It was only when they had the opportunity to compare themselves to the real world that these self-concepts became more realistic. In consideration of the above, I offer the following suggestion for enabling standards:

Suggestions for Standards and Enactment Activities

Enabling standards that include a heterogeneous classroom organized into within-class small groups that have both individual accountability and interdependence are desirable because they increase the potential to accomplish content and performance standards. Moreover, the content and performance standards themselves may need to include the skills necessary for collaborative effort.

Where possible and when needed, enactment activities may be further differentiated to meet individually diagnosed student needs.

The Setting: Allocations of Time

The research base that would provide a firm rationale for deciding enabling standards of time and space is very slim, but schools have been sensitive to their influence and responded. In a previous publication on the role of time in effecting school change (Solomon, 1995), I defined time in three perspectives, as a resource, in its passage, and in its sense of timeliness. It may be useful to pursue these perspectives here as well. In respect to time as a resource for learning, a well-circulated government publication called *Prisoners of Time* (National Education Commission on Time and Learning, 1994) outlines how schools are constrained by the inherited schedules of an agrarian society and illustrated how little time is allocated to actual instruction. Although it is difficult to manage changes in structures that are firmly entrenched in our national culture, some schools are attempting to increase allocated time by experimenting with radically different calendars such as the 12-month school year. Until such changes are widespread, plans and specifications for the best use of allocated time may be a critical part of the enabling standards.

Allocated time is itself subject to the actual engagement or attention of the student to the task that is designed to help construct knowledge. The attention of students within planned activities will be discussed in the sections below in reference to the management of goals and dialogue, but school routines and time schedules are external variables that can be adjusted to guarantee that interruptions in the enactment activities will be at a minimum. Elementary schools have tried inviolate time periods when no students are pulled out for special classes and all interschool messages are withheld in an attempt to maintain momentum and maximize allocated time. Interruptive low priority activities that have little impact on learning can also be evaluated and made more efficient or eliminated (Saphier & Gower, 1997).

At the secondary level, a major difficulty has been the disruptive nature of short time periods and the constant movement of students from one place and subject to another. In response, innovative middle school schedules with four longer period days in a six-day schedule and class sequences where concept development classes are followed by individual progress groups have been attempted and proven successful (Canady & Rettig, 1995). High schools have tackled the time problem with longer blocks of time that treat fewer subject classes in a single day, but cover all the content subjects by the end of a trimester school year (Edwards, 1995; Stumpf, 1995).

There is no doubt that spending more uninterrupted and engaged time on teacher- or peer-mediated learning activities will increase the rate of construction of the knowledge expected by the new standards, but we must also consider time from the perspective of its passage. Students develop over time; they may not be ready to add new perceptions or discard old ones. Some students will need more time than others to make new constructions. The stretch across the *zone of potential construction* may have to occur in small increments. The enactment activities must recognize and provide for these variations. The relatively short brain-processing lifetime of the goals of the rational band that control learning may have to be considered.

Some interesting new cognitive research has demonstrated the impact of time on the control of memory by goals. In explanations of cognitive processing, scientists use the term *goal* to refer to a mental representation of an intention to accomplish a task, achieve some specific state of the world, or take some mental or physical action. Educators alternately refer to goals as those dispositions, the previously stored attitudes and interests that motivate the learning process, that may affect the intention to accomplish a task. The strength of a particular primary goal to engage the brain activity in cognitive processes varies over time, quickly reaching a crescendo of power before losing strength and becoming more vulnerable to being subsumed by distractions and other different goals (Altmann & Trafton, 2002). Small and carefully focused goal-directing scaffolds that grab attention quickly and defer distractions may be the most effective. Old-fashioned teacher tricks, such as hitting the desk with a ruler to emphasize an important idea or as a signal to elicit a related question from students, work. The research now tells us why.

Timeliness is another factor to consider. Receptivity to the acquisition of new knowledge varies over the school day. For the brain to work at its optimum in processing new perceptions and adapting prior constructs, it must be well-nourished, untired, and uncluttered. Elementary teachers have always recognized this, and because they usually consider reading as their highest priority, they teach that in the early morning. If students are expected to reach higher standards in math, then the allocation of some of that early morning time may have to become an enabling standard.

The effectiveness of enactment activity choices may also be governed by timeliness and its connected cultural relevance. The occurrence of a startling weather phenomenon is the best time to study weather. The Olympic events are a good time to study the history of Greece or its influence on our culture. A presidential election is the time to consider our democratic processes, the statistical processes in poll taking, or the power of the written or spoken words of our media. Teachers have always capitalized on such high-interest events. Situational interest is a motivating goal that positively mitigates the cognitive process.

In contrast, anachronistic and culturally irrelevant connections can be dysfunctional. Children's goals change rapidly in response to their own development and cultural influences. Their culture is more than the home environment; it is their peers, the latest TV commercial or show, Disney film, or for teenagers, pop record, movie star, or athlete. The Pokemon toys that were an excellent foil for math problems and reading activities last year may not work today, but Harry Potter books and Star Wars applications might. Timeliness, in respect to the receptivity of students at a particular stage of development and within their current culture, is one of the many reasons why teachers should have flexibility in the creation of enabling activities—and another reason why quickly outdated and externally designed curriculum materials packages don't always work.

Suggestions for Standards and Enactment Activities

Adequate, engaged, uninterrupted and high-energy time must be provided and guarded. Students need some flexibility in the time it takes to achieve the standards. Performance standards should reflect these differences. Enactment activities should be developmentally appropriate, timely, and responsive to changing culture, student goals, and interest.

The Setting: Allocations of Space and Place

The concept of open schools and classrooms had a brief period of enthusiasm in the 1960s. Some new schools were built without walls between classrooms and with open shared spaces. The theory behind them was that this openness would provide students and teachers with greater flexibility and freedom in their learning space. Classrooms would change from the pattern of a single teacher in front of the whole class into a more student-centered learning environment. Unfortunately, the teaching methods did not change with the change in environment, and teachers in these new settings attempted to teach in their ordinary teacher-directed and isolated way. They suffered feelings of anxiety and frustration with the lack of privacy and the increased distractions of their colleagues' classes. Good teacher-to-teacher peer relationships sometimes deteriorated.

Flexible arrangements of space are necessary for classrooms that nurture student needs for autonomy and support their differing intelligences and learning styles. Some children need to have a private and undistracted space in which to study. The need for privacy may itself be a controlling human goal, and some students may require the diminished distractions of a private place to process new perceptions. I remember one particular classroom with a study loft that was a favorite place for students to retreat with a book to read or for small groups to prepare a presentation in private. A similar loft for small-group work that doubles as a puppet theater is described by George (1995). Arrangements of classroom space into activity centers that challenge the many senses and allow for student choices have been effectively used for a number of years because they are congruent with cognitive processing and the preemptive goal management I discuss below.

If content and performance standards call for students to work in teams, to assume greater responsibility for their own learning, and to have the ability to apply knowledge to the real situations of our rapidly changing technological society, the spaces of the traditional classroom may not work. If the promises of educational technology are to be realized, it must be accessible to every child. Cooperative learning requires spaces for groups to work with face-to-face interaction. Research centers and demonstration preparation centers will be necessary to meet the more authentic performance indicators (see Chapter 6). The provision of instructionally functional space has become a critical enabling standard.

In some cases it may be advantageous to move outside of the classroom into the other spaces in order to create the appropriate setting. There is no better place to study the environment than an outdoor setting. A recent visit to a Challenger Space Center had me and a group of fifth graders in awe. We were transported in separate groups into the control center and into the space-ship. Communication was via computer, and teams of students performed duties such as medical monitoring, communication, probe launching, and environment control. We were completely absorbed in solving one problem after another and depended upon each other for solutions. In a math and science enrichment program that I manage for secondary students on

Saturday mornings, the place for instruction is where science happens: a pharmaceutical laboratory set up with robotics or a geological research facility actively recording seismographic readings. We may not be able to create such simulations in our classrooms, but we do have a growing number of props to help us.

Suggestions for Standards and Enactment Activities

Enabling standards for learning environments should provide space for face-to-face interaction between students working in small groups, and space for activities that support and nurture variations in intelligence and student goals. Enactment activities should, where possible and indicated, move outside of the classroom into more realistic spaces.

The Setting: The Props of Materials and Technology

Within the classroom space setting are the many props of materials and technology that create new perceptions, lead to dissatisfaction with prior concepts, and develop plausibility and comfort with new or adapted ones. They are a vital component of enabling standards, but need to be carefully chosen. Commercial interests promote a variety of materials that easily appeal to overburdened and anxious teachers who do not have the time to create their own. Critical questions to be asked before deciding on materials include: What evidence is there that these materials will provide enactment activities that can help students reach our chosen content and performance standards? Do we know how to use them? Can they be easily replaced with more cost-effective, more culturally relevant, or more interest-stimulating substitutes?

My own program evaluation research as an educator in school and university settings as well as that of so many others demonstrates the value of using concrete materials that increase perception and nurture varied intelligences, but too often the props are seen as the entire solution. For example, the omnipresent elementary science kits with hands-on materials for student exploration have intrinsic value in that they satisfy children's goals to use all of their senses, and the resulting new perceptions can lead to new constructions. But to ensure the development of complex new concepts in the consensual domain—the set of universal or commonly held beliefs that constitute the **content standards**—the teacher mediator still needs to set the stage for the stretch across the *zone of potential construction* with appropriate dialogue. This may be difficult for many elementary teachers, who are themselves uncomfortable with science concepts. Even high school science teachers sometimes neglect to make the necessary connections between the content they wish their students to learn and the cookbook labs they schedule because they are convenient and familiar.

The many new manipulatives for mathematics instruction are wonderful—I cannot envision working without them. The manipulatives are motivating and necessary because they respond to the often-neglected kinesthetic intelligence, create new kinesthetic and spatial perceptions, simulate realistic problems, facilitate reasoning, and promote the construction of conceptual knowledge. But they, too, are analogies for the real thing and are only as good as the meaningfulness of the problems they are meant to solve and the reasoning that goes into their solutions. The teacher still has to do some instructional mapping for students as they use the material in order to stretch them to a new concept and generalization that then works in new situations without the presence of manipulatives. I have discovered, moreover, that some children quickly reason abstractly and become annoyed with manipulatives; others, and some adults, need them longer.

Although modern textbooks are designed for eye appeal and rarely do a good job of unaided concept development, they do respond to the needs of those with linguistic and spatial intelligence and they can be useful as one source of new perceptions. Single-topic trade books with good narrative form and other types of children's literature may be better choices to engage students and allow them to independently construct new knowledge in their interaction with what is, after all, a social artifact. Written texts nurture and are needed for the further development of linguistic intelligence. They are not, however, an adequate or complete substitute for the teacher's dialogue, peer interactions, or for the other kinds of more realistic experiences (see Chapter 2). Enactment activities that combine the reading of text and writing are more effective. Mediation of the reading of texts and other literary artifacts by teachers using dialogue constructions are a necessary adjunct for most students. Particular constructions such as those used in reciprocal teaching have been proven effective. I discuss these below.

Interactive technology offers much promise. The substantive research evidence that would prove the effectiveness of technology applications to the instructional process is not yet available. Most of what we have are descriptions of students and programs in action. But when these observations are related to what we already know about what works, it is easy to predict the outcomes. Interactive technology combines goal-satisfying student control with stimulation of spatial, linguistic, and kinesthetic intelligence. It provides the immediate feedback that verifies efficacy and helps create disequilibrium if the new perceptions do not agree with prior knowledge. By offering choices at varying levels, it allows for developmental differences.

As I watched my grandson, Edward, play with a computer learning game, I was amazed. Without any formal reading instruction, he learned to read the necessary instructions and choices in a program meant for slightly older children. Some of it was trial and error, but when the problem was not easily surmounted he became only momentarily frustrated, discovered a way out, and tried something else. He was also persistent with follow-up attempts to correct the same stumble. There was no one to deride his mistakes and instant gratification for his successes. He punctuated and communicated them with a resounding "yessss!" He preferred to have me or a peer at his side as he worked and called for my help sometimes, but readily accepted the challenge to discover how to do it himself.

Short of worldwide travel, what better way is there to learn about our vast world culture than to correspond over the Internet with students in other countries or to access, at will, video clips that depict the places they live in? I watch third and fourth graders use the PowerPoint presentation to prepare a social studies report for the class. They have researched the Internet, used an on-line encyclopedia, pulled in some video clips and their own photographs, and word-processed their original coordinating dialogue. The challenge for us now is to ensure equity for all students by making the enabling standards of technology a requisite adjunct to the content and performance standards, and we need to learn how to work them into our overall plans for constructing the classroom environment.

Technology will help us meet the challenge of new content standards and help us prepare our students for life in a technologically rich world. It must be considered as a high-priority enabling standard, but not the only one. Not all of the new software is good, and we need to avoid overdependence on it. It is all too new for us to reach any firm conclusions, but it is my prediction that technology will never completely eliminate the need for teacher mediation of the learning process, replace the mind-stimulating experience of face-to-face peer interaction, or be a substitute for counting individual pieces of candy to achieve the concept of one-to-one correspondence.

In summary, the props of the educational theater must place the teacher and the student in the center of the enactment. The materials should not be in control, or as Ball and Cohen (1996) suggest: the traditional boundaries between teachers' teaching and the material's presentation of content may need to be redrawn. One of the most powerful uses of props in theater (with devastating effect) has been the use of the cigarette. Those of us old enough to remember the scene in *Now Voyager* in which Bette Davis and Paul Henried share cigarettes, will also recall, however, that it was the involvement of the performers and the power of the script that made the props work.

Suggestions for Standards and Enactment Activities

Enabling standards should include opportunities for teachers to learn how to *choose and use* educational materials (texts, packaged curriculum guides, manipulatives, and technology). Materials need to be provided and carefully articulated with the content and performance standards as well as with varying student interests and abilities. The presence of educational technology may be a critical enabling standard. However, the enactment of curriculum by teachers and students, not the materials, should be at the center.

THE ACTORS

The Director

Continuing the metaphor of classroom environment as theater, our attention is now drawn to the actors. In addition to the aspects of classroom management that were described above as components of the setting, it is the responsibility of the teacher-director to manage and control the actors so that they are engaged and attentive to the tasks prescribed. One key to success for this endeavor may be the effective management of student goals. As I have stressed a number of times, human goals control learning. They can promote it, but they can also undermine it. In addition to considering the prior knowledge of the learner, and reflecting on previous instructional experience with a selected activity, teacher-directors must pay attention to student goals as they set up the zone of construction. For example, there is, undoubtedly, a strong human need to control the environment. If it appears to the individual that new knowledge is required for this control, then the learner will probably "go for it." If learning what others have prescribed appears to the individual to have nothing to do with personally desired control of the environment, or more significantly that the prescription for learning interferes with other personal goals, there is, instead, resistance.

A third grader who has not met with much success in learning mathematics experiences little sense of power or efficacy when that subject is being taught, and may make an effort at that time to satisfy more personal goals. The time may be used to gain the attention and approbation of peers with a joke, or to play with a more interesting new toy; the student satisfies a competing social goal and is disengaged. Other goals such as social compliance can, for a while, overcome this distraction; goal revision via experiences of success, planned and strengthened by effective teaching, will over time work the best.

A hungry elementary child may be dealing with physical urges that wipe out other stimuli. An emotionally insecure middle school preadolescent or a high school student concerned with personal safety may find it difficult to put aside the retrieval of conflicting memories and ideas. In each case the zone of construction of new knowledge is too wide or nonexistent. Prior relevant knowledge is not retrieved and new perceptions are unprocessed.

Preemptive Goal Management

The techniques that teachers may employ in the task of nurturing goals that positively mediate learning can be divided into preemptive and contingent/corrective categories. Preemptive goal management can be embedded in the enactment activities, but contingent/corrective management of students' goals usually boils down to the behavioral punishment and reward procedures of traditional classroom discipline. Both require an understanding of human goals.

New knowledge gained from recent research has added to extensive prior findings that explain how goals control the learning process, but also require some theory revision. Early emphasis in the investigation of the relationship between motivation and achievement focused on the influences of human needs such as the need for power, the need for achievement, and the need for affiliation (Murray, 1938, cited in Urdan & Maehr, 1995). Later research examined the differential achievement of students motivated either by task (mastery) goals, which value the outcome of learning for its intrinsic value of knowing, or by performance (ability) goals, which, more egotistically, value the social prestige that higher grades or other evidences bring from comparisons with others. In these studies, task goals were associated with more effective performance, greater retention, and more in-depth knowledge (Dweck & Leggett, 1988; Pintrich, Marx, & Boyle, 1993). The two kinds of goals appeared at first to be dichotomous and mutually exclusive—students motivated by either one or the other.

Recent evidence has shown the influences of goals to be much more complicated. A variety of social goals has the potential for both positive and negative effects on achievement depending upon the cultural norms, and the particular context (Wentzel, 1989, 1993). For example, in cultures where achievement is valued as a contribution to the group rather than as an accomplishment for the individual, the more social-performance goals have the same effect on learning as task-mastery goals. Goals based on compliance with parents and teachers may be more effective in societies or ethnic groups where the sense of self is derived from affiliation with parents. A strong task-mastery goal orientation may even be dysfunctional in a society where group rather than individual efforts are rewarded.

Even within heterogeneous populations, the desire by an individual for affiliation with a high-performing peer group can result in greater achievement.

In contrast, the need for acceptance by a low-performing peer group can have the opposite effect. In some situations, it may be beneficial to have a combination of task-mastery and ability-performance goals. Cooperative learning environments that provide structures for individual accountability and group interdependence are examples of multiple goals acting in tandem.

A substantial body of research has investigated the relationship between achievement and self-concept (Anderman & Maehr, 1994). A strong self-concept has been generally associated with better performance. Recently, self-concept has been recognized as a complex construct that can be subdivided into sub-categories such as self-worth, self-esteem or sense of self in relation to others (how do I compare), and self-efficacy or the "beliefs in one's capabilities to organize and execute the courses of action required to manage prospective situations" (Bandura, cited in Pajares, 1996, p. 2). Feelings of self-efficacy that are related to a specific task (I can learn to skate well) seem to have a greater effect on the ultimate performance than more general feelings of positive self-esteem (I am a capable person).

Many researchers seek to demonstrate that variations in general self-esteem explain the differences between performances, but find ambivalent evidence that it does. Those who hypothesized that differences between various ethnic groups can be attributed to differences in self-esteem have in recent studies found these differences to be changing over time and less significant or ambivalent predictors of varying performance then previously believed (see Cooper & Dorr, 1995; Graham, 1995).

Teachers should, however, be interested in the considerable effects of self-efficacy on the construction of knowledge. Self-efficacy is much more specific in that it relates to a specific task rather than an overall feeling about one's ability. That specificity makes it a stronger predictor of ultimate performance (Pajares, 1996).

The motto "believe you can achieve" is posted all over a school I visit frequently, and I am sure that it has some positive self-esteem effect, but it is Melinda O'Neill, a teacher who provides carefully chosen, step-by-step, developmentally appropriate transitional experiences and supportive dialogue, who reinforces students' confidence to achieve a particular task and ensures the best performance. She begins her build-up of self-efficacy by giving students choices for activities within their cooperative groups; when they successfully complete the easier ones, she slowly cajoles them with cautious encouragement to try harder ones. Curriculum should include a range of enactment activities that reinforce competence and challenge students further. Enabling standards may have to include opportunities for teachers to learn how to assess, manage, and change student goals preemptively, just as they have done correctively in the past.

Suggestions for Standards and Enactment Activities

Content standards should include step-by-step progressions that allow students to gain self-efficacy in particular tasks. Matching performance standards should allow for multiple assessment forms that will not undermine self-efficacy. Task-mastery goals are more effective than performance goals and have longevity. We want our students to attempt new tasks because they feel good about achieving the tasks—not merely because they want to be better than their peers. Nevertheless, cultural and micro-social variations in the weight of task-mastery and performance goals and in social-compliance goals should be considered. Combinations of these goals may be a viable alternative. Cooperative learning can provide this kind of preemptive goal management.

Contingent-Corrective Goal Management

Gold stars have been around for a long time. They have been somewhat replaced by happy face stickers and other tokens. My grandson, Edward, received them on his nursery school papers all of the time. He never pointed them out to me. Instead, he proudly displayed the new letter he has written all by himself on the back of the ditto sheet that required him to trace the letter. Although teachers have consistently used contingent extrinsic rewards such as gold stars with apparent effect as a means of controlling student goals, there is some evidence that, when expected, these rewards may not be the most effective form of goal management in that they undermine the pursuit of intrinsic rewards and consequent self-motivation for further engagement in similar tasks (Deci, Koestner, & Ryan, 2001; Kohn, 1993, 1996; Lepper, Keavney, & Drake, 1996; Ryan & Deci, 1996).

The strength of this negative effect of extrinsic rewards on the development of intrinsic motivation is, however, questioned by Cameron (2001). Cameron suggests that policymakers reserve judgment on limitations of the use of extrinsic rewards in schools until the evidence is more substantial. My own hunch is that in some cases where the culture or the home environment is itself highly structured with contingent rewards, the child's expectations of such rewards may be so great that they are the teacher's only recourse, but other tactics should be tried.

Unexpected contingent rewards do not seem to affect intrinsic motivation. Some teachers detach rewards from specific tasks and instead surprise students with little tokens from time to time. I watched some third graders quickly open their desks after lunch to see if there was a surprise for someone from their teacher. These tokens seem to be a way of establishing an affiliation with the teacher, who rewards them in a general way rather than for a specific task. Verbal reinforcement can be also be used profitably if it addresses the content more specifically than if it is a general expression of praise. For example, the teacher comment, "Using the Internet to get some information really helped your report" may be more supportive of intrinsic motivation than, "That was an excellent report."

It is beyond the intended scope of this chapter and book to discuss the various methods of correction that have been used to control student goals, but these methods have been a standard response to the constant struggle for power that exists in any classroom. Teachers' goals for controlling the learning process and their imperative to construct new knowledge conflict with student needs for autonomy and for the satisfaction of other social goals that may not be learning directed. Time for teacher-designed learning tasks will be curtailed by student disengagement, either in pursuit of these other goals or by the other distractions of today's schools. Even in my graduate classes and in the halls of Congress, an order to *cease and desist* activity that takes time from the task intended is sometimes needed. It works if it is used infrequently—like an extrinsic reward diminishing in its effectiveness with every use. Enabling standards that are preemptive goal managers, that establish time-saving routines, and that protect the space of the learning environment from unnecessary and extraneous interference are more effective. Enactment activities that grab the student's attention with interest and nurture the satisfaction of intrinsic goals offer the greatest promise.

Suggestions for Standards and Enactment Activities

Corrective goal management works best if it consists of specific verbal reinforcement of the content task, or surprise contingent rewards that promote a general sense of affiliation and recognition. General verbal reinforcements and task-specific contingent rewards such as gold stars have only a transitory effect. They may, however, be necessary and useful at some times with some students and in some classrooms. Other forms of correction may also be necessary to gain attention, but they lose effectiveness with increased usage. Enabling standards and activities should provide for the more effective correctives so that attention and momentum are assured.

THE SCRIPT

The Overall Plot

The third pivot in our metaphor of constructing learning environments as theater is the script: the overall plot and the dialogue. These are at the heart of the enactment activities that match and accomplish content and performance standards. They are often not adequately planned for. I am not recommending that teachers walk into every class with prescribed inflexible scripts (a direct instruction method that was suggested at one time), but there are patterns that work and should become part of every teacher's repertoire. For overall plot there are proven effective models such as inquiry, jurisprudential inquiry, role playing, reciprocal teaching, synectics, concept attainment, and induction (see Joyce & Weil, 1996, for descriptions of these models). They can be copied as a whole or combined in different ways to meet varying needs. What they have in common is a problem-solving organization that builds upon intrinsically motivating goals, and a structure that maps new perceptions and that challenges students to make new complex connections instead of simply recalling what they hear or read. These connections enable the student to construct new or adapted knowledge. When combined with cooperative learning, these models can promote the intersubjective construction of new knowledge, knowledge that is new to all of the interacting learners: students and teachers (Lerman, 1996).

What I miss most about teaching only science classes is the ease with which I could motivate my students to pursue the solution to a problem and the thrill of discovering something new along with them. I still try to use the presentation of anomalous data or a discrepant event whenever I can. Like scientists, students (and most adults in everyday situations) are intrinsically motivated by the need to solve a problem or explain something that has unexpectedly happened or that does not agree with previous perceptions. Problem solving can be an effective framework for the overall script plot in any domain. The problem can be posed by the teacher, by students in response to an experience planned by a teacher, or it can arise spontaneously from student needs and experiences.

Planning for a field day can evolve into the following: How can we predict the weather for our field day? How should we lay out the baseball field so that the sun is not in anyone's eyes when we play? How can we discover what soft drink most kids would prefer? How can we elect judges for the contests who are representative of the whole school? What should we say in our invitations to parents and the community and how can we advertise it best? What artifacts should we choose for the time capsule we bury?

In the Saturday morning enrichment program that was part of the teacher network I describe in Chapter 7, each curriculum unit was organized around a specific relevant problem, such as, "What are the chances for an earthquake in our county?" Students collected data from observations in the field and from current and historical seismographic reports, and then they interpreted the data and made projections. This kind of problem solving is different from the historical application of word problems at the back of a chapter in math or physics books. Those follow teacher-demonstrated rules, procedures, and previously practiced algorithms. Instead, teachers in problem-centered math programs do not "expect all children to use a particular algorithm," and they allow their students to "spend a great deal of time working out their own procedures for solving problems and sharing and discussing alternate strategies with their classmates" (Carpenter et al., 1994, p. 4). Ultimately, after making the necessary connections between the problems and the physical representations that can be used to solve them, students design their own algorithms.

A problem-solving structure works in other subject areas as well. Recent studies of the reading and writing connection illustrate that the need to synthesize and analyze information from texts when it is required for writing analytic essays enhances the comprehension of the read material. Simple summaries that do not require synthesis are less effective (Greene & Ackerman, 1995). Smagorinsky (2001) provides a more in-depth description of what happens in the process of reading text. The author suggests that meaning is generated as the reader repeatedly reflects upon and reconstructs the text. The transaction process through which this occurs is furthermore subject to the reader's prior knowledge, and the context and culture in which it occurs. Meaning is then not simply extracted from the text, but from the interaction of the reader and the text. Smagorinsky cautions, therefore, against prescriptions that limit the variety of reading interpretations by a student.

This does not preclude the role of the teacher in constructing activities that promote reflection and reconstruction. When learning about the models of teaching that were described above, my students must cooperatively demonstrate one of the models. Their absorption and long-term retention of the model that they actively demonstrate is evidenced by its appearance and clarity in later portfolios and in their student teaching. In contrast, they have some difficulty with the models for which they merely read descriptions and observe others demonstrating, but a graphic organizer that requires them to analyze the similarities and differences between the models has proven very helpful. It is a "double bubble" or intersecting Venn diagram, but other forms of concept mapping are also useful. This brings us to the dialogue.

The Dialogue

The settings and props may frame the script, and patterns such as those of the models mentioned above can develop the themes of the plot, but the enacted curriculum as the performers experience it is essentially improvisational. Classroom ethnographers have documented what we educators always knew:

that "students' goals and their understanding of the objectives of the task can transform the task to the point that it is no longer the same as what was intended by the teacher." In addition, the teacher "can wittingly (or unwittingly) change the nature of tasks by stressing less- or more challenging aspects of the task or by altering the resources" (Stein, Grover, & Henningsen, 1996, p. 460).

If the teacher has clear outcomes in mind, there is less chance of loss of learning opportunity as control is shifted to the student performers. Instead, the improvisations can be made to work as effectively as any planned script! In reciprocal teaching, for example, metacognitive strategies for attacking the text—such as question generation, summarization, predictions, and clarification—are first purposely modeled, but then students are encouraged to challenge each other's interpretations with self-constructed elaborations, reflections, and questions. This method has been demonstrated to increase comprehension. You have to listen in order to respond.

The teacher-director does not abdicate in the discourse. This is the opportunity for scaffolding of the algorithmic level of brain processing addressed in Chapter 3. This is where attention is captured to heighten new perceptions; cues are offered to help retrieve prior knowledge, including previous generalizations; questions are asked to help make connections and new generalizations; and learning-supporting goals are managed to mitigate the construction. This is where we get to higher-order thinking.

Clarity for the student in the task itself and in the new constructions of knowledge are the teacher's constant responsibility. Actions are reflective of what is happening at the moment and of previous teaching experience. Many of the actions are assessments, which I discuss in detail in Chapter 6. The director interprets and responds to the assessments and aims for the further stretch across the zone of construction. In reciprocal teaching and in other forms of scaffolding or instructional mapping, the tasks and dialogue are set up by the teacher, and as it progresses it is fermented[2] by further discourse tosses (questions, paraphrases, etc.) from the teacher (see Cohen, 1994; Rosenshine & Meister, 1994).

The script can include the materials and proven techniques such as advance and graphic organizers. The dialogue tosses can consist of directions, questions, and requests for questions. There may also be nonverbal cues such as: a puzzled look, pointing to another child to ask for a response or reaction, a smile, thumbs up, tap on the desk, or hand motions asking for additions.

The research on instructional mapping in mathematics education is especially strong. Educators are recording the thinking processes of students as they confront problems and use materials to try to solve problems, but they are also examining the effects of various forms of questions and dialogues. Here are some of the direction and question patterns I encourage future math teachers to use:

- How did you get your answer?
- Show us how you used your materials to get your answer.
- Is there another way to get that answer?
- Does anyone have another answer?
- Can you prove your answer?
- Can you think of another problem that can be solved in the same way?
- Try this problem with smaller quantities.
- Act out this problem, or make a picture of it.
- Share your reasoning with your partner.
- Write about what you just learned so that someone else can learn from it.

A quote from Vygotsky (1962, p. 104, cited by Rosenshine & Meister, 1994, p. 484) also seems most appropriate here:

> In the child's development imitation and instruction play a major role. . . . Therefore, the only good kind of instruction is that which marches ahead of development and leads it; it must be aimed not so much at the ripe, but at the ripening functions.

This is not far from the high expectations our new standards are calling for. The only thing keeping us from a sellout performance is the right setting, motivated performers, a good script, and the best director we can find. I offer some overall suggestions for enabling standards and activities below, and criteria for predicting their overall success in Table 5.1. Table 5.2 shows how two

Suggestions for Standards and Enactment Activities

Enabling standards should provide professional development for teachers to share overall patterns or models of teaching that provide a framework for metacognitive strategy development, task-mastery goals, self-constructed knowledge, and maximum active interaction. Problem-solving frameworks, inquiry designs, and reciprocal teaching and concept attainment forms, especially effective in combination with cooperative learning, are examples. Enactment activities within these models should allow for some student task control, question generation, syntheses, and reflective evaluations. Teachers should direct the enabling activities with supportive dialogue, instructional mapping, or scaffolding—constantly stretching students toward levels higher than those already attained.

Table 5.1 Criteria for Assessing Enabling Standards and Enactment Activities (Teachers should add their own criteria to this list)

Enabling standards and activities address the learning environment, the within- and outside-of-school experiences, and the materials and personnel they require.
The enabling standards and enactment activities (Check all that apply and comply)
Articulate with content and performance standards (are designed to help students meet them)
Provide for the necessary allocations of space and time
Provide the teacher with necessary skills and support
Group students heterogeneously in small within-class groups that are interdependent
Provide opportunities for students to develop self-efficacy in terms of specific tasks
Reflect multicultural differences and changes in student needs for affiliation, their motivations to achieve, and their interests
Provide for greater preemptive goal management and less contingent rewards and corrective discipline
Provide for carefully selected, proven-effective curriculum materials that reflect all of the above
Have structures that are built around finding solutions to student-relevant problems, and use constructive models such as inquiry, concept attainment, role-playing, and induction
Are flexible or varied enough to meet the needs of all student intelligences and learning styles
Have teacher-directed dialogues that encourage students to reflect, synthesize, and evaluate new perceptions and ideas and respond with their own self-generated questions
Are designed to constantly stretch the student from present levels of knowledge to new generalizations at higher levels

enactment activities address the general commencement and more-specific unit content standards of a social studies unit. It is the work of teacher Patricia deNoble and is used with her permission. The table does not represent the entire unit; other activities are planned. An assessment rubric that matches the standards is presented in Chapter 6.

Table 5.2 Sample Curriculum Unit Standards and Activities

Commencement content standard(s)

What students should know and be able to do when they graduate

New York State Social Studies Standards:

Standard 7: All students will acquire geographical understanding by studying spatial terms.

Standard 8: All students will acquire geographical understanding by studying human systems in geography.

Elementary Benchmark Level Performance Indicators

Students will be able to:

- Use maps, globes, graphs, diagrams, and computer-based references and information to generate and interpret information
- Use mental maps to identify the locations of places within the local community and nearby communities
- Use mental maps to identify the locations of the earth's continents and oceans in relation to each other
- Use mental maps to identify the locations of major physical and human characteristics in the United States
- Demonstrate understanding of the spatial concepts of location, distance, direction, scale, region, and movement

Unit Content standards and performance indicators
Content standards (what you want your students to know)
Performance indicators (what you want your students to be able to do)

Students will be able to:

Describe how to get from one location to another in their school and or classroom environment

Identify related locations by familiar landmarks, e.g., school, stores, or parks

Locate and identify land and water forms on a map or a globe

Identify the cardinal directions of North, East, South, and West

Verbally explain and understand the relationships to function and spatial location that are present among their neighbors and community helpers

Locate or move from one location to another on a map or globe

Identify and use the terms *right, left, straight, forward, up, down,* and *backward.*

Enactment Activities

The learning experiences that are designed to help students achieve the standards stated for this unit

Lesson Four: ***This activity addresses Commencement Standard 7***

Materials: Globe, Flat Map

Procedure: Introduce the students to both the globe and the flat map.

1. Ask the students:
   What are the *differences* between the globe and a map? (one is round and one is flat)
   What are the *similarities* between the globe and a map? (they both have oceans and land)
   Do they both use the directions North, South, East, and West? Can you identify and point to the water on the map and then on the globe? Can you identify and point to the land on the map and then on the globe? Are these the same or different on both the map and globe?
2. Divide the class into two cooperative learning groups. Give one group a flat map and the other group a globe to look at.
   - Group 1 will be given the task to list why it is better to use a globe. (provide a globe for this group to examine)
   - Group 2 will be given the task to list why it is better to use a map. (provide maps for this group to look at)
3. Allow the students time to discuss and construct their responses to the assignment. Then regroup into the whole class and discuss the [singular?] group's answers.

Lesson 10: ***This activity addresses the Commencement Standards 7 and 8***

Materials: Computer and Internet access

Procedure: To conclude and review the concepts of the unit study on map and spatial terms, log on to mapmachine@nationalgeographic.com. This will allow students to view the various types of maps available through the Internet. It will also familiarize the students with using the computer as a valuable resource. Model an example for the students to see before asking them any questions concerning the activity.

1. Ask the students: How can the Internet help us find our location? Can the Internet help find the directions to some place that we need to go? How is finding our location on the Internet different from using a map to find a location? How is using the Internet the same as using a map?
2. Then allow small groups of students to use the computers to find the map directions from their address to the school. Give the students the school address to aid in their search. After the students have completed this task, allow them to print out the directions.
3. Once the students have their map directions printed out, have them circle the terms *right, left, North, South, East, West, straight, up,* and *down*. These are all terms that the students have been introduced to during the two-week unit.

NOTES

1. Even in states that do not have laws that mandate curriculum, there are some exceptions to this. By special legislative action, for example, the state of New York prescribes the teaching of some specific curriculum fragments such as Arbor Day, the humane treatment of animals, drug education and, recently, the potato famine in Ireland.

2. *Fermenting* is a term used in cooperative learning. It implies that the teacher or the group must make the discourse go beyond simple recall into higher-order thinking skills such as analysis, synthesis, and evaluation.

6 How Are We Doing?

Measuring Success

ABOUT THIS CHAPTER

My friend, who is a drama coach, questioned my use of the theater as a metaphor for creating the classroom environment. Her point, which was well taken, was that the performers in a drama put on masks, and classrooms should be places where students are themselves. Upon reflection, I am not so sure that this is what really exists. Even as they are evaluating themselves, much of what students and their teachers do in schools is for the purpose of demonstrating to others. On the classroom stage the teacher- and student-performers constantly demonstrate what they know to each other and productively use the demonstrations to help direct and motivate further actions. Schools also have off-stage and demanding audiences, parents and the public at large, for whom they must demonstrate that the time and resources spent on education are effective. Like good theater, a well-communicated demonstration for others, whether it is within the action on stage or directed toward the audience, sometimes involves putting on a special face or mask.

When demonstrations go beyond the purpose of communicating with others and are measured and compared to a standard, they become quality or quantity indicators of what the performer knows, has accomplished, or can do. Because they have different standards or criteria, theater critics and teachers often disagree on the same performance. Among educators today there is even some disagreement about the meaning of the term *standard.* Wiggins (1995, p. 189) has defined standard in the singular as "an exemplary performance serving as a benchmark," and in the plural as "specific and guiding pictures," and when modified to "high standards" as "a set of mature, coherent, and consistently applied values." The widely adopted standards of the National Council of Teachers of Mathematics (1989, 2000) and the statements of standards developed by states represent this description. These usually begin with the more general principles or values, and then attach more specific expectations to a particular grade level or span of grades. What is missing in the descriptions of standards in most cases are clearly discriminated "levels of the bar" or models of exemplary performance. Instead the models are embedded in the assessment items, and the "levels of the bar" are represented as test proficiency expectations, which, in reality, are percentages of correct responses.

In previous chapters I distinguished among the various statements of standards, designating the standards that describe the knowledge or skill to be attained without reference to a level for the purpose of measurement as content standards or performance indicators, and those that have inherent statements of levels of achievement as performance standards. This chapter adds greater detail to the meaning and role of content and performance standards in framing instruction, and to the actions and instruments that measure them.

STANDARDS AND THEIR MEASURES

Standards may be defined, interpreted, applied, and measured in many different but often overlapping ways. To begin with, it is important to remember that there is a strong human imperative to judge oneself. Standards may be the performer's own, and the measure may be one of self-evaluation. An infant takes great pleasure in his first successful attempt to reach for something or stand, not because he measures himself against an external standard, but because he has a strong human need to have power over the environment in which he finds himself. Our ability to control the environment is an internal standard that is with us always. Although we may make revisions and modifications in response to other goals, we measure ourselves against this standard until we die.

The common connotation for performance standards is that they are externally imposed measures. This may be the case if we don't create environments in which students are motivated to set their own performance standards and take their own measures—or at least measure themselves against a standard that they understand and accept. Nevertheless, we live in a social world and respect externally imposed standards because they represent the consensual domain of knowledge and skills. The revisions we make in our own standards are most often based on what we observe others able to do, and on the judgments of others. Schools and their students owe their audiences clearly communicated evidence that they are meeting their expectations. It is our own constant measure of how we ourselves are progressing, however, that directs us and drives us over a lifetime to ever-higher levels of achievement.

When Gary Kasparov walked away from his final defeat in his well-publicized chess tournament with IBM's "Big Blue" computer, he did so in a huff. It was a simple win-or-lose measure that disappointed him for the moment, but did not discourage him from quickly issuing a new challenge. He admitted that he had underestimated the abilities of his opponent, but a more carefully prepared rematch would prove his human invincibility. Kasparov then busily engaged himself in studying his own errors and the skills of his computer opponent in anticipation of another challenge. Unfortunately, educators' measures of students' progress are not always precisely revealing and, more often than not, they do not challenge us or our students to try harder or motivate us to find out exactly why we were unsuccessful. Although we constantly assess students in informal ways as we teach them, we rarely openly attribute the students' lack of success to our own performance. How often have you heard a teacher say, "I am sorry you didn't understand, perhaps I didn't do a good job of explaining what was needed." Nor do we often enough engage and encourage students to methodically and consciously evaluate themselves. Modeling of self-assessment by teachers and more structured opportunities for self-evaluation by students such as the one in Table 6.1 might be helpful. It is part of a unit by teachers Pam Deming and Eva Simons. The entire unit may be retrieved at www.stac.edu/mcc/deming/htm.

The standards or levels of the bar against which we most frequently measure ourselves in schools are socially determined. And though we usually accept the results as personal, these measured demonstrations are often designed for the benefit of another audience, and for different purposes. It is important to understand the differences in the purpose of measured demonstrations or *assessments*, as they are commonly referred to when they are more systematically applied (Herman, Aschbacher, & Winters, 1992), because even though they may overlap, different purposes require different measures.

THE PURPOSES OF MEASURES OR ASSESSMENTS

Students' various on- and off-stage audiences—themselves, their peers, their teachers, their parents (at times in the role of teacher), and the public at large—represent different purposes for assessment. As they interact with the environment, students need to measure themselves in terms of personal goals such as the ability to control that environment. The interactive responses they get from their peers and the informal and formal assessments by their teachers are among the measures they use. And depending upon the strength of affiliate goals such as self-efficacy, social compliance, and task or performance motivation (see Chapter 5), these assessments may or may not positively affect their learning process. The assessments may also frame new goals or modify existing ones.

Table 6.1 Grade 2 Dinosaur Project: Self-Assessment Activity

Culminating Assessment: As a final project, each student will be asked to do research on a dinosaur of choice. The student must answer the following questions:

1. **During which period did your dinosaur live?**
2. **What does its name mean?**
3. **What did it eat?**
4. **What was its length?**
5. **Where have its bones been found?**
6. **What other facts have you learned about this dinosaur?**

Children will be given a choice, if available, of using Hyperstudio or PowerPoint as a method of presenting their research information to the class. If a scanner is available, children will be required to find a picture of their dinosaur and include it in the presentation. This project will be assessed using the attached rubric, which the children will be given in advance.

Self-Scoring Rubric

	4	3	2	1
Knowledge Learned	I answered all six of the questions completely.	I answered five of the six questions completely.	I answered four of the six questions completely.	I answered three or fewer of the questions completely.
Technological Presentation	I used at least four slides. I used graphics and fade-outs.	I used fewer than four slides. I used graphics and fade-outs.	I did not use slides or I did not use graphics and fade-outs.	I did not use slides and I did not use graphics and fade-outs.
Oral Presentation	I spoke in a clear, loud voice. I shared my facts and answered questions.	My voice was loud and clear most of the time. I shared my facts and answered most questions.	My voice was NOT loud and clear. I did NOT share my facts. I answered some questions.	My voice was NOT loud and clear. I did NOT share my facts. I did NOT answer questions.

Teachers in the students' on-stage audience take constant informal measures within activities and classroom discourse, reflect on these measures, and then adjust the discourse or the learning environment in response. This most important purpose for measurement has also been the most unrecognized. The standards against which teachers make informal classroom assessments are not usually stated in written form: They are more often subliminal and intuitive, based on teachers' knowledge, their prior experience with children, and on their own learning experiences. The informal assessments may be systematized, however, in oral questioning patterns and in the materials within the enactment activities. Teachers may at times also assess themselves in relation to their informal assessments of students, but their self- and student measures usually place greater weight on more formal assessments such as oral and written tests, probably because these can also have the purpose of informing a different audience: school administrators, parents, and the public at large.

Parents and the public have an important investment in the education of our students. They are a critical and demanding audience. Formal HSSB assessments and traditional standardized tests are meaningful to this audience because they believe that the tests are controlled, reliable, and valid. Although only broadly assessing the child's individual progress and rarely diagnosing specific needs, they provide comparison to a norm and allow parents to position their children and their schools in relation to others. Educated parents recognize the highly competitive culture in which we live and worry about their offspring's chances for success. Better assessments of individual progress matched to clarified performance standards might be able to sway parents from preoccupation with these incompletely revealing measures. They may also have greater meaning for the many uninformed parents who do not understand standardized and normed[1] tests and may consider them unfair and biased when they are used to measure children whose cultures may be different from the norming sample.

On a broader scale, the public audience demands accountability for the dollars spent on education, and attributes some of the country's socioeconomic problems to school failure. The purpose of assessment in this case is to evaluate the system rather than the individual child. Although system measures require the levels of objectivity, validity, and reliability that we have endowed upon our traditional standardized tests, we may not need to use them in such a pervasive and controlling way. They also need careful interpretations.

Much of the recent effort on the part of political entities to instill higher standards and uniformity has been based on unfavorable comparisons of the children of this country with the performance of children from other nations on international tests. Although the results of the Third International

Math and Science Study (TIMSS) showed some improvement over previous studies (more so in science than in math), the results are still disappointing (Schmidt, McNight, Raizen, 1996). Concerns about our students' performance continue. Even though our own assessments, the National Assessments of Educational Progress (NAEP), show some improvement since the early 1980s, the white/minority achievement gap persists (Barton, 2002). Reports of the most recent results can be retrieved at www.negp.gov/reports.

Some educators believe that we have exaggerated the international deficiencies and perhaps incorrectly attributed them to poor performance on the part of schools and educators (Bracey, 1997). They suggest that we have neglected to examine other contributing factors such as the wide disparities in our own population, and failed to consider the perhaps unfavorable emphasis on tests and resulting pressures on students in other countries. This may be true if one considers the *jukus*[2] of Japan, but even our neighbor Canada gets better results.

Follow-up studies responding to the TIMSS results elucidated some possible causes, such as unfocused curriculum and materials and less time for teachers to prepare. They also found that the typical goal of U.S. mathematics teachers is to teach students how to do something, whereas the goal of Japanese teachers is to help students understand mathematical concepts (Stedman, 1997). These diagnosed differences need to be addressed, but I agree with Baker (1997), who believes that fixating on national achievement as "some sort of educational olympiad" is problematic. He admits that ranking may be useful in a limited way, but suggests that "international studies are most useful . . . when they are used to shed light on why a country produces a particular pattern of achievement" (p. 16). Light and clarity help us communicate with our public audience.

Although Kasparov's actions in achieving his goal were extremely complex, the goal itself was clear and the win-or-lose measure an objective and simple dichotomy. Clarity in the standards we use in schools as informal and formal benchmarks or levels of the bar are rarely so objective or simple. The results of formal assessments like standardized tests are often openly reported, but the content standards on which they are based are unclear. Informal standards are rarely stated. If standards are to serve us as a guide for instruction and for our self-measures, greater clarity is necessary. For the measurements we make for other audiences it is a sine qua non.

THE CONSEQUENCES OF HIGH-STAKES ASSESSMENTS

Greater clarity is particularly critical when assessments are designed for a public audience and are "high-stakes" measures. Any evaluation of performance that has long-term and psychological consequences, such as class placement or college acceptance, can be a high-stakes measure. In Chicago and in Massachusetts (see Chapter 1), students were not allowed to go on or graduate until they passed tests that measured their achievement of higher standards. They would have to go to summer school and retake the tests. In New York City, hundreds of Community College students were told two weeks before graduation that they would not receive diplomas because they had not passed an English Proficiency Test that was mandated just before their graduation was scheduled.

These highly publicized incidents were met with similarly mixed reactions. There was support from the unaffected public that applauded the implementation of "higher standards." Some teachers were pleased that they now could use the real threat of nonpromotion or nongraduation to get students to work harder. Students and their friends and relatives, however, were emotionally traumatized. Their personal expectations and feelings of self-efficacy were greatly affected. In response, there was some reneging on the part of the colleges, in that students went to graduation but did not receive diplomas. Interestingly, letters from City University faculty members published in the *New York Times* mostly found fault with the test itself.

As was described in Chapter 1, officials in several states also made critical changes in their expectations for student performance when faced with the reality of the federal sanctions of NCLB legislation and the consequences of hastily produced state assessment instruments. National testing experts have cautioned states that unreliable instruments administered without sufficient time for development could backfire and create negative public attitudes—some of that has happened.

In North Carolina, confidence in the state's testing system was undermined when the state Board of Education tossed out results of the spring 2002 writing exam. Experts said that test was poorly designed and was an unreliable measure of students' writing skills. The action came one year after state testing officials were embarrassed by inaccurate passing scores on a new set of math exams (Silberman, 2002).

In New York State, school administrators, teachers, and parents were so concerned with the surprisingly low scores on the 2002 high school physics Regents exam that they decided to send messages with college applications asking the colleges to ignore the physics scores (Associated Press, 2002). This followed a summer of hastily arranged coaching sessions and retests for these very competent students. Teachers complained that the test did not articulate with previously published state curriculum standards.

The public distress caused by these incidents could have been avoided if there had been greater clarity in the standards themselves and then careful matching of the standards and the assessment instruments. High-stakes standards-based tests (HSSBs) need to be *transparent,* not in that they are not visible, but in that they are *free of deceit.* After-the-fact impositions of standards via tests with high-stake consequences are unfair and may in the long run even be unproductive. Those who make decisions about high-stakes measures can benefit from listening to the voices of those affected (Solomon, 1995).

IMPROVING HSSB TESTS

Matt Gandal (2002) of Achieve, Inc., a nonprofit agency dedicated to assisting states in standards implementation, reports on the following useful list of principles for HSSB tests that were adopted by attendees at the 2001 Education Summit Governor's Conference. Many of these recommendations apply to all assessments and will be addressed in the sections ahead.

> *Quality:* State tests should be designed to measure student progress against clear and rigorous standards. Reports sent to schools and parents should indicate how students perform against the standards—not just how they compare with other students. Tests developed for other purposes cannot meet this need. The tests should measure the full range of knowledge and skills called for by the standards, from basic to most advanced.
>
> *Transparency:* In a standards-based system there should be no mystery about what is on the test. Students, parents, and teachers should know what is being tested. They should be confident that if students are taught a curriculum that is aligned with state standards, they will do well on state tests. The best way for states to ensure transparency is to publicly release questions from previous years' tests, along with sample student answers at each performance level.
>
> *Utility:* Ultimately, it is the clarity of the results and the manner in which they are used that will make a difference in schools. Test results should be returned to schools and parents as quickly as possible without compromising the quality of the test instrument. Score reports should be clear, jargon-free, and designed to guide action.
>
> *Comparability:* The goal of state assessment programs is to create measurement systems that can accurately track and compare student and school progress from year to year. To accomplish this, the tests from one grade level to another must be aligned with state standards, and the results must be comparable from grade to grade so that student progress can be tracked from year to year.

> *Coherence:* State tests are only one piece of a comprehensive data system. Local and teacher-developed assessments are important too. States must work with districts to ensure that all tests serve a distinct purpose, redundant tests are dropped, and the combined burden of state and local tests remains reasonable.
>
> *Strategic Use of Data:* Closing the achievement gap can occur only if student achievement data are disaggregated by race and income, and if schools are required to show that all groups of students have made reasonable progress. By regularly reporting how every school is performing against state standards, states can focus attention on the problem, on the progress that some communities and schools are making in response, and on areas where additional work is needed.

The results and form of high-stakes measures are not always made public. The measures that determine placement in gifted programs, special education, or acceptance to college are usually private and sometimes secret. A recent *New York Times* article (Medina, 2002) described the tension and anxiety created among eighth-grade students competing for placement in New York City's highly selective special schools. Some students taking the exam believe that the results of this one test will determine the nature of the rest of their lives—college admission and career. There is no set of standards on which the test is based, and only those wealthy enough to take private preparation courses have the opportunity to practice general test-taking skills.

High-stakes measures for students, such as placement exams and SATs, may not be high stakes for teachers, and the opposite may also seem to be true. A test becomes high stakes for teachers when administrators use test results to help them make tenure or class assignment decisions, when results are published, and when students are transferred to a higher-performing school. The concern about poor results on a high-stakes measure may seem to be immediate only for a teacher up for tenure, but it may already have had an immediate, although indirect, effect on students. End-of-the-year individual student scores on state-produced HSSB tests may seem of little direct consequence for students—the test scores may not even be recorded until the following school year. Nevertheless, because of the teachers' concerns, the students' educational experience may have already been deeply affected.

Knowledgeable parents also tend to evaluate the quality of their children's schools and teachers on the basis of publicly shared results. States issue public *report cards* that advertise results in an open and dramatic way. Individual school scores are posted on state Web sites and published in local papers. Schools are now subject to the sanctions of failure to make adequate yearly progress (AYP) as I described in Chapter 1. In several states, low-performing schools or districts are actually taken over by the state education departments.

High-stakes measures may also have a negative and limiting effect on curriculum. A study of the time spent by elementary teachers in preparing their students for standardized tests (Madaus et al., 1992) revealed that teachers in minority schools spent considerably more time at this than teachers in nonminority schools. Teachers at different levels are also affected differently. With the exception of teachers in the few states that have HSSB tests at the secondary level, elementary and intermediate school teachers are more likely than high school teachers to be concerned about their students' performance on HSSB tests. The recent legislation calling for tests at Grades 3–8 has made them very sensitive to the possible consequences of high-stakes measures. Our team of teachers engaged in writing a new science curriculum may have just such a test on their minds.

WHERE SHOULD MEG, APRIL, AND BRAD BEGIN?

We left the science curriculum writing team in Chapter 5, as they began their task. Not too far into the task Brad brought up a real concern. "Well, these content and performance standards we are writing are fine for your kids, but what about my ESL students? They're having a hard enough time with the state test now." Meg and April were not exactly without anxiety either. Although their students had usually done fairly well on the tests, each new administration or version brought some trepidation that perhaps they as teachers hadn't covered everything. Parents always seemed more interested in these results than in other things the kids were bringing home. And the annual press releases comparing their school with others in the region was sometimes an embarrassment.

April, always the most concerned with content coverage, quickly suggested, "Let's look at all the old tests and write our new curriculum based on them." Where high-stakes tests are mandated, it may be helpful to look carefully at previously administered samples. Teachers owe their students preparation for these, but it is a mistake to allow such measures to limit what they want to do. As the common aphorism, "what gets tested gets taught" tells us, tests can drive the curriculum (Resnick & Resnick, 1989). They can also narrow it, calling our attention away from what may be more important but not tested. HSSB tests can distract us from some consideration of the individual needs, goals, learning styles, and current culture of students that we have previously discussed. Nevertheless, they are very much a part of the culture of schools today. We can, perhaps, use them more effectively.

Preparation for HSSB Tests

The current practice in most schools in response to the frenzy created by HSSB tests is for teachers to bombard students with practice tests. Popham

(2001), however, distinguishes between preparation for a test that is *item teaching*, which is focused on practice with actual or similar test items, and preparation that is *curriculum teaching,* which is directed at the content and skills represented by the test. A more effective way to deal with the immediate compulsion to focus just on item teaching is to carefully identify the standards and embedded concepts that the tests measure, and then examine the curriculum standards and activities to make sure the standards tested are addressed. The curriculum may have to be responsively adjusted; new enactment activities may have to be planned.

The next step for the curriculum team would be to design their own "proximal" measures, measures constructed by those close to the subjects to be measured (their own students). Proximal measures can tell us whether students know what we want them to know before we measure them using the more "distal" measures of HSSB tests, produced far away from those they measure. As soon as the team identifies the content standards they wish to achieve—including those that are mandated or tested and those that team members feel are worthy—they can immediately write end-result levels of achievement into their performance standards. These will help the team know where they want their students to go. Well-written performance standards are easily translated into assessment measures. These can be informal components of enactment activities or more formal assessment instruments.

Some teachers have developed systematic assessment patterns that they use all of the time. Journal writing is an example of this. If the journal goes beyond a recording of events and requires the student to reflect on what has been learned, it can be a documented self-assessment measure and also work to guide further instruction. Questioning patterns that are purposely directed toward assessing results can be routinely inserted into classroom dialogues. Videotaping the students as they work in small groups allows teachers to review dialogue at their leisure, or share it with students as a self-assessment experience. Combinations of self- and peer assessments can be used to stimulate reflective interaction and improve the skills of each peer involved. Computer managed instruction will help monitor progress, and presentation software adds easily documented and shared products. Table 6.2 contains a beginning assessment template our curriculum writing team can follow. I will add to it as we proceed.

The steps in Table 6.2 are only a beginning. Day-to-day informal measures that aim for the end-result level will have to be incorporated into dialogues and other enactment activities, and more formal intermediate measures of levels of performance will have to be designed. Individual adjustments in the forms will be needed. Brad may allow his ESL students to demonstrate what they know in different ways than Meg and April. Meg may have to examine her hands-on activities, identify the science concepts

Table 6.2 Getting Started on Assessment

- Decide on your content standards (what you want your students to know or be able to do). Base these on criteria, including any mandated curriculum and needs analyses of previous HSSB tests (see below and Chapter 4).
- Describe the end-result level that will tell you that your students have accomplished each content standard. This becomes your performance standard.
- Make a list of the audiences who will be interested in measures of how your students achieved the end results. Be sure to include the students themselves, yourself, supervisors, parents, and other publics.
- Clarify the purposes of the measures for each audience.
- Clarify the consequences of the measures for each audience.
- Decide where you will place more formal systematic assessments and what form they will take.
- Plan to include some assessment in each enactment activity. Developing a pattern that can be repeated in each is a good way to monitor informal measures.
- Use technology to help whenever you can.

that are embedded within them, and make sure they are measured. April will need to reconsider her dependence on texts if the new standards require students to analyze data and solve realistic problems. New forms of assessments will be needed to match their new curriculum. Among the questions on their minds will probably be, "How can we make our assessments authentic?"

A HISTORY OF ASSESSMENT FORMS

The concern for "authentic" or "alternative" assessments began at the end of the twentieth century. These frequently interchanged terms distinguished a more complex and revealing form of assessment from the form overwhelmingly in use at the time. Many of the things our three teachers may already have in mind are authentic, but some clarification of differences and history is needed. To begin with, we need to consider the source of the assessment. Like the many influences on curriculum, the origins of tests fall on a continuum from very distal (produced far from where they are applied) to closely proximal (generated at the site of application). Examples at the distal end include the globally applied TIMSS, national tests such as the NAEP, and commercially produced instruments such as the College Board's Scholastic Aptitude Test (SAT), Stanford Achievement Test, and California Achievement Tests that are widely used across the country. In the middle of this continuum are the statewide assessments. At the proximal end of the continuum are the small-group or individual teachers' classroom tests.

The form of the distally produced tests of the latter part of the twentieth century was generally limited (with some variation) to multiple-choice items because these are easy to standardize, norm, and validate. Although middle range statewide instruments such as Regents exams originally required extensive essay answers, they were shifted to strictly short answer and multiple-choice formats in the 1950s and 1960s. Some of the teachers' own tests tended to follow the same pattern. Commercially produced accompaniments to texts and electronic scoring facilities made this format easy to apply and score. Tests that asked only for unconstructed choices and with little opportunity for student-generated answers became the conventional form.

Unfortunately, a multiple-choice test is out of sync with the more constructive demands of real life. In personal living and in the workplace, picking the right answer from four or five stated choices is a rarely used skill. For the potential employer, the ability to create answers is what is highly prized. For the teacher, multiple-choice testing does not lend itself easily to the kind of individual analysis that would help guide instruction. For the student test taker, it does not provide the kind of specific feedback that might strengthen task-mastery goals.[3] Therefore, even when they have been high-stakes measures, the traditional formal measures of standardized tests have not been productively used. Teachers either discounted them as unrelated, or were so intimidated by the high-stake consequences of these measures, that they abdicated their rights to make better decisions about what their students needed and just "taught to the test." In both cases, they saw the tests as a separate entity: separate from what they taught or separate from what they wanted to teach.

As part of the general reform movement to improve education, this form of testing was identified by some educational leaders (e.g., Wiggins, 1989, 1996/1997) as a source of some of our educational problems. Assessment was identified as the driving force in curriculum (what gets tested gets taught); the multiple-choice tradition was lambasted as unrelated to real-life situations and demands, and declared dysfunctional as an appropriate guide for instruction. *Alternative* and *authentic* are terms that have been synonymously used to describe a variety of assessments that are performance- based or require a student to demonstrate or construct an answer instead of simply making a choice. As opposed to conventional multiple-choice tests, performance-based assessments are envisioned to require students to "actively accomplish complex and significant tasks, while bringing to bear prior knowledge, recent learning and relevant skills to solve realistic or authentic problems" (Herman et al., 1992). They are more subjectively scored, but also promise to be more useful instructional elements themselves and more efficient as guides for instruction.

States have taken some leadership in reform efforts to make assessments more authentic. Most now include a variety of performance items in their

Table 6.3 Comparing Conventional and Alternative Assessment Options

Option	*Response Type*	*Objectivity of Scores; Scorer*	*Classification*
True-False Item	Responses are selected	Objectively scored: answers predetermined by educators	Conventional assessment
Multiple-Choice Item			
Matching			
Modified Objective		Subjective scoring: may also be scored by self and/or peers.	
Completion	Constructed responses • open • free		
Short Answer			
Essay			
Papers			
Lab Reports			
Poster-Board Session			Alternative assessment
Portfolios			
Discussion			
Interviews			
Skills Checklist			
Performance Testing			
Lab/Field Practicals			
Projects			
Observations			

measures. Unfortunately, a majority of today's teachers, having grown up with multiple-choice questions, are themselves uncomfortable with preparing their students for performance measures and constructed responses. Many more efforts are being made at the school district level (Hartenbach, Ott, & Clark, 1996/1997) and individual schools and teachers are producing examples such as those at the end of this chapter.

Although the major difference between alternative and conventional tests is the requirement of student-generated answers or performances rather than a choice from already prepared ones, there are some major constructive, implementation, and consequential differences as well—and these present renewed assessment challenges for educators. Table 6.3 compares some of the conventional and alternative options and I discuss some of the challenges of alternative assessments below. The table is adapted from one produced for the New York State Education Department by Reynolds, Doran, Allers, and Agruso (1996).

CHALLENGE 1: ESTABLISHING VALIDITY

One of the important criteria used by professional conventional test makers to judge the quality of assessments is the test's validity. Establishing validity requires us to ask these questions: Does the question or the performance task measure what you want it to? Does it limit itself to measuring what you want it to: the desired concept or skill, and does it not require unaccounted-for additional concepts? This second question has been particularly significant in the condemnation of conventional tests as biased. For example, a question that is set in the suburban mall experience might contain the requirement of unrelated prior knowledge that may be missing from inner-city or rural students. Wide-scale alternative testing that is based on realistic problem solving may present a greater challenge in establishing this kind of validity. What is realistic in terms of experience for one student may be not be realistic for another. We may have to come to consensus first on what is in the experience of most children or discount the particular situation and expect the student to be able to generalize from one situation to another—a worthwhile skill. But then we have to prepare our students for this and count the ability to generalize as well.

Before we can ask whether the assessment measures what we want it to, we must know what we want. Among the advantages of multiple-choice testing is its ability to get at very specific embedded concepts with relative ease. Although in their focus on the actions of the enactment activities teachers often forget to identify concepts, they are less likely to forget them when they are constructing tests. I have often suggested that teachers might try developing their tests before they develop their curriculum. Simultaneous construction may be the best!

Applying this to our current curriculum ideas and terminology, the content and performance indicators as well as performance standards should also be articulated and constructed in tandem. Notwithstanding this primary importance of the articulation between the content and the performance that will be used to measure it, I believe that the distinction between them is also valuable. Although it may seem redundant to some readers to make this distinction and state each separately, this procedure may help us overcome our past failure to either carefully clarify the embedded concepts that we wish our students to attain or match them with appropriate measures.

CHALLENGE 2: TASKS OR PERFORMANCES VERSUS CONCEPTS

In the quest to develop more meaningful alternative measures of performance there may be other unexpected outcomes. Just as assessments in the past have focused inordinately on the content without attention to the applications of knowledge, we can make the corresponding mistake of placing too much emphasis on the applications and not enough on the embedded concepts described in Chapter 4 as chunks of declarative knowledge. Teachers like Meg, who are motivated to use activities that are "doing" kinds of things, sometimes forget to map embedded concepts, even as those like April are so focused on the content that they may forget that knowledge is as good as our ability to use it.

Therefore, while not overlooking the reality that unapplied knowledge is also unrevealed and that any measure of what is known requires a demonstration, I agree with McTighe (1996/1997, p. 7) and others that it is important to set clear *performance targets* in terms of *performances of understanding.* Although the performance may be as simple as a choice of true or false or as complex as an original musical composition, I think we must start with what that understanding is. Others, who are measurement specialists, agree. In the design of what he calls "cognitively designed assessment," Nichols (1994) describes the need for a substantive base that includes a description of the "cognitive mechanisms a performer . . . would use," and may include "how the cognitive mechanisms develop and how more competent performers differ from less competent performers."

Porter (2002) also recognizes the need for a common language that would enable educators to properly align curriculum and the assessments that measure them. He generalizes the processes of mathematics into five forms of "cognitive demand" and suggests mathematical indices for evaluating curriculum alignment based on the forms. I have found these indices very helpful in the construction of well-balanced assessment instruments. Nevertheless, the ability to perform the processes of mathematics with meaning depends upon knowledge of the related embedded concepts. I believe we also need clarity, common language, and consensus on the embedded concepts needed to perform the processes. The curriculum design procedures described in previous chapters can lead us to the achievement of this goal.

In a related perspective, Messick (1994) debates the issue of where the assessment focus should be. He distinguishes between *task-driven* performance tests, which require the students to perform complex tasks and focus on the ability to perform the task itself, and performance evaluations with a *construct-driven* approach that focus on the knowledge learned. He carefully examines the merits and deficiencies of each, but his conclusion is that when we are assessing the constructs (or concepts) that the performance demonstrates (in math, for example) rather than the performance itself (in some artistic endeavors), the construct-driven approach is best because it helps guide the selection or construction of the measurement tasks and because it focuses attention on the validity of the measure.

Messick implies that because a task-driven measure may be less focused on the embedded concept, it is less clearly subject to the criterion of validity. I agree that the validity of such assessments may be more difficult to justify, but would not want the criterion of validity to be overlooked in them. I also question the implication that performances themselves are not as dependent on concepts. The illustration that I often offer for this is that almost anyone can follow a recipe and produce a quality roux or cream sauce, but a real chef understands the concepts that explain how to balance fat, flour, and liquid, add them in the right order, and alter them to make interesting variations and additions.

I have observed that many of the newly produced alternative performance assessments do appear task-driven and neglectful of concepts. This may, however, be because it is more difficult to break concepts down to developmental levels that can be observed in a performance than it is to break tasks down. In the analysis of different forms of rubrics (see Table 6.11 ahead), developmental rubrics are judged the most difficult. Conventional testing rarely required us to break concepts down into developmental levels. Instead it looked at concepts quantitatively rather than qualitatively. The highest score belonged to the individual who got the most items correct rather than the individual who was functioning at the highest level. Some tests did build in different levels of difficulty so that only those who reached the highest level on each construct could achieve a very high score, but discriminating where the weaknesses were was difficult. Interestingly, recently initiated computer-administered forms of tests like the GMAT and SAT[4] do attempt to sequence questions at increasingly higher levels. A student who reaches the highest level quickly may have to answer fewer questions.

The Importance of Embedded Concepts: Some Examples

The tendency for teachers to overlook concepts that are not clearly stated was demonstrated to me in two recent events. In the first case, it was the sudden realization of a graduate student art teacher as she reflected on the value of clarified concepts. Just that day she had taken great pride in the fact that her students were able to differentiate with clarity the positive and negative space in their drawings, and that she had related the terms *positive* and *negative* to other applications of the terms. But to her astonishment she realized that although they performed this distinction with skill, she had forgotten to help her students construct the major artistic concept that too much negative space was boring and too much positive space distracting.

The second event occurred as we reviewed an otherwise excellent curriculum unit published in a New York State resource guide that was designed to provide examples of enactment activities articulated with the content standards from the state curriculum (University of the State of New York, 1997).

The teacher-produced unit is one example of several in the resource guide. It is an interesting and complex one based on the topic of seed dissemination that describes creatively designed, performance-based enactment experiences and measures in great detail. With some additions and adjustments the teacher used it for classes in both the seventh and 10th grades.

The unit begins with reference to the state standards it is designed to address. Although within the document there are separate sections of content area standards that address broad themes and more specific concepts, there is a stronger and more specific focus on interdisciplinary general processes. The teaching unit is a clear manifestation of this emphasis. Processes addressed by the unit include data gathering and interpretations, design, question development, decision making, working effectively with others, analysis of ideas, and presentation skills. The enactment activities in the unit are designed to develop many of these. Included is an opportunity for students to design their own seeds, and redesign them based on collected data. There are also suggestions for students who are fast-paced learners or academically challenged, and space and time recommendations as well as safety precautions.

The assessments of performance of these processes are thorough and I use them as illustrations in our discussion of rubrics ahead. There are cooperative group measures as well as individual student reflections and self-evaluations with directed questions that ask the students about the purpose of the experience and their personal outcomes.

The only weak part of this otherwise remarkable unit is its lack of explicit specification for the science concepts involved in seed dissemination. These may be needed for the majority of elementary teachers whose subject concentration in preparation for teaching is in nonscience areas. The statement of content standards at the beginning addresses them only generally as follows: *Through the observations of seed structures and methods of seed dispersal, students will construct knowledge on:*

- adaptive advantages for seed dispersal to distribute seeds away from the parent plant
- adaptive advantages to intermittent dispersal of seeds as opposed to dispersing seeds all at once
- the beneficial impact of humans and animals on seed dispersal
- the close relationship between structure of seed and its function for seed dispersal

(University of the State of New York, 1997, II.1, p. 2)

Although the above provides an organizational outline for the concepts needed, there are no specific descriptions of the advantages, impact, and relationships. Some embedded concept statements are needed to clarify what the advantages of seed dispersal are, and how humans and animals help in the process. Such specifics would guide teachers as they scaffold and assess the development of the concepts by their students. They would also help students make connections to important themes or generalizations that would enlarge understanding. For example, the adaptive dispersal advantages of the seeds are for the purpose of minimizing competition and assuring species survival. The beneficial impact of humans and animals on seed dispersal is an example of the interdependence of plants and animals. Even though these ideas may arise in the activity discussion, they are just as likely to be missed. They were not made transparent as a content or performance standard, and therefore do not provide complete guidance either for the dialogues of enactment activities or for the construction of assessment items.

The assessment of the concepts that are stated consists of four open-ended questions (University of the State of New York, 1997, p. 5) that may have a variety of correct answers, but do not demand connections to the themes mentioned above. There are also other difficulties with the questions that further illustrate the need to clarify concepts and the considerable difficulty of structuring open-ended questions. For example, although the best question, "What are some advantages of seeds getting away from the parent plant?" hints at the major concept of species survival, it can be answered simply with "in order to get more light and water" without ever getting to the competition or survival concept. Limiting the space for answers to two or three lines also encourages minimal responses. The second question, "Why do plants not drop all their seeds at exactly the same time?" could also get to the survival concept, but it can also be answered with a simple "they ripen at different times." The third question, "What would happen if all seeds dropped together and fell in the same spot?" could be interpreted as repeats of the first two. The last question, "How might humans and animals help disperse seeds?" is also repetitive (and leading) if it is answered simply with, "they can move them away from the parent." To get at the idea of interdependence in a less leading way the question could be simply reworded: "What did you learn about seed dispersal that tells you something about the relationship between plants and animals?"

An example of the value of clearly stated and understood embedded concepts and the need for better task-driven measures as a basis for developing meaningful assessments was illustrated in the implementation of a successful long-term elementary math program change in which I was personally engaged (Solomon, 1995). To document the new curriculum, teachers produced a written K–6 curriculum with explicit content standards stated first as embedded concepts that we named as *teleologic,* or *bottom-line* (Van Lehn, 1986), and then translated into matching *criteria* or performance indicators. It was quite different from traditional curriculum documents at the time, in that for each of the conventional titles or subtopics covered, the document stated exactly what we wished our students to know (see Solomon, 2000).

The curriculum document attempted to do what Nichols (1994) suggests: predict the cognitive processes of a competent performer. The concepts and cognitive processes were grounded in ongoing research in mathematics that explored how children learn. Although teachers may have been comfortable with the procedures required by the performance indicators, many would not have previously been able to state the concepts that they depended upon. The challenge to verbalize them was a revealing experience, quickly transferred to their classrooms.

Each of the concepts was articulated with specific assessment criteria or performance indicators and median grade-level expectations based on our own experience as teachers. Instead of identifying a single grade level as the benchmark for achieving each concept, we projected a three-stage developmental sequence range over three grades: procedural exploration, concept mastery, and procedural or algorithmic mastery. The median expectations then can become the performance standard. For example, as sampled in Table 6.4 for Concept 17, by the end of the first grade we would expect most first graders to be at the concept mastery level, able to identify the parts in a single digit addition problem, construct the algorithm, and identify the whole. By the end of the second grade we would expect that they would be at the procedural mastery level, capable of computing multidigit addition algorithms and perhaps generating an original word problem from an algorithm. Although the original written document projected the three levels, it did not designate a specific performance standard level for each concept. These level standards could be decided upon as state expectations, but I believe that realistically they depend upon the very individual circumstances of the school and its students.

Included in the performance indicators were many informal measures such as observations by the teacher of how the children used manipulative materials and reasoned their estimates and solutions to problems. Basically, these measures were embedded within classroom activities (Solomon, 2000).

There was, however, also a formal end-of-the-year teacher-constructed grade-level written test with each item matched to the specific concepts tested. Table 6.4 is an edited excerpt from the written document. Table 6.5 illustrates an item that was designed to match Concept 17. In order to address the validity criterion of not measuring unintended concepts, we also read the problem to children who were not yet reading at a second-grade level. Note how the stated concepts of addition are measured by the performance indicators and then embedded in the test item. Essentially, the grade-level test

Table 6.4 A Sample from a Concept: Clarifying Scope and Sequence

Title	*Performance Expectation for Grade Level**			*Teleologic Embedded Concept (content standard)*	*Performance Indicator*
	A	B	C	<u>*What students will know:*</u>	<u>*How will we know what they know:*</u>
17. Addition: Related Facts/to eighteen	**K**	**1**	**2**	Addition is a combining of parts to form a whole, the size of the parts and the whole can be represented by symbols representing the real amounts (numbers). The symbol for the combining operation is (+).	Ability to identify parts and whole in change/result unknown combine problems Ability to construct a symbolic algorithm from the problem
18. Addition: Related Facts/to eighteen	**1**	**2**	**3**	We combine parts by adding on from one part. (Cardinal principle [*knowing that the last number counted is the size of the part]* must be in place.)	Correct new number by counting on. Two development levels: counting from first number in problem (COF) or largest number (COL)
30. Subtraction: One digit from two digits without trading. Related Facts/to eighteen.	**1**	**2**	**3**	We use subtraction to find the value of a part when we know the whole value and the value of another part. The part we <u>don't</u> know is the <u>difference</u> between the part we know and the whole. <u>To find the difference we count up from the part or down from the whole, whichever is easier.</u>	Identification of whole, known part, and difference sought from real or story problems (include comparison, change unknown, start unknown, referent unknown problems). Using real or representative materials, observed evidence of "choice" of counting up or down.

***Performance Expectation Levels:**
A. Procedural Exploration; B. Concept Mastery; C. Algorithmic or Procedural Mastery

Table 6.5 Assessment Item for Embedded Concept 17

After Halloween, Ed counted his candy lollipops. He had eight (8) red ones and five (5) green ones. Make a picture that shows the whole number of lollipops. Draw a circle around the part of the lollipops that was green and another circle around the part that was red. Then fill in the missing symbols for this problem.

8
( )( )
———
(   )

became our performance standard for the grade. In the section on rubrics ahead there will be an example (Table 6.6) of how the results of the testing can be reported for each item.

Achieving a Balance: Concepts and Performances

As history reveals, when assessments are too focused on concepts, they may be less meaningful and detached from the real-life applications in which the concepts will be needed; they draw our attention away from these applications. As some current examples of performance measures reveal, if assessments are mainly task-driven and encourage extensive preparation for a specific task, they may overlook important concepts. The repetition of a task in a particular context without the accompaniment of a generalizing concept limits the learning. Potentially, the concentration on specific tasks may even diminish the creativity and flexibility of the activities teachers plan, and promote just what we are trying to avoid, *teaching to the test.* This further narrows the curriculum. Although the negative results of "teaching to the performance test" can be lessened if worthy concepts are embedded in the task-driven measures, the inclination to make the measurement vehicle primary would remain. Clear statements of equally important content and performance indicators can avoid this consequence. If we value the concepts and the performances themselves, it is important to clarify and measure each and measure them well.

Curriculum assessed by HSSB distally prepared tests needs to have the transparency of clearly stated concepts and expected levels of performance ahead of time, and the HSSB test items in turn should come with attached connections to the concepts and expected levels of attainment. The results also need to be disaggregated in terms of these connections. I discuss the process of disaggregation in sections ahead.

CHALLENGE 3: WRITING RUBRICS

An evaluation of a student's achievement of a standard can be in terms of levels of progress toward the "level of the bar" or end result, or in terms of the overall quality of the achievement when compared to the quality of others. In either case, descriptions of the performed behaviors that mark the intervals or comparative characteristics and provide evidence of that achievement will need to be delineated. These descriptions, which are called **rubrics**, can be defined as a set of guidelines for distinguishing between performances or products of different quality. A rubric is an assessment tool that verbally describes and scales levels of student achievement on performance tasks, but it can also be associated with more conventional alphanumeric and numeric scores or grades. Rubrics should be based on the end results of stated performance standards, and be composed of scaled descriptive levels of progress toward the end result. They may also have levels above the stated standard end result. Among other criteria for creating rubrics are the following:

- They are understandable to students.
- The scores of the scale are equidistant on a continuum (at least four scores are suggested).
- Descriptors are valid (test what you want them to) and scores are reliable (consistent).
- The highest point (level) may be above the end result of the performance standard.
- Scores relate to empirically validated actual levels of student performance.
- The scale types include holistic (overall performance) and analytic dimensions; the assessment of a student performance should include both types.
- They make explicit to students, parents, and administrators the criteria for student achievement.
- They can be used by students to assess their own performance and the performance of other students.

Depending upon purposes and the standards being assessed, there are several different forms of rubrics being used by teachers. A report by The Council of Chief State School Officers (1995) defines three basic types: task specific, developmental, and relative, but there are variations and combinations. Their report also identifies strengths and weaknesses. Examples of these three types are in Tables 6.6, 6.7, 6.8, 6.9, and 6.10, and descriptions of their strengths and weaknesses are in Table 6.11. The tables are adapted from various sources.

I found the developmental type the most difficult to find a good sample for, but there are three examples here. Table 6.6 is a developmental rubric based on the named, but not clearly defined, levels in the math scope and sequence I discussed above, although only three developmental levels, attached to median grade level expectations, were described in the scope and sequence. Four levels with the top level above standard have been suggested as desirable. I believe that the top and fourth level in the case of the math concepts would be that the student is capable of applying the concept in creative ways.

For each concept as delineated in Table 6.6, the median expectation or standard of development for the grade level will be different. In essence, based on median expectations, each student can then be below, at, or above standard for each concept, but the expectations and the judgments are ordered by the developmental sequence for the concept. For example, a student may be at Level 2 (concept mastery) of the developmental sequence, but the expectation for that grade is for her to be at Level 3 (algorithmic mastery), and therefore the student is below standard.

A similar and comparative analysis can be made for the entire class.

If scored grades were desired, the report could be adapted to provide a numerical equivalent for achievement of the standards. For example, meeting the standard for the grade on Item 17 could earn a 3, surpassing it a 4, not achieving it a 1 or 2. The item scores could then be collated and translated to letter or percentage grades. Table 6.7 (adapted from Meisels, 1996-1997, p. 60) is a simple language and literacy developmental rubric used in the early grades, and Table 6.8 (The University of the State of New York, 1997) is a more definitive one that was used to assess participation in the group activities for the seed dissemination unit described earlier.

Table 6.11, which was developed by the Council of Chief State School Officers, compares the different forms. A final example of a task-specific rubric (Table 6.12) is useful for evaluating a curriculum itself. It is presented at the end of this chapter as a summary of the preceding chapters. Although the examples of a task-specific rubric (Table 6.9) and a relative rubric (Table 6.10) may be easily shared with students, the negative descriptors may have to be changed. Additional adjustments would also have to be made in the developmental rubrics for this purpose. Children might respond to math levels called: Touching, Touching and thinking, Thinking without touching, Thinking of new ways.

Table 6.6 A Developmental Math Rubric

Explanation of Levels			
Level 1	*Level 2*	*Level 3*	*Level 4*
Procedural exploration:	**Concept mastery:**	**Procedural or algorithmic mastery:**	**Application mastery:**
Can solve problems based on this concept using the real or concrete representative materials, but unable to explain concept.	Can solve problems and explain the concept used; may still need concrete material.	Can generalize the concept and use it to solve problems without concrete material.	Can generate an original problem using concept or apply it in an unusual way.

Individual Student and Class Assessment of Levels			
Concept	Expected Level For Grade	Student's Level	Class Level
17. (See standard list)	Level 2	Level 3	Level 2
18. (See standard list)	Level 1	Level 2	Level 2

Table 6.7 A Developmental Rubric

Language and Literacy: Grade 1: Fall, Winter, Spring		*F*	*W*	*S*
Listens for meaning in discussions and conversations.	Not yet In process Proficient			
Speaks easily, conveying ideas in discussions and conversations	Not yet In process Proficient			

Adapted from Meisels (1996/1997, p. 60)

Table 6.8 A Developmental Rubric: Class Participation Criteria Checklist

Level	*Speaking/Reasoning*	*Listening*
4	• Understands questions before answering • Cites appropriate evidence from background information • Expresses in complete thoughts • Displays logic and insight • Synthesizes ideas	• Pays close attention and records details • Responses include comments of others • Identifies logical errors • Overcomes distractions
3	• Responds to questions voluntarily • Comments indicate thought and reflection • Ideas draw interest from others	• Generally pays attention • Responds thoughtfully to others • Questions logical structures • Self-absorption may distract the ideas of others
2	• Responds when called upon • Comments indicate little effort in preparation • Comments may be illogical and may ignore important details • Ideas may not relate to previous comments	• Attention wavers • Classifies ideas inappropriately • Requires inordinate repetition of questions • Shows interest in own ideas
1	• Extremely reluctant to participate • Comments are illogical and meaningless • Has incomplete thoughts • Makes little relationship between comments and text	• Acts uninvolved in discussion • Misinterprets previous comments and ideas • Shows ambivalence toward any ideas presented

SOURCE: University of the State of New York, 1997.

Table 6.9 A Task-Specific Rubric

Skill	*Above Standard*	*At Standard*	*Below Standard*
Use of simple machines	Involves more than 4 kinds of machines	Involves 3-4 kinds of simple machines	Involves fewer than 3 kinds of machines
Understanding of simple machines	Can clearly and in detail explain how it works Can clearly and in detail explain how it helps us do work	Can generally explain how it works Can generally explain how it helps us do work	Has difficulty explaining how it works Has difficulty explaining how it helps us do work

SOURCE: Egeland (1997, p. 45)

Table 6.10 A Relative Rubric

Language and Literacy			
Skill	**Exceeds Standard**	**At Standard**	**Below Standard**
Listening			
Speaking			

CHALLENGE 4: DISAGGREGATING THE ASSESSMENT RESULTS

In the case of the proximal tests designed to match the curriculum and assessments described above, in addition to looking at overall results, we disaggregated the assessment responses based on the concepts tested. Separate summaries of concept mastery were generated for individual students, classes, and schools. At the beginning of the year, every teacher received a mastery-level report on the skills of incoming students to avoid unnecessary repetition and highlight needed redevelopment. Careful analysis showed us where we needed more effort. When deficiencies were analyzed, we shared responsive group and individualized instructional strategies at grade-level meetings. Modeling by the more experienced teachers for others was directed at ensuring that every child attained mastery.

This program experience offered us an additional rationale for clarifying the embedded concepts in content standards separately from the performance standards. Although the teachers engaged in implementation used a textbook at first, the clarified concepts soon became the basis for a wide range of original teacher-crafted enactment activities. If the concepts are separate and well clarified for the teacher and the student, they not only can guide the construction of planned measures, but they can be embedded with great flexibility into the enactment activities. These may then proffer unplanned and unpredicted measures of attainment.

The performance-based rubrics for newly administered state HSSB tests can allow for similar disaggregation if the items are attached more specifically to curriculum concepts. If the rubrics are also written to assess specific developmental levels of performance, the test can then be collated for individuals and smaller groups in terms of attainment of the expected levels of performance for each concept. Another form of disaggregation, however, has proven very enlightening and may be most useful in achieving equity for the schools across our nation.

Table 6.11 Rubrics: Comparing Types

Type	*Strengths*	*Weaknesses*
Task-Specific	• High inter-rater agreement • Faster to learn • Direct measure of a task	• Measures small part of a skill domain • Must develop, verify, and train a new rubric for each question or task • Poor generalizability or transferability to other real-world tasks • Doesn't indicate what to teach next
Developmental	• Increases understanding of what is meant by the concept and what to do next • Increases teaching to the skills • Direct measure of the skill • Can tell what is being assessed by looking at the rubric • Different rubrics do not have to be developed • Improved generalization of skills • Same examples can be used across different grade levels or groups	• May take longer to develop • Needs consensus from users on what skills come next • May be harder to learn, but is easier to use
Relative	• Fastest to learn • Good for the big picture • Will work for most accountability needs	• Can't always tell what is being assessed by looking at the rubric • Reliability is not always high • Rubric doesn't always help to define the concept • Dependent on different examples, i.e., anchor samples, at different grades or for different target groups • Doesn't communicate to students what to do differently at different points in time

Disaggregating for Noninstructional Differences

In our multicultural country it is important that we consider insights from multiple perspectives and learn, appreciate, and grow from these in ways that will contribute positively to policy, practice, and social justice. The search for ways to close the gaps between our many subcultures may be helped by greater understanding of the causes of those gaps. Proper treatment depends on accurate diagnosis. States are now disaggregating test results by race and geographic location and have found that even though overall results may be better, the gap between white and minority students still exists. Suburban students also still seem to be more successful than urban and rural students.

In mathematics we have long been concerned by the gender discrepancy and much effort has been expended to overcome it. A recent longitudinal study of early age-gender differences revealed the disappointing results that, despite careful reform emphases and supportive professional development for the teachers involved, girls' problem-solving strategies lagged behind those of boys (Fennema, Carpenter, Jacobs, Franke, & Levi, 1998). In our reform efforts we were similarly concerned about this difference, and disaggregation of the data gave us some interesting insights.

Our data on student achievement were also disaggregated for the variables of gender and socioeconomic status (SES). At the time the school district was a rather homogeneous suburb of New York City with a middle-income population that included many families of civil service employees. Pre-reform performance by students in mathematics, especially at the secondary level, was well below expectations. Following several years of reform, the total test scores were reassuring, but the score distributions were not entirely normal. There was a double bell curve, with a group of students well above the mean and another smaller, but noticeable group below the mean. We were anxious to discover why some groups were progressing better than others and decided to disaggregate the total scores. Gender differences were a possibility, but we also hypothesized socioeconomic variations. Because of the apparent homogeneity of the population in terms of income level, the data were also disaggregated by the mother's level of education—previously proven as an affecting socioeconomic variable. This information was also accessible because it was part of the school enrollment record. There were two categories of socioeconomic (SES) status for the first through fourth graders who took the tests. Students whose mothers had only a high school education or less were placed in one category and those whose mothers had some college were placed in another category.

We noted that, even in the first grade, there was a difference between girls and boys, but in the lower socioeconomic group the girls were slightly better than the boys, while in the higher socioeconomic groups the boys were better. As predicted, both genders of the higher SES group outscored the lower SES group. The most interesting result in our disaggregation, however, was that the significant SES differences among the boys was somewhat overcome by the end of the fourth grade. The lower SES girls, on the other hand, lost ground while the girls whose mothers had a college education caught up to their male counterparts at the same socioeconomic level.

Apparently the new program worked really well at achieving equity for everyone except the lower SES girls. There was one exception. At the second grade level a group of experienced teachers, dedicated to the new approach, seemed to have achieved greater equity. It is my hypothesis that the "pictures in the heads," the motivating goals, of the lower SES girls, which were placed there by mothers and teachers, were not easily overcome—except by particularly strong teaching. Gender, socioeconomic status, curriculum, and teaching are interactive variables. Disaggregation of scores can tell us what may need attention, and explain patterns of success and failure.

CHALLENGE 5: LEVELS OF PERFORMANCE, GRADING

It was in the process of developing formal test items for the math curriculum that the teachers and I began to struggle with the need for indicators of the achieved performance levels for specific concepts. Although we could judge fairly well whether the student had developed the concept of part, part, whole, and could generate the algorithm, it would be difficult to tell whether the children could generalize without manipulatives or a picture (see Table 6.4) or whether they had already made such a complete shift to the algorithmic procedural level that the picture making was unnecessary. Facing the challenge of constructing formal items made us realize that even for the informal classroom observations it would have been helpful if there was a way to determine at what level of concept construction the student was functioning. It may be that once concepts are so clearly stated and organized in a developmental sequence that level specificity for performance assessment is not necessary, but the benefits of thinking about the levels and measuring them are worth the effort.

Because we prepared this test not only for ourselves but also for a public audience with some anxieties about change, we did employ a quantitative substitute for explicit levels of a construct that has been frequently used by professional test makers. Having more than one item matched to a specific concept helped us decide on classifications of mastery, partial mastery, or nonmastery for the concept. This may be useful for public audiences, but it has less value as a true diagnostic for the teacher.

The requirements of a public audience remind us to consider the connection between assessment and grading. Our embrace of conventional assessments has much to do with their commonly understood comparison grades. Most of us can interpret the apparent meaning of an "A" or a 100%—it means we got all the questions right and did better than someone with a 90% or a "B." However, in general, even though these grades may be based on an objectively scored test, they are still subjective measures against a standard. Conventional test questions are, after all, based on the expectations and skills of the test maker. They may or may not be valid measures of standards.

Nevertheless, getting a grade makes us feel a sense of accomplishment; it may also allow us to close the door on a piece of work and comfortably go on to the next. My own students were apprehensive when instead of giving them grades on a long-range project I gave them ungraded, ongoing, extensive feedback on what was good and what still needed to be done. They wanted to know "where they stood." A recent survey of high school math teachers in schools that were supposedly using new assessment forms in response to the NCTM standards revealed similar findings. They wanted to grade assessments because, "Kids don't like to do things that aren't graded" (Senk, Beckman, & Thompson, 1997). Although forms of assessment used included portfolios, notebooks, interviews, and oral reports, only 7% of the grade was derived from these items. The reason for this skewed computation may be that graded assessments of performance items are more difficult to design and justify. Well-written rubrics are critical if we wish to add some objectivity to performance measures.

CHALLENGE 6: SHARING RESULTS WITH STUDENTS, PARENTS, AND THE COMMUNITY

Many educators and parents are anxious about the shift toward more authentic assessment and grading. Teachers are overwhelmed by the complex task of developing rubrics that can be translated into grades. Although it seems much easier to describe levels of task-driven performance tests than it is to define developmental levels of constructs, as evidenced by the great variation in quality of the samples above we have hardly developed mature skills in our new endeavors. As I mentioned previously, different audiences will require us to make different kinds of assessments. Reporting of the results and the consequences will vary. Reporting forms will need revision, and re-education of audiences may be necessary.

It will take time for students to develop skills and positive attitudes toward self- and peer assessments. Parents may need to be involved in the creation of new assessments or at least informed of the systems and the standards they match before they get report cards. Some audiences will insist on familiar grades. Comparative grading seems to be built into our society and many of us feel uncomfortable without it. Almost any good set of scaled rubrics can be converted to grades. But audiences need to know how the qualitative basis of rubric-based grades can be used by the teacher to inform instruction, by the parent to provide guidance and motivation, and by the student to help plan the next step.

The community may be suspicious of changes from familiar patterns, especially those that avoid the wide-scale comparisons that make them secure in their investments in home and property. Parents and public officials may be reluctant to abandon their comfortable standardized tests. It may be necessary to occasionally reassure them with the most authentic version of a national or internationally normed test (this is suggested in new NCLB legislation). Teachers may also want to construct some traditional tests so that students are prepared for these.

Among the advantages of assessments are that they cause us to focus clearly on what we wish to accomplish, and that they can be more squarely situated as a part of the instructional process. Changing assessment practices can help us do better, but there are some cautions we must take as we progress in this endeavor. We should not allow formal assessments to overpower our other goals. We cannot forget the power of the informal measures that are an integral part of the discourse we have with our students and they have with each other. The true value of any assessment lies in its ability to promote the best possible learning environment.

Meg, Brad, and April have to plan for this environment and include their assessment elements. Here are some things for them to consider as they complete their task.

- Identify which standards are mostly procedural or processes. These can usually be more easily generalized and yet individually assessed with a relative rubric.

- Identify major concepts or ideas that may be acquired gradually in a developmental sequence. These will require some developmental rubrics if you wish to measure progress levels through performance tasks. Once that is done, use the concept levels to design a conventional test as well. Occasionally compare results.

- Engage students in the process of self-assessment as much as possible. Establish patterns such as journal writing and peer editing.

- Task-specific assessments may be most helpful if they are an integral part of enactment activities. Make them work for the teacher and the students, but unless they are connected in some way to more general outcomes, it may be a waste of time to report these to distal audiences. Do not overuse them in the classroom environment either; they may interfere with other student goals. No one wants to feel that everything done is constantly assessed. Try getting students to create them.

- Make personal reflection on the results of students' assessments a routine. Be a teacher-researcher. Take the time to do an analysis that compares results of different activities. Try to discover why some activities work better than others (see Chapter 7).

- Use technology whenever possible. Use a camcorder to provide data for you and feedback for other audiences. Consider constructing performance tasks that require the students to use a computer (e.g., a PowerPoint or Hyper Studio presentation), and that can then be saved in a file for you to see and respond to when you have time, or buy a program that does that, or have the students construct the tasks for each other. Grab ideas from other teachers over the Internet. Share your ideas with other teachers. Share them with me at psolomon@stac.edu

Table 6.12 A Rubric for Evaluating Curriculum

Level 4: (Above Standard)
State standards clearly defined as content standards and performance indicators
Designed-down unit standards articulated with state commencement standards and show clear and appropriate developmental levels toward reaching them
Unit enactment activities articulated to accomplish standards and inspire students to go beyond the standards
Performance standards and assessments designed to diagnose deficiencies in achievement and direct students and teachers toward remediation measures
Assessment instruments designed to measure concepts and performances in alternate and authentic ways
Activities clearly outlined, creative and inspiring for others to follow
Technology creatively employed

(Continued)

Table 6.12 (Continued)

Level 3: (At Standard)
State standards clearly defined as content standards and performance standards
Designed-down unit standards appropriately articulated with state commencement and benchmark standards
Unit enactment activities articulated to accomplish standards
Performance measures adequately measure standards
Assessments provide some alternate and authentic measure of performance
Activities clearly outlined for others to follow. Activities are original or appropriate adaptations.
Technology employed
Level 2: (Approaching Standard)
State standards clearly defined as content standards and performance standards
Some designed-down unit standards not appropriately articulated with state commencement and benchmark standards
Some unit enactment activities not articulated well enough to accomplish standards
Performance measures not articulated well enough to adequately measure standards
Assessments provide no alternatives and measure a narrow range of skills
Some activities not clearly enough outlined for others to follow. Some originality.
Technology not adequately employed
Level 1: (Below Standard)
State standards not clearly defined as content standards and performance standards
Designed-down unit standards not appropriately articulated with state commencement and benchmark standards
Unit enabling activities not articulated well enough to accomplish standards
Performance measures not articulated well enough to adequately measure standards
Assessments measure only a limited number of skills or concepts
Enabling activities not clearly enough outlined for others to follow. Little originality.
Technology not applied

NOTES

1. Standardized tests are tests that are designed to be administered under controlled and uniform conditions, including time allocations and support from teachers and other materials. Standardized tests are usually normed. Normed tests are tests that have been administered to methodically selected sample populations (the norming sample). Scores reported for test takers are then comparatively based on the performance of participants in this sample.

2. *Juku* is an after-school intensive test preparation practice that many Japanese children attend regularly.

3. Test developers do sometimes offer item analyses that would be helpful, but they are not well used. Even criterion referenced tests have not been adequately applied by teachers.

4. Graduate Miller Analogy Test and the Scholastic Assessment Test (formerly Scholastic Aptitude Test). Computer-based forms of these commonly administered test have not proven popular with students.

7 Where Do We Go From Here?

ABOUT THIS CHAPTER

Although they had made some good progress with their project, and were having some fun doing it, it was soon evident to Meg, Brad, and April that the task of writing a curriculum based on the state science standards was indeed daunting. They were using the outline Brad had brought back from the summer workshop as a template, and the unit he had already produced with his working group fit right into what they were planning. It was interpreting the standards themselves and matching them with activities that was difficult. "How do you do scientific analysis and interpretation of data in third grade, I'm not sure even I can do that?" April wondered out loud to her colleagues. Brad responded by telling her about his experience at the summer workshop where he had an opportunity to try out some new-generation software at an IBM facility. "Well, the kids can collect data about the temperature each day with these probes that connect to a computer—or they can even use a special calculator."

Meg loved the idea of kids going out to collect data, but was still somewhat confused about what the computer could do with it once it was collected. She had always done data collection with her science kit. Her students made tables and graphs of the data they collected without using any technology except for a thermometer, a pencil, and a ruler. One of the things that concerned them all was the fact that there were only a few computers in the whole school and most of these were slow and able to use only the drill and practice software that was not that exciting to the kids anymore. A recent budget referendum that would have gotten them new computers was turned down by the community. And they had lost out to a nearby city for some federal grant money for technology.

"Do we have to use computer technology? Is that mandated by the state?" April asked. Perhaps they could find a way to get around the mandates. She remembered other times when they had ignored state curriculum guides. Brad then reminded them about the new performance tests based on the standards that their students would have to take. "I think it might be different this time," he said.

It needs to be different this time! The new millennium has brought us changes in our culture and society that will require profoundly different approaches to education—and the children, born to those for whom new technology is already as basic as the pencil and text were to us, are different. And they will have to survive and compete on a global basis with many others. This chapter is about what we need to do to build the curriculum bridge to the future.

WHERE WILL THE LEADERSHIP FOR NEEDED CHANGE COME FROM?

President Bill Clinton used the charismatic approach, not a new policy, in encouraging schools to participate voluntarily in his call for administration of national tests based on national standards. President George W. Bush has a different approach: federally determined sanctions for required state tests and instruction based on scientific research. Will these factors work to improve education in this country? Will they close the achievement gaps? There are some different opinions.

After reviewing conclusions reached by researchers who studied how education had been influenced by the relationships between different levels of government over the past decade, Michael Kirst (1995) reports that, "Power and influence in education's intergovernmental relations is not a zero-sum game whereby one level gains and another loses the ability to influence policy." Kirst suggests that state and federal initiatives can "galvanize more local curriculum policy-making and leadership at the local level, so that policy making impact of all government levels can increase simultaneously" (p. 18). This is just as it happened in Brad, April, and Meg's case. There is strong evidence that local school districts are responding broadly to the new government policies.

Kirst also proposes that even if the curriculum standards are in general form—most of the new state documents have been—they still can have an effect on practice by shaping attitudes about content and performance. He suggests that policymakers use a combination of *push* and *pull* factors to help implement new policies. Push factors include the mandated assessments, graduation requirements, and federal sanctions discussed in previous chapters. Pull factors include incentives such as grants, bonuses for principals, and demonstrations of effective practice. Based on his interpretation of the data, Kirst admits, however, that state education agencies are neither well structured nor prepared to help implement systemic reform. He identifies local school central offices as similarly fragmented, with a lack of ability to work intensively on curriculum in all subjects at one time; in agreement with many others he identifies the need for teacher capacity-building. His main conclusion is that policy can "create a skeleton or shell in which classroom practice can change" (p. 21). We need such a skeleton or shell to give better form to our restructuring efforts.

In related articles on systemic reform Cohen (1995) identifies the need for coherence in direction at all levels as a major problem, and Corcoran and Goertz (1995) find the current systems fragmented and suggest that we need to address the total system's capacity to carry out reform. These needs were illustrated in the summer workshop that Brad attended. Everyone was confused by the terminology. The state documents differed from those issued by professional organizations. Proficiency standards were widely disparate and changed in response to new legislation. New documents combined the new terms with the old ones in unexplained ways. Some had recently written new curriculum using the older terminology of goals and objectives or outcome-based education terms and had used different templates.

Corcoran and Goertz identify inappropriate sequencing of implementation as a common problem. New assessments were introduced too soon after the standards, with little time to make the necessary curriculum changes and provide needed professional development. A few teachers in Brad's workshop reported that central office and building administrators had different opinions on how to address the new standards and assessments. Because of this lack of coherence, teachers receive fragmented messages and policies are implemented with great variation. Corcoran and Goertz also suggest that we look more broadly at "the quality and quantity of the resources available for teaching" (p. 27), which I have defined as enabling standards, and more carefully at "exaggerated claims about the effectiveness of various strategies" (p. 30).

Cohen (1995) identifies teachers (and their administrators) as both the problem and the solution, and urges us to look at teachers' professional development and instructional practice if we wish to change instruction. Even if policy becomes more coherent, "coherence in policy is not the same thing as coherence in practice" (p. 16). Porter (2002) agrees that knowing the content of instruction, educational materials, content standards, and professional development is key to the implementation of education reform and the monitoring of its effects. He also suggests, however, that "there are questions about how well a particular reform of educational content is reflected in the policy environment in which teachers operate and in the supports that teachers receive to make their jobs manageable" (p. 3).

Based on a limited but intensive examination of the effects of state tests on teaching practice, Grant (2002) questions whether reformers should pin their hopes on high-stakes standards-based (HSSB) tests. He argues that they may be an "uncertain lever," and faith in them may be difficult to maintain (p. 398). Like Porter, he also questions the alignment of the tests and curriculum, as well as the intention of reform—needs I have already addressed. Although these authors identify the problems and make valid recommendations for overcoming the identified impediments to systemic reform, they offer little in the way of suggestions for the role of leadership in providing coherence for either policy or practice.

Can Research Lead Us?

This brings us back to the repeated stipulations in the 2001 revision of the Elementary and Secondary Education Act. The "No Child Left Behind" (NCLB) legislation calls for instruction that responds to "scientifically-based" research (SBR) over 100 times (Feuer, Towne, & Shavelson, 2002; Traub, 2002). It is obvious from these repetitions and attached fund allocations that research is supposed to lead the reform endeavors. The response of the educational research community to this emphasis is a mixture of gratitude and anxiety. Researchers are glad that their endeavors are recognized and are hopeful of the possibility of forthcoming funds to support their work. They are, however, anxious about the danger of a concurrent attempt to impose rigid constraints on the nature and methods of what may be classified as SBR. They see the culture of educational research as a mixture of different research cultures such as pure science and social science, and subject to the many interactions and variations of practice. They also question the commonplace, but perhaps inaccurate, impression of pure science as a rigid, invariable form. In its function, each culture has its own norms or standards of what is acceptable research practice, and these variations are worthy of respect (Berliner, 2002; Erickson & Gutierrez, 2002; Feuer et al., 2002).

Educators have traditionally responded erratically to the finding of educational research. Sometimes critical new knowledge is ignored because of inadequate dissemination and translatable connections to practice. At other times, however, sketchy findings have been catapulted to fame by clever merchandising or a talented guru who speaks the teachers' language. This kind of fame has been mostly fleeting, however, quickly replaced by some other promising new solution to the problems facing those engaged in learning and teaching.

There are some important differences between the cultures of research in pure sciences such as physics and most educational research. A critical element in proving your hypothesis in pure science research is control of all of the variables except for the one you are testing. There are so many difficult-to-control variables in the practice of education that it is almost impossible to identify one particular variable as significant and unaffected by other variables. It is, consequently, difficult to generalize that what works with one group of children and one teacher in one school environment is going to work for every child in every classroom.

Most significantly, educational research always involves human subjects. Drugs can be tried on animals whose biological systems are similar, but effective teaching methods for chimpanzees are not always the best for humans. Human subjects are also very difficult to control. I remember one incident in which I piloted a new math program with a sample of teachers in order to compare class results with comparable classes that were not piloting the program. The children, the teachers, and the parents loved the new manipulatives attached to the program so much that nonpiloting teachers begged, borrowed, and stole them for their own classes. This diminished the differences in the variables we were testing. It's called the "John Henry effect," and is common in educational research settings. A related phenomenon is the "Hawthorne effect." Its manifestation is improvement of performance or a measurable effect of change only because of newness or novelty. Unfortunately, the Hawthorne effect quickly fades.

Another difference between the two research cultures is that the chemist or biologist clearly identifies ahead of time, and with great specificity, what the goal of the research is—although there are sometimes unexpected findings. This has not always been the case in educational research. An experimental trial may reveal that the same teacher using either direct phonics instruction or whole word approaches with the same group of students is more successful at teaching new word attacks with direct instruction. Nevertheless, if the desired and assessed curriculum standard is reading with understanding, a reading program based solely on direct instruction will not achieve that standard. Furthermore, if a publicly shared test only measures program improvement as indicated by improved student performances on decoding of new words, are we willing to sacrifice the untested standard of developing appreciation for the joy of reading books within every student? And on the other hand, can we overlook the need for every individual to be able to interpret complex meaning from expository text?

As an example of the confounding complications of the NCLB legislation's controlling emphasis on SBR, the board that supervises the NAEP (National Assessment of Educational Progress) testing program is considering revisions of its tests to emphasize the phonics and basic skills approach that has been guiding some state and local reading policies and practices in recent years. This is a shift in the existing NAEP assessments, which primarily test comprehension and critical-thinking skills. A perhaps unpredicted outcome of this is that previous tests would then become useless as a baseline to judge adequate yearly progress (Manzo, 2002).

Other unrecognized variables may also be at work. A particular group of children may have short-term memory limitations that benefit from the attention-focusing methods of direct instruction; consequently, that approach proves to be more effective in teaching phonics. A teacher who is more successful with direct instruction may be uncomfortable with the diminished level of student control required for more constructivist approaches. A teacher who teaches students to use symbolic algorithms with ease, but avoids the nonroutine problems that require embedded concepts, may not be personally comfortable with the embedded math concepts. Traub (2002) also suggests that it may be a preexisting value system that affects the outcomes. Like the effect of "task-specific rewards" (Chapter 5), a teacher's belief in the efficacy of a particular method of instruction may affect the outcome.

The above does not preclude the potential value of educational research, and certainly not the importance of the scientifically structured cognitive research on learning that I described in previous chapters. We need coherence in how we structure educational settings, and part of that coherence can come from constant updating of the teacher's knowledge of how learning happens and what factors affect learning. New and useful knowledge can come from cognitive researchers in controlled settings, but it can also come from the teacher, engaged in the process of ongoing action research.

Teachers as Researchers

Teachers, in the practice of their craft, have always been researchers. Research is not in their written job description, but effective teachers always search for methods and materials that work in their classrooms and for their students. Unlike the protocols of the practice of science, however, their findings are rarely shared with others and teachers sometimes become so comfortable with what they have done in the past that they are unaware of the changed culture or nature of the students they serve. Perhaps we need to include a more formal research protocol in the teachers' job description. It may help to gain greater respect for what they do as individuals, while it informs the process of educating all of our students.

Like the scientist, before engaging in the task of finding out what educational strategy works best for our particular children, educators need to come to some kind of general consensus on what we want students to know. Beginning with broader national and state standards that represent a national consensus, the specifics of the content standards and embedded concepts must be designed down as I described in Chapter 4. This process may require choices and interpretations. There are many books that can be used to show how history was influenced by literature or vice versa, and many incidents in history that reflect the events of the current time. How do we generalize these concepts? Which books should we use? Which ones will work the best with our students, who live in their culture and at the present moment in history?

Teachers need to be engaged in consensus building on the specifics of the content, and they then need to be engaged in a process of action research that formalizes constant reflection on the effects of their instruction. This research could begin with integrated analyses of the results of state assessments and their own informal and formal assessments that can reveal what their students are, or are not, learning. Using this data, the findings of cognitive science research, and their own awareness of their students as a framework or knowledge base, teachers can hypothesize what factors of the educational environment, enabling standards, and enactment activities may have affected their students' learning.

Responsive recommendations for adjustments in the enactment of their curriculum should then be considered in interactive shared collegial discussions and tried. As Hiebert, Gallimore, and Stigler (2002) suggest, teachers' knowledge base differs from the scientific in that it is less generalizable and less independent of the context, but it might be very worthwhile to accumulate, verify, and share practitioner knowledge in a scientific manner so that it gains in its credibility to others and in the end provides us with some needed answers. Documentation of the teachers' findings may help us find answers for others. Perhaps the strength of the collation of these answers will even generate changes in HSSB assessment instruments and policies. From the researchers' point of view, when too many variables other than the tested variable affect the outcome of a scientific experiment, a very large sample size can overcome the effects of intervening variables and convey validity. No one made a particular group of human beings smoke for 20 years for the sake of finding evidence for smoking as a cause for cancer, but the size of the population of cancer victims who smoked helped confirm the results of animal research.

Figure 7.1 shows the possible multi-interactive and responsive elements of a research-based design for informing educational practice. All the arrows are bidirectional, allowing for feedback and renewal as we face the ever-changing human environment of schools. The line around the enabling standards and enactment activities is dashed because these must be responsively flexible. Research takes time, energy, and knowledge. In the university environment it is respected and separately funded. There is little counterpart effort or funding support for this endeavor in public schools. Teachers will have to learn how to be researchers, and, most important, they must be rewarded or compensated for the effort.

Figure 7.1 Interactive Design for Educational Research

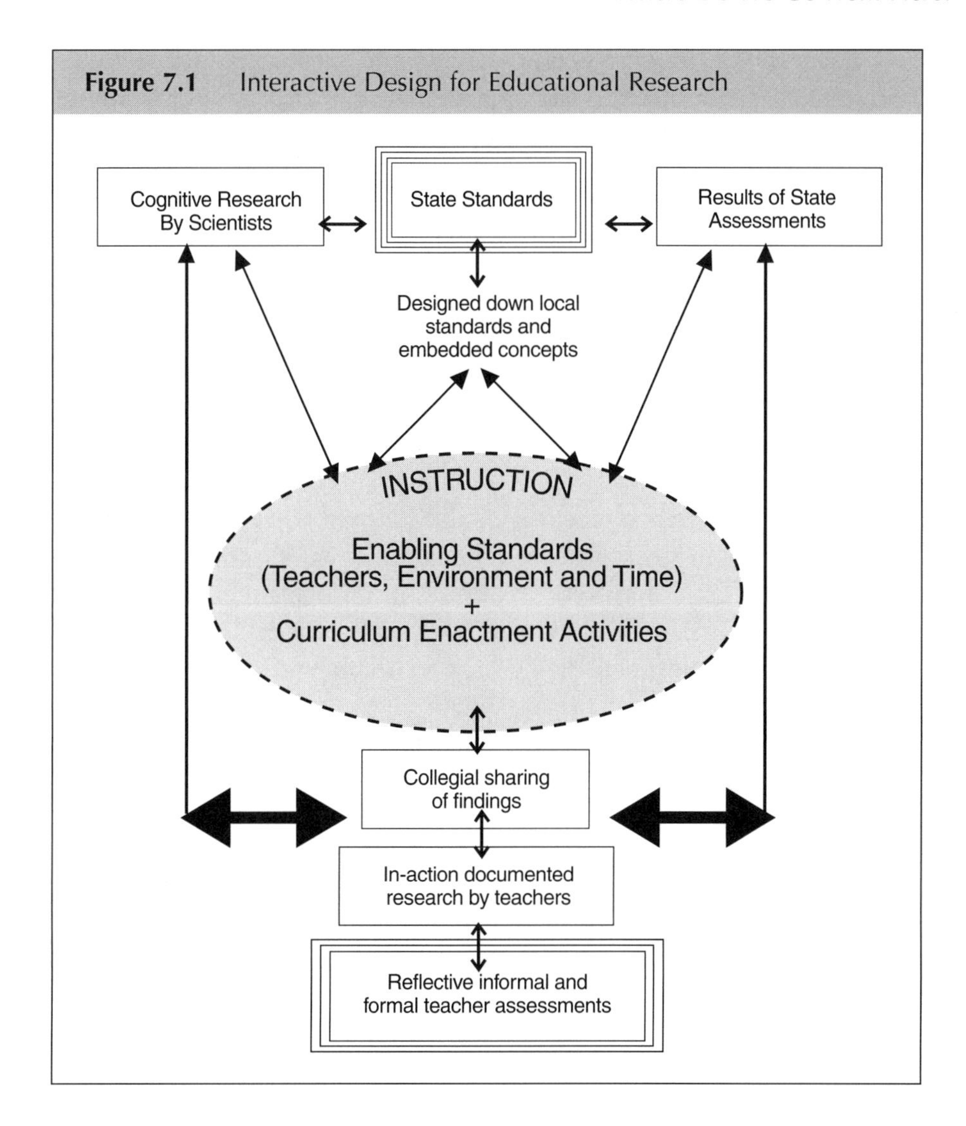

PROFESSIONAL DEVELOPMENT FOR TEACHERS

Many researchers have identified the professional development of teachers as the key to educational reform. They have also recognized that it will not be an easy task. Little (1993) explains that although traditional forms of delivery of professional development might work for the skills training components of reform, especially if transfer of knowledge from experts is followed up with opportunities to practice and is supported by coaching, the presently called for reforms go beyond skills. They require that persons in local situations grapple with what broad principles look like in practice. Teachers as researchers would need to grapple with principles and a perspective that they may not be prepared for. Little quotes Deborah Meier[1] as saying that these reforms require us to reinvent teaching and schooling.

This was exactly what Brad's curriculum writing team was struggling with. They could easily write daily lesson plans, but they had great difficulty in connecting lessons to the broad commencement standard that:

> Students will use mathematical analysis, scientific inquiry, and engineering design, as appropriate, to pose questions, seek answers, and develop solutions.[2]

Teachers need intensive professional development programs to help them accomplish this reinvention. Designing a curriculum down from a commencement content standard, constructing matching content and performance standards, and then assessing them in alternative forms at your grade level are demanding and very different tasks. Responding differentially to disaggregated analyses of test results is not something teachers have traditionally done—at least not in a systematic and formal way. Understanding and implementing a constructivist approach to teaching is a departure from the way most of us learned in school. Dealing with multiple intelligences, student goals, and building classroom dialogues that encourage metacognitive strategies and generalizations at the algorithmic level require us to learn and practice all of the new knowledge we have begun to read about in previous chapters. Just reading about these new ideas may not be enough. Like our students, we must construct new concepts. Time for interactive reflection with our peers and time for guided practice may be necessary.

Why would teachers bother to participate in professional development that would help them learn these challenging new techniques? Stout (1997) identifies some motives that have encouraged them in the past.

- Salary enhancement. Eligibility to compete for extra increments or to climb a career ladder is often tied to participation in staff development.
- Certificate maintenance. Some states have a maintenance policy.
- Career mobility. Teachers take courses and earn degrees and participate in workshops to build résumés. Having done so, they attempt to leave education for other occupations or to pursue other careers within education, administration being the notable example.

Stout maintains that none of these three motives, in itself, necessarily leads to better performance by teachers because existing systems do nothing to ensure or encourage it. He believes that a fourth motive—their intrinsic wish to gain new skills and knowledge to enhance their own classroom performance—offers the greatest promise. I agree with Stout that this fourth motive is the critical one and that programs that engage teachers more directly in plans for overall school improvement have a greater potential for success. I disagree with his minimization of the current existence of this motive. I believe that the vagueness he sees in teachers' commitment is because the extrinsic rewards of the first three motives have clouded the issue and teachers have not been given the venues in which to develop intrinsic goals. Harken back to our discussion of gold stars versus intrinsic goals in Chapter 5 when I suggest that we should give this approach a chance for teachers as well. I have seen teachers' intrinsic goals at work for a half century in my own engagement as an educator in many different roles—and as I describe below, I saw them again this summer.

If intrinsic motivation to improve their own performance is to take over from the other three motives, the nature of traditional engagement of teachers in professional development may need a whole new approach. Smylie (1996, p. 10) identifies some "best practices" in professional development that have worked. They resemble the things that work with students. They have: "a focus on the concrete tasks of day-to-day work" and opportunities to learn that are grounded in inquiry, experimentation, and reflection. They involve interaction with other teachers, and are coherent, intensive, and ongoing. We may need to get away from the present marketplace concept of professional development for teachers in which competing graduate programs are disconnected from real needs, and from the one-shot conference days and haphazard inservice programs. Engagement, documentation, and respect for teacher research can help. It may require better articulation with traditional researchers. Teacher networks and professional development school relationships offer this promise. They may also offer a new and different form of leadership.

Teacher Networks and Professional Development Schools

Teacher networks have appeared in several different forms. There are privately funded and university affiliated networks such as New Standards and the Center for Research on Evaluation Standards and Student Teaching (CRESST), which I have mentioned in previous chapters. Other successful networks include the Philadelphia Alliance for Teaching Humanities in the Schools (PATHS), the Urban Mathematics Collaboratives, and the Bay Area Writing Project. The strength of these groups is based on several aspects that include capacity for teacher support over and above the district or university, norms of informed experimentation, a system of mutual aid (mentoring) that compensates for uneven preparation of teachers, connections to the classroom, and engagement of teachers in professional discussion and debate (Little, 1993).

A more focused variant or component of a teacher network is the professional development school or PDS. In this arrangement, one district interacts in a systematic and interactive relationship with a university that prepares teachers. McConnell, Bruneau, Barbour, and Ambrose (1991) define the professional development school in its broadest interactive sense as one "in which classroom teachers and university faculty work collaboratively to better understand teaching and learning." In a truly progenerative or self-renewing educational web or network we can try to reach beyond limits of the individual place to a shared space where each educator has the potential to learn and respond to the other. The teacher-educator reflects with and learns from the inservice teacher (and principal) and vice versa.

After a study of networks that are part of the National Center for Restructuring Education, Schools, and Teaching (NCREST), Ann Lieberman (1996) reports that the opportunity for sharing among teacher participants "has the effect of dignifying and giving shape to the substance of educators' experiences. . . . Networks are particularly good at helping school-based educators discuss and work on current problems . . . teachers and administrators find it easier to question, ask for help, or tell it like it is." She describes leadership in networks as making phone calls, raising money, arranging meetings, brokering resources and people, and negotiating time commitments for university-based and school-based educators.

Our small network started as an outreach from the St. Thomas Aquinas College graduate education program to the surrounding schools. As the Marie Curie Math and Science Center, our first agenda was in math, science, and technology education; we provided inservice support and an enrichment program for secondary students.[3] Now in its 12th year, with increased funding, the network's activities have been expanded beyond these subjects. The network has several important distinguishing characteristics:

- An advisory board comprises school district administrators, teachers, parents, students, college faculty, and industry representatives.
- Through peer coaching in the inservice programs, teachers learn how to engender trust and interact with each other for the purpose of instructional improvement.
- In most cases, teachers must sign up with colleagues. The districts recruit participants in what we call PIPs or peer interactive partners. PIPs are made up of an experienced teacher and a novice.
- Cooperation with local industry. Industry has provided us with venues, materials, and personnel for the student and teacher programs.
- Many connections exist between the program elements. For example: Follow-up, school-site reflective meetings are held in the districts with college faculty members, teachers, and school administrators.
- College course practicums are held at school sites where preservice teachers work with district students.
- Teacher participants from the schools practiced in a Saturday morning science enrichment program for secondary students.
- The teachers taught on teams with scientists and college faculty at the College, at home schools, and at science industry sites. It became a learning laboratory.
- Experienced teachers who participated became paid supervisors for student teachers in the College's teacher-education program.

The broader role of the network includes all of the school districts within an entire county, local teachers centers, and the college. There is also a more intensive professional development school (PDS) relationship with one large district that has a high minority enrollment (see Solomon, 2002, for descriptions of this component). Our support comes to us from some private sources, the districts, the college, and the state (using federal sources), and we are accountable to each policy-making entity to some degree, but essentially we have designed our agenda, shared it, and received approval.

Following a study of state-supported teacher networks, Firestone and Pennell (1997) present three propositions that offer suggestions for the design of networks. I will use our Marie Curie Center experience as confirmation, elaboration, or correction of their propositions.

Proposition 1. *Capacity-building networks contribute more directly to teacher learning, motivation, and empowerment than do policy-supporting networks.*

Although most of our program has involved teacher capacity-building, we work closely with school administrators to provide policy support as well. Several administrators and college faculty have become involved in our programs, either as participants or as supporting faculty. Everyone needs to be informed of their responsibilities toward meeting the standards, and they need the capacity to deal with them and the new technology they demand. It may be a good idea to combine the groups. The discomfort we observed in the beginning was with accepting and understanding the standards, and with the requirement for a product of written curriculum that matched them. A few participants had a hard time accepting this responsibility, probably because of previous, less-rigorous staff development experiences. After they got going, they were all fine. Like Brad, most participants not only enjoyed the technology components but immediately worked some of them into their curriculum units.

Proposition 2. *Extrinsic incentives can attract teachers, but teachers are most likely to continue participating when they receive the intrinsic incentives that come from learning that is useful in the classroom.*

Our network provides monetary incentives in the form of stipends, but these rarely match regular pay. Another incentive is the opportunity for graduate credit at a reduced cost, which can then be used as Stone has defined above. Some teachers opt for this. They are mostly the novices in the PIPs, who needed the credits. Even though some teachers complained at first about having to work in groups to write their own curriculum units (a task they had previously viewed as an isolated one), they ended up loving the opportunity to share the experience with colleagues outside of their districts and created high-quality units (see the anecdote below).

Proposition 3. *Networks reach a greater variety of teachers by offering a mix of constructivist and directive activities.*

We have done just that! Programs begin with a formal, more directive course (nondirective activities are embedded), but they are followed by specific time for interaction back at the home school. It was in this time that teachers intersubjectively constructed new knowledge (see Chapter 3). The summer curriculum writing challenge usually begins with some direct instruction that includes embedded constructivist activities as models (colleagues often present the models). This is followed by additional days spread out over the school year for teachers to interact with their working group and try their units with their students.

In the more concentrated effort of our PDS component we have piloted the teachers' newly constructed curriculum units and materials and then engaged reorganized teams of teachers in the process of review and decision making. An interesting finding was that it was in the process of constructing their own matching proximal (local) assessments for each unit that teachers reflectively began to achieve clarity and take ownership of the content standards and embedded concepts.

Assessments of achievement of the content standards we planned for the teachers in previous programs were based on self-assessment questionnaires and follow-up interviews with them and their principals during the following year as they practiced what they had learned. They show growth in the use of the particular skills, but even greater all-around impact on their professional relationships with colleagues. And this is of significant value in that it sets the stage for long-term improvement.

Teacher Networks as Leaders

The real evidence for the leadership value of teacher networks is in the long-term improvement of practice and in the consequent improved achievement of students; that remains to be measured. I disagree, however, with one of Firestone and Pennell's (1997) conclusions. They state that most teachers are not ready for challenging instruction or complex thinking about instruction and that they would benefit more from direct instruction. Thinking such as this is tantamount to having low expectations for your students and then having them realized. High standards mean high standards for teachers as well, and this means giving them greater responsibility for complex thinking and decision making. Ready or not, they must face the challenge of learning how to provide this kind of instruction for their students and this is the model we should use for them!

Teacher networks can help them do this in that they overcome the fragmentation that exists between schools and districts, and between schools and higher education institutions. Given the right policy support, networks can also relieve the burden of overextended state education and central office personnel. A word of caution, however, is that the network must be seen as part of the overall district staff development program, not as a separate entity. Its efforts must be integrated into whatever is happening on a local level. I have tried to deal with this potential problem by maintaining close contact with state- and district-level policymakers and demonstrating the quality of our efforts. For example, Brad came to the McExtend program at the suggestion of his principal to prepare for the curriculum work with April and Meg. He came back with ideas, shared knowledge, and a template for beginning his design that reflected a common vocabulary that reached beyond his own setting—and made his work assume greater importance and prestige. As noted above, we also try to limit our program instructional staff to all levels of network participants. But I think the following personal anecdote gives us another aspect of the value of teachers learning together and the value of networks.

* * *

Kathy and John came in to my office today. Kathy is a Biology teacher (and new department chairman) at a network high school. John is a professor of Biology at the college. Both of them had worked in the Marie Curie program for secondary students, but they did not really know each other until they joined the same working group this summer. I had earlier asked Kathy to again join us in the kids program, but she had hesitated because of her new responsibilities.

At this moment in time they might both have been unrecognizable to their students. They were covered in mud! Their curriculum writing had taken them to a nearby stream to find out what was there for their students to find. They were quite animated and joked with each other about a big fish and turtle that almost nipped Kathy's leg. Spontaneously, they blurted out how much fun it had been to work on this project together—and to my surprise suggested that they could team up and try their new curriculum units with the kids on Saturday mornings.

* * *

The curriculum units and the relationships formed may take us beyond this little episode into even greater opportunities for learning by sharing. The units are posted on the Web for the benefit of teachers all over the world: www.stac.edu/mcc/indexrev.htm. And this brings us to another kind of network and another promise for the future.

USING TECHNOLOGY AND ITS NETWORKS FOR SHARING CURRICULUM AND RESEARCH

Interactive sharing among today's teachers is no longer limited to the place in which they work. The possibility for new knowledge based on technology exists for them as it does for their students. The Web already offers much that can be helpful to teachers. From their own classroom or home computers they can access curriculum documents and sample assessments that teachers have produced all over the world. They can discuss them with the writers and with other colleagues who have used them. Their discussions make the owner/originator feel a sense of efficacy (they can count the hits) and perhaps inspire the users to return the sharing favor. Preservice teachers (and experienced teachers) practicing in the field in a rural environment can access these materials, and can communicate regularly with professors and classmates back at their far-away institutions.

Teachers can use technology to record and pool their research findings, disaggregate the data, and translate them into more friendly graphic presentations. In my vision, based on computer-managed assessment analyses, teachers would be able to generate a slate of curriculum enactment activities appropriate to the needs of a class or smaller group of students within the class. And then of the most value to us all would be a follow-up report on the effect of those enactment activities. Technology can be used to communicate with others who share our responsibilities. It can also be used to communicate with the public that judges what we do.

TECHNOLOGY FOR COMMUNICATING WITH OUR PUBLIC

Technology can help us do a better job of communicating with parents and the public. It can also bring us help from others. Parents with computers no longer need to ask, "What did you do today?" if they can get an online report from the teacher. Many schools and classes now have Web pages where students can post and share their work. Students out ill can get assignments and interact with classmates back at school. The school district in which I live has many students who come from economically deprived homes without computers. We planned to put them in community centers and local businesses that want to help with access for the children. The libraries and churches already have them. We also planned for a volunteer corps of community online homework helpers. Greater involvement by these individuals may engender greater knowledge of what we do, and greater trust in our efforts may be the unexpected result. School report cards online may still be requested, but reading students' stories and viewing their artwork may be more convincing, and more meaningful. We will, however, have to be careful what we send!

And this brings us to a word of caution. The virtual nature of the Internet demands that we all learn new information filtering skills, skills that were always necessary but are more so now that the forms of communication are so expanded. We need to learn how to evaluate what others say. We cannot accept everything on the Internet as truth. It doesn't even have a librarian to help screen the stuff we see. Because it is virtual, we still need teachers to make the decisions about when and how to use technologically based experiences and information, and we still need the human social learning requirement of face-to-face interaction with other human beings. Even the techies flock to computer conferences, and my computer scientist daughter prefers a phone call to e-mail. Most students prefer to have a friend at their side as they explore the world with their computers. Brad, April, and Meg can read this book and access the standards of many states, and the curriculum units of many teachers including those in our network. But as they implement the standards that others may have agreed upon and that they have been given responsibility for, they will still need to use real spoken words; smiles of understanding, approval, and satisfaction; quizzical looks of confusion; and other human exchanges as they learn with each other and with their students across the curriculum bridge.

NOTES

1. Deborah Meier is the principal of the Central Park East School in New York City. The school has been very successful using a restructured curriculum and alternative assessments with diverse populations of students.
2. Standard 1 of the New York State Standards in math, science, and technology.
3. The Marie Curie program is validated by the State of New York for dissemination purposes.

References

Allan, S. D. (1991). Ability grouping research reviews: What do they say about grouping and the gifted? *Educational Leadership, 48*(6), 60–74.

Altmann, J., & Trafton, J. G. (2002). Memory for goals: An activation-based model. *Cognitive Science, 26,* 39–83.

American Association for the Advancement of Science. (1989). *2061: Science for all Americans.* Washington, DC: Author.

American Association for the Advancement of Science. (1994). *Benchmarks for science literacy.* Washington, DC: Author.

American Federation of Teachers. (1999). *Making standards matter 1999.* Washington, DC: Author.

Anderman, E. M., & Maehr, M. L. (1994). Motivation and schooling in the middle grades. *Review of Educational Research, 64*(2), 287–309.

Anderson, J. R. (1983). *The architecture of cognition.* Cambridge, MA: Harvard University Press.

Anderson, J. R. (1990). *The adaptive character of thought.* Hillsdale, NJ: Lawrence Erlbaum.

Anderson, J. R. (2002). Spanning seven orders of magnitude: A challenge for cognitive modeling. *Cognitive Science, 26,* 85–112.

Anderson, J. R., & Betz, J. (2002). A hybrid model of categorization. *Cognitive Science, 26,* 39–83.

Anderson, J. R., & Douglass, S. (2001). Tower of Hanoi: Evidence of the cost of goal retrieval. *Journal of Experimental Psychology: Learning, Memory, and Cognition, 27*(6).

Anderson, J. R., Matessa, M., & Lebiere, C. (1997). ACT-R: A theory of higher level cognition and its relation to visual attention. *Human Computer Interaction, 12,* 439–462.

Anderson, J. R., Reder, L. M., & Simon, H. A. (1996). Situated learning and education. *Educational Researcher, 25*(4), 5–11.

Anderson, J. R., Reder, L. M., & Simon, H. A. (1997). Rejoinder: Situated versus cognitive perspectives: Form versus substance. *Educational Researcher, 26*(1), 18–21.

Apple, M. (2001). Markets, standards, teaching and teacher education. *Journal of Teacher Education, 52*(3), 241–247.

Associated Press. (2001, September 23). Lawmakers move ahead on education. *[Rockland County, N.Y.] Journal News.*

Associated Press. (2002, November 8). N.Y. superintendents urge colleges to overlook scores. *Washington Post,* p. A14.

Ausubel, D. P. (1963). *The psychology of meaningful learning*. New York: Grune & Stratton.

Ausubel, D. P. (1968). *Educational psychology: A cognitive view*. New York: Holt, Rhinehart & Winston.

Bailey, S. M. (1996). Shortchanging boys and girls. *Educational Leadership, 53*(8), 75–79.

Baker, D. F. (1997). Response: Good news, bad news, and international comparisons: Comment on Bracey. *Educational Researcher, 26*(3), 16–17.

Ball, D. L., & Cohen, D. K. (1996). Reform by the book: What is—or might be—the role of curriculum materials in teacher learning and instructional reform. *Educational Researcher, 25*(9), 6–8, 14.

Barksdale-Ladd, M. A., & Thomas, K. F. (2000). What's at stake in high-stakes testing: Teachers and parents speak out. *Journal of Teacher Education, 51*(5), 384–397.

Barlow, J. P. (1991). Coming into the country. *Communications of the ACM, 34*(3), 19–21.

Barton, P. E. (2002). Raising achievement and reducing gaps: Reporting progress toward goals for academic achievement in mathematics. *National Educational Goals Panel Report*. Available online at: http://www.negp.gov/reports/Raising AchievementReducingGaps

Berliner, D. (2002). Educational research: The hardest science of all. *Educational Researcher, 31*(8), 18–20.

Berliner, D. C., & Biddle, B. J. (1995). *The manufactured crisis: Myths, fraud and the attack on America's public schools*. Reading, MA: Addison-Wesley.

Bert, A. (2001, May 17). Rally rips state exams. *[Rockland County, N.Y.] Journal News*, p. A1.

Blakesley, S. (1995, March 21). How the brain might work: A new theory of consciousness. *New York Times*, pp. C1, C10.

Bornfield, G. (2000). In: Agora: The impact of high-stakes testing. *Journal of Teacher Education, 51*(4), 289–292.

Borthwick, A., & Nolan, K. (1996). Performance standards: How good is good enough. *Pre-Summit Briefing Materials: 1996 National Education Summit*. Palisades, NY: Governors' Commission Report for New Standards.

Bracey, G. W. (1996). International comparisons and the condition of American education. *Educational Researcher, 25*(1), 5–11.

Bracey, G. W. (1997). On comparing the incomparable: A response to Baker and Stedman. *Educational Researcher, 26*(3), 19–26.

British Broadcasting System (BBC). (2002, October). *"Never again" says exams chief*. The System: Online at http://news.bbc.co.uk/2/hi/education/2314299.stm

Bruni, F. (2001, August 2). Bush promotes education, and in a calculated form. *New York Times*, p. A14.

Bryant, A., & Houston, P. (1997). The roles of superintendent and school board in engaging the public with public schools. *Kappan, 78*(10), 756–759.

Cameron, J. (2001) Negative effects of reward on intrinsic motivation—A limited phenomenon: Comment on Deci, Ryan & Koestner. *Review of Educational Research, 71*(1), 29–42.

Canady, R. L., & Rettig, M. D. (1995). The power of innovative scheduling. *Educational Leadership, 53*(3), 4–10.

Carpenter, T. P., et al. (1994, April). *Teaching mathematics for learning and understanding in the primary grades.* Paper presented to the American Educational Research Association, New Orleans.

Cattell, R. B. (1963). Theory of fluid and crystallized intelligence: A critical experiment. *Journal of Educational Psychology, 54,* 1–22.

Checkley, K. (1997). The first seven . . . and the eighth: A conversation with Howard Gardner. *Educational Leadership, 55*(1), 8–13.

Chubb, J. E., & Moe, T. M. (1990). *Politics, markets, and America's schools.* Washington, DC: Brookings Institution.

Cobb, P. (1990). Multiple perspectives. In L. P. Steffe & T. Wood (Eds.), *Transforming children's mathematics education: International perspectives* (pp. 200–215). Hillsdale, NJ: Lawrence Erlbaum.

Cobb, P., & Bowers, J. (1999). Cognitive and situated learning perspectives in theory and practice. *Educational Researcher, 28*(2), 4–15.

Cochran-Smith, M. (2000). Gambling on the future. *Journal of Teacher Education, 51*(4), 259–261.

Cohen, D. K. (1995). What is the system in systemic reform? *Educational Researcher, 24*(9), 11–17.

Cohen, E. G. (1994). Restructuring the classroom: Conditions for productive small groups. *Review of Educational Research, 64*(1), 1–35.

Cohen, E. G., & Lotan, R. A. (1995). Producing equal status interaction in the heterogeneous classroom. *American Educational Research Journal, 32*(1), 99–121.

Cooper, H., & Dorr, N. (1995). Race comparisons on need for achievement: A meta-analytic alternative to Graham's narrative review. *Review of Educational Research, 65*(4), 483–508.

Corcoran, T., & Goertz, M. (1995). Instructural capacity and high performance standards. *Educational Researcher, 24*(9), 27–31.

Council for Basic Education. (1996). *History in the making: An independent review of the voluntary national history standards.* Washington, DC: Author.

Council of Chief State School Officers. (1995). *State collaborative on assessment and student standards year-end report.* Washington, DC: Author.

Darling-Hammond, L. (1990). Instructional policy into practice: "The power of the bottom over the top." *Educational Evaluation and Policy Analysis, 12*(3), 233–241.

Deci, E. L., Koestner, R., & Ryan, R. M. (2001). Extrinsic rewards and intrinsic motivation in education: Reconsidered once again. *Review of Educational Research, 71*(1), 1–27.

Dewey, J. (1973). Education as a social function. In S. D. Sieber & D. E. Wilder (Eds.), *The school in society.* New York: Free Press. (Original work published 1916.)

Doll, W. P. (1993). *A post-modern perspective on curriculum.* New York: Teachers College Press.

Dossey, J. A., Mullis, I. V. S., Lindquist, M. M., & Chambers, D. L. (1988). *The mathematics report card: Are we measuring up?* Princeton, NJ: Educational Testing Service.

Dweck, C. S., & Leggett, E. L. (1988). A social-cognitive approach to motivation and personality. *Psychological Review, 95,* 256–273.

Edmonds, R. R. (1983). Programs of school improvement: An overview. *Educational Leadership, 40*(4), 4–11.

Edwards, C. E. (1995). The 4 x 4 plan. *Educational Leadership, 53*(3), 16–19.

Egeland, P. (1997). Pulleys, planes and student performance. *Educational Leadership, 54*(4), 41–45.

Erickson, F., & Gutierrez, K. (2002). Culture, rigor, and science in educational research. *Educational Researcher, 31*(8), 21–24.

Fennema, E., Carpenter, T. P., Jacobs, V. R., Franke, M. L., & Levi, L. W. (1998). A longitudinal study of gender differences in young children's mathematical thinking. *Educational Researcher, 27*(5), 6–11.

Feuer, M. J., Towne, L., & Shavelson, R. J. (2002). Scientific culture and educational research. *Educational Researcher, 31*(8), 4–14.

Firestone, W. A., Fitz, J., & Broadfoot, P. (1999). Power, learning and legitimation: Assessment implementation across levels in the United States and the United Kingdom. *American Educational Research Journal, 36*(4), 759–793.

Firestone, W. A., & Pennell, J. R. (1997). Designing state sponsored teacher networks: A comparison of two cases. *American Educational Research Journal, 34*(2), 237–266.

French, H. W. (2002, September 23). Educators try to tame Japan's blackboard jungles. *New York Times,* p. A6.

Fullan, M. (1990). Staff development, innovation, and institutional development. In B. Joyce (Ed.), *Changing school cultures through staff development* (pp. 3–25). Alexandria, VA: Association for Supervision and Curriculum Development.

Fuson, K., Wearne, D., Hiebert, J., Murray, H., Human, P., Olivier, A., Carpenter, T. P., & Fennema, E. (1997). Children's conceptual structures for multi-digit numbers and methods of multi-digit addition and subtraction. *Journal for Research in Mathematics Education, 28*(2), 130–162.

Gandal, M. (2002). Multiple choices: How will states fill in the blanks in their testing systems? In *No child left behind: What will it take?* Thomas B. Fordham Foundation. Available online at www.achieve.org

Gardner, H. (1983). *Frames of mind: The theory of multiple intelligences.* New York: Basic Books.

Gardner, H. (1993). *Multiple intelligences: The theory in practice*. New York: Basic Books.

Gardner, H. (1995). Multiple intelligences: Myths and messages. *Kappan, 77*(3), 202–209.

George, J. (1995). A loft-y idea for learning. *Educational Leadership, 53*(3), 56–57.

Gerstner, L. V. (2001, October 9). Paper presented at the National Education summit, Palisades, New York. Retrieved January 15, 2002, from www.ibm.com/lvg/1009.phtml

Ginsburg, H. P. (1989). *Children's arithmetic: How they learn it and how you teach it.* Austin, TX: Pro.Ed.

Glass, S. R. (1997). Markets & myths: Autonomy in public and private schools. *Education Policy Analysis Archives*, *5*(1). Available online at http://olam.ed.asu.edu/epaa/v5n1/problem.html

Glasser, W. (1986). *Control theory in the classroom.* New York: Harper and Row.

Glenn, J. (2000). *Before it's too late. A report to the nation from the National Commission on Mathematics and Science Teaching for the 21st Century*. Jessup, MD: U.S. Department of Education, Education Publishing Center.

Goodnough, A. (2002, September 25). If test scores of students swell, so may superintendents' wallets. *New York Times,* p. A1.

Graham, S. (1995). Narrative versus meta-analytic studies of race differences in motivation. *Review of Educational Research, 65*(4), 509–517.

Grant, S. G. (2002). An uncertain lever: Exploring the influence of state level testing in New York State on teaching social studies. *Teachers College Record, 103*(3), 398–426.

Greene, S., & Ackerman, J. M. (1995). Expanding the constructivist metaphor: A rhetorical perspective on literacy research and practice. *Review of Educational Research, 65*(4), 383–420.

Greeno, J. G. (1997). Responses on claims that ask the wrong questions. *Educational Research, 26*(1), 5–17.

Gross, J. (2002, September 25). Paying for disability diagnosis to help on college boards. *New York Times,* pp. A1, B5.

Gutwillig, R. (1996, June 24). Kids, teachers offer thoughts on education. *Rockland Journal News,* p. 5.

Hartenbach, D. L., Ott, J., & Clark, S. (1996/1997). Performance based education in Aurora. *Educational Leadership, 54*(4), 51–55.

Hartocollis, A. (2001, October 16). Scarsdale warned not to boycott state tests. *New York Times*, p. A3.

Hayward, E. (2001, September 25). Appeals process blueprint to go to ed board. *Boston Herald,* p. 21.

Heid, M. K. (1988). Resequencing skills and concepts in applied calculus using the computer as a tool. *Journal for Research in Mathematics Education, 19*(1), 3–25.

Herman, J. L., Aschbacher, P. R., & Winters, L. (1992). *A practical guide to alternative assessment.* Alexandria, VA: Association for Supervision and Curriculum Development.

Hiebert, J., Gallimore, R., & Stigler, J. W. (2002). A knowledge base for the teaching profession: What would it look like and how can we get one? *Educational Researcher, 31*(5), 3–15.

Hoff, D. J. (1997, February 12). Clinton gives top billing to education plan. *Education Week on the Web.* Available online at www.edweek.org

Hoff, D. J. (2002, October 9). States revise the meaning of proficient. *Education Week on the Web.* Available online at www.edweek.org

Horn, J. L. (1985). Remodeling old models of intelligence. In B. B. Wolman (Ed.), *Handbook of intelligence* (pp. 267–300). New York: John Wiley.

House, E. R. (1996). A framework for appraising educational reforms. *Educational Researcher, 25*(7), 6–14.

Immerwahr, J., & Johnson, J. (1996). Americans' views on standards. *Pre-Summit briefing materials*: *1996 National Education Summit*. Palisades, NY: Governors' Commission Report for Public Agenda.

Japan Society of Mathematical Education. Excerpts from Mathematics program in Japan. (1990). In Pre-Summit Briefing Materials: 1996 National Education Summit. Palisades, NY: Governors' Commission Report for New Standards.

Johnson, D. W., & Johnson R. T. (1989). *Cooperation and competition: Theory and research.* Edina, MN: Interaction Books.

Johnson, D. W., Johnson R. T., & Holubec, E. J. (1987). *Revised circles of learning: Cooperation in the classroom.* Edina, MN: Interaction Books.

Joyce, B., & Weil, M. (1996). *Models of teaching*. Boston: Allyn & Bacon.

Kirshner, D. (2002). Untangling teachers, diverse aspirations for student learning: A cross-disciplinary strategy for relating psychological theory to pedagogical practice. *Journal for Research in Mathematics Education, 33*(1), 46–58.

Kirst, M. W. (1995). Recent research in intergovernmental relations in education. *Educational Researcher, 24*(9), 18–22.

Kohn, A. (1993). *Punished by rewards: The trouble with gold stars, incentive plans, A's, praise, and other bribes*. Boston: Houghton Mifflin.

Kohn, A. (1996). By all available means: Cameron & Pierce's defense of extrinsic motivators. *Review of Educational Research, 66*(1), 1–4.

Labaree, D. F. (1997). Public goods, private goods: The American struggle over educational goals. *American Educational Research Journal, 34*(1), 39–81.

Lehmann, S., & Spring, E. (1996). High academic standards and school reform: Education leaders speak out. *Pre-Summit Briefing Materials: 1996 National Education Summit.* Palisades, NY: Governors' Commission Report for New Standards.

Lepper, M. R., Keavney, M., & Drake, M. (1996). Extrinsic motivation and intrinsic rewards: A commentary on Cameron and Pierce's meta-analysis. *Review of Educational Research, 66*(1), 33–38.

Lerman, S. (1996). Intersubjectivity in mathematics learning: A challenge to the radical constructivist paradigm? *Journal for Research in Mathematics Education, 27*(2), 133–150.

Lezotte, L. W. (1981). Search for and description of characteristics of effective elementary schools: Lansing public schools. In R. R. Edmonds (Ed.), *A report on the research project: Search for effective schools* (pp. 6–15). East Lansing: Michigan State University.

Lieberman, A. (1996). Creating learning communities. *Educational Leadership, 54*(3), 51–55.

Linn, R. L. (2000). Assessment and accountability. *Educational Researcher, 29*(2), 4–16.

Linn, R. L., Baker, D. F., & Betebenner, D. W. (2002). Accountability systems: Implications of requirements of the No Child Left Behind act of 2001. *Educational Researcher, 31*(6), 3–16.

Little, J. W. (1993). Teachers' professional development in a climate of educational reform. *Educational Evaluation and Policy Analysis, 15*(2), 129–151.

Lohman, D. F. (1989). Human intelligence: An introduction to advances in theory and research. *Review of Educational Research, 59*(4), 333–373.

Longstreet, W. S., & Shane, H. G. (1993). *Curriculum for a new millennium.* Needham, MA: Allyn & Bacon.

Lou, Y., Abrami, P. C., Spence, J. C., Poulsen, C., Chambers, B., & D'Appolina, S. (1996). Within-class grouping: A meta-analysis. *Review of Educational Research, 66*(4), 423–458.

Madaus, G., West, M. M., Harmon, M. C., Lomax, R. G., Viator, K. A., Mungal, C. F., Butler, P. A., McDowell, C., & Simmons, E. (1992). *The influence of testing on teaching math and science in grades 4–12.* Boston: Boston College, Center for the Study of Testing, Evaluation, and Educational Policy.

Mann, D., MacLaughlin, M. W., Baer, M., Greenwood, P. W., Prusoff, L., Wirt, J., & Zelman, G. (1975). *Federal programs supporting education change.* Santa Monica, CA: RAND.

Manzo, K. K. (2002). NAEP board initiates reading-test overhaul. *Editorial Projects in Education, 22*(10), 25, 28.

Marzano, R., Brandt, R., Hughes, S., Jones, B. F., Presseisen, B. Z., Rankin, S., & Suhor, C. (1988). *Thinking: A framework for curriculum and instruction.* Alexandria, VA: Association for Supervision and Curriculum Development.

Mayer, R. E., Sims, V., & Tajika, H. (1995). A comparison of how textbooks teach mathematical problem solving in Japan and the United States. *American Educational Research Journal, 32*(2), 443–460.

McCaslin, M. (1996). The problem of problem representation: The Summit's conception of student. *Educational Researcher, 25*(8), 13–15.

McConnell, J., Bruneau, B., Barbour, N., & Ambrose, R. (1991). From collective entrepreneurship to collaborative professional development: Thoughts on the professional growth of teacher educators. In R. Hawthorne & J. G. Henderson (Eds.), *Collaborative reflections: Colleges of education as professional development schools.* Salem, OH: Kent State University and Graduate School of Education.

McInerny, D. M., Roche, L., McInerny, V., & Marsh, H. (1997). Cultural perspectives on school motivation: The relevance and application of goal theory. *American Educational Research Journal, 34*(1), 207–236.

McNight, C. C., Grosswith, F. J., Dossey, J. A., Kifer, E., Swafford, J. O., Trevers, K. J., & Cooney, T. J. (1987). *The underachieving curriculum: Assessing U.S. school mathematics from an international perspective.* Champaign, IL: Stipes.

McREL Institute. (1993). *Conference materials.* Aurora, CO: Mid Continent Regional Educational Laboratory.

McTighe, J. (1996/1997). What happens between assessments? *Educational Leadership, 54*(4), 6–12.

Medina, J. (2002, October 28). Stress just part of the test for selective high schools. *New York Times,* pp. B1, B8.

Meisels, S. J. (1996/1997). Using work sampling in authentic assessments. *Educational Leadership, 54*(4), 60–65.

Messick, S. (1994). The interplay of evidence and consequences in the validation of performance assessments. *Educational Researcher, 23*(2), 13–23.

Mosle, S. (1996a, October 27). The answer is national standards. *New York Times Magazine,* pp. 44–47.

Mosle, S. (1996b, September 12). Scores count. *New York Times Magazine,* pp. 41–45.

National Art Education Association. (1994). *A priority for reaching high standards.* Reston, VA: Author.

National Center for Policy Analysis. (2000). *Extra SAT test time given those claiming learning disabilities.* Retrieved November 17, 2002, from http://www.ncpa.org/pi/edu/pd011100a.html

National Commission on Excellence in Education. (1983). *A nation at risk.* Washington, DC: U.S. Department of Education.

National Council for the Social Studies. (1994). *Curriculum standards for the social studies: Expectations of excellence.* Washington, DC: Author.

National Council of Teachers of Mathematics. (2000). *Principles and standards for school mathematics.* Reston, VA: Author.

National Council of Teachers of Mathematics, Commission on Standards for School Mathematics. (1989). *Curriculum and evaluation standards for school mathematics.* Reston, VA: Author.

National Education Commission on Time and Learning. (1994). *Prisoners of time.* Washington, DC: Government Printing Office.

National Research Council. (1996). *National science education standards.* Washington, DC: National Academy Press.

Natriello, G. (1996). Diverting attention from conditions in American schools. *Educational Researcher, 25*(8), 7–9.

New Jersey Educators Association. (1996, March). Commentary: Making the standards work. *NJEA Review,* p. 76.

New York State School Boards Association. (1990). *School boards & curriculum: Special focus on science and mathematics—A position paper.* Albany, NY: Author.

Nichols, P. D. (1994). A framework for developing cognitively diagnostic assessments. *Review of Educational Research, 64*(4), 575–603.

Ogawa, R. T. (1994). The institutional sources of educational reform: The case of school-based management. *American Educational Research Journal, 35*(3), 519–548.

Ohanian, S. (2002). In: Agora: The impact of high-stakes testing. *Journal of Teacher Education, 51*(4), 289–292.

Orton, R. E. (1995). Ockham's razor and Plato's beard. *Journal for Research in Mathematics Education, 26*(3), 204–229.

Pajares, F. (1996). Self-efficacy beliefs in academic settings. *Review of Educational Research, 66*(4), 543–578.

Peeno, L. N. (1995). *Status of arts in the states.* Reston, VA: NAEA.

Piaget, J. (1926). *The language and thought of the child.* New York: Harcourt Brace.

Piaget, J. (1977). *The development of thought: Equilibration of cognitive structures.* New York: Viking.

Pintrich, P. R., Marx, R. W., & Boyle, R. A. (1993). Beyond cold conceptual change: The role of motivational beliefs and contextual factors in the process of conceptual change. *Review of Educational Research, 63*(2), 167–169.

Popham, W. J. (2001). Teaching to the test. *Educational Leadership, 58*(6), 16–20.

Popkewitz, T. S. (2000). The denial of change in educational change: Systems of ideas in the construction of national policy and evaluation. *Educational Researcher, 29*(1), 17–29.

Porter, A. C. (2002). Measuring the content of instruction: Uses in research and practice. *Educational Researcher, 31*(7), 3–14.

Public Agenda. (2002, Summer). *Students say they take standardized tests in stride.* New York: Author. Also available online at www.publicagenda.org

Purdie, N., & Hattie, J. (1996). Cultural differences in the use of strategies for self-regulated learning. *American Educational Research Journal, 33*(4), 845–872.

Qin, Z., Johnson, D., & Johnson, R. (1995). Cooperation, competition, and problem solving. *Review of Educational Research, 65*(2), 129–143.

Ravitch, D. (2002). Seven lessons for the schools. *Educational Leadership, 60*(2), 6–9.

Resnick, L. B. (1983). A developmental theory of number understanding. In H. Ginsburg (Ed.), *The development of mathematical thinking* (pp. 110–149). New York: Academic Press.

Resnick, L. B. (1989). *Education and learning.* Pittsburgh, PA: University of Pittsburgh, Learning, Research and Development Center.

Resnick, L. B., & Resnick, D. (1989). Tests as standards of achievement in schools. *The uses of standardized tests in American education.* Princeton, NJ: Educational Testing Service.

Reynolds, D. S., Doran, R. L., Allers, R. H., & Agruso, S. A. (1996). *Alternative assessment in science: A teacher's guide.* Buffalo, NY: New York State Education Department.

Rogers, H., & Saklofske, D. H. (1985). Self concepts, locus of control, and performance expectations of learning disabled children. *Journal of Learning Disabilities, 18,* 273–277.

Rosenshine, B., & Meister, C. (1994). Reciprocal teaching: A review of the research. *Review of Educational Research, 64*(4), 479–530.

Rosko, K. (1996). When two heads are better than one. *Journal of Teacher Education, 47*(2), 120–129.

Rothstein, R. (2002, September 18). How U.S. punishes states that set higher standards. *New York Times,* p. B8.

Ryan, R., & Deci, E. L. (1996). When paradigms clash: Comments on Cameron and Pierce's claim that rewards do not undermine intrinsic motivation. *Review of Educational Research, 66*(1), 33–38.

Saphier, J., & Gower, R. (1997). *The skillful teacher.* Carlisle, MA: Research for Better Teaching.

Sarason, S. B. (1983). *Schooling in America.* New York: Free Press.

Sarason, S. B. (1990). *The predictable failure of educational reform.* San Francisco: Jossey-Bass.

Schmidt, W., McNight, C., & Raizen, S., in collaboration with six others. (1996). *A splintered vision: An investigation of U.S. science and mathematics education* (executive summary). Lansing: Michigan State University, U.S. National Research Center for the Third International Mathematics and Science Study.

Sedlak, M. W., Wheeler, C. W., Pullin, D. C., & Cusick, P. A. (1986). *Selling students short: Classroom bargains and academic reform in the American high school.* New York: Teachers College Press.

Senk, S. L., Beckman, C. E., Thompson, D. R. (1997). Assessment and grading in high school mathematics classrooms. *Journal for Research in Mathematics Education, 28*(2), 187–215.

Sharan, S., Kussel, P., Hertz-Lazarowitz, R., Bejanaro, Y., Raviv, S., & Sharan, Y. (1984). *Cooperative learning in the classroom: Research in segregated schools.* Hillsdale, NJ: Lawrence Erlbaum.

Silberman, T. (2002, July 15). In schools, a test of patience: State trying to restore confidence in exams. *Raleigh, North Carolina News & Observer.* Available online at http://newsobserver.com

Slavin, R. E. (1987). Ability grouping and student achievement in elementary schools: A best evidence synthesis. *Review of Educational Research, 57,* 293–336.

Slavin, R. E. (1990). Achievement effects of ability grouping in secondary schools: A best evidence synthesis. *Review of Educational Research, 60,* 471–499.

Slavin, R. E. (2000). *Educational psychology: Theory and practice.* Boston: Allyn & Bacon.

Smagorinsky, P. (2001). If meaning is constructed, what is it made from? Toward a cultural theory of reading. *Review of Educational Research, 71*(1), 133–169.

Smith, N. (1996). *Standards mean business. Pre-Summit briefing materials: 1996 National Education Summit.* Palisades, NY: Governors' Commission Report for National Alliance of Business.

Smylie, M. A. (1996). From bureaucratic control to building human capital: The importance of teacher learning in education reform. *Educational Researcher, 25*(9), 9–11.

Solomon, P. G. (1995). *No small feat: Taking time for change.* Thousand Oaks, CA: Corwin Press.

Solomon, P. G. (2000). *The math we need to know and do.* Thousand Oaks, CA: Corwin Press.

Solomon, P. G. (2002). *The assessment bridge: Positive ways to link tests to learning, standards, and curriculum improvement.* Thousand Oaks, CA: Corwin Press.

Sousa, D. A. (2000). *How the brain learns.* Thousand Oaks, CA: Corwin Press.

Spady, W., & Marshall, K. (1990). *Vail leadership seminars.* Santa Cruz, CA: High Success Program.

Stedman, L. C. (1997). International achievement differences: An assessment of a new perspective. *Educational Researcher, 26*(3), 4–15.

Steffe, L. P., & D'Ambrosio, B. (1995). Toward a working model of constructivist teaching: A reaction to Simon. *Journal of Mathematics Teaching, 26*(2), 146–159.

Stein, C. (2002, September 17). Being nice but being firm. *Boston Globe,* p. B1.

Stein, M. K., Grover, B. W., & Henningsen, M. (1996). Building student capacity for mathematical thinking and reasoning: An analysis of mathematical tasks used in reform classrooms. *American Educational Research Journal, 33*(2), 455–488.

Steinberg, J. (2001, October 10). National education talks languish in shadow of war. *New York Times,* p. A15.

Sternberg, R. J. (1985). *Understanding and increasing intelligence.* New York: Harcourt Brace Jovanovich.

Sternberg, R. J. (1988). *The triarchic mind.* New York: Viking.

Sternberg, R. J., Okagaki, L., & Jackson, A. S. (1990). Practical intelligence for success in school. *Educational Leadership, 48*(1), 35–39.

Stevenson, H. W., & Stigler, J. W. (1992). *The learning gap.* New York: Summit.

Stout, R. T. (1997). Staff development policy: Fuzzy choices in an imperfect market. *Education Policy Analysis Archives, 5*(4). Available online at http://epaa.asu.edu/epaa/v5n11.html

Strike, K. A. (1993). Professionalism, democracy, and discursive communities: Normative reflections on restructuring. *American Educational Research Journal, 30*(2), 255–275.

Strike, K. A. (1997). Centralized goal formation and systemic reform: Reflections on liberty, localism and pluralism. *Education Policy Analysis Archives, 5*(2). Available online at http://epaa.asu.edu/epaa/v5n11.html

Stumpf, T. (1995). A Colorado school's un-rocky road to trimesters. *Educational Leadership, 53*(3) 20–22.

Tobias, S. (1994). Interest, prior knowledge, and learning. *Review of Educational Research, 64*(1), 37–54.

Tomlinson, C. A. (2000). Reconcilable differences: Standards-based teaching and differentiation. *Educational Leadership, 58*(1), 6–18.

Traub, J. (2002, November 10). Does it work? *New York Times*, Sec. 4A, p. 24.

Tyler, R. W. (1949). *Basic principles of curriculum and instruction.* Chicago: University of Chicago Press.

Tyree, A. K. (1993). Examining the evidence: Have states reduced local control of curriculum? *Educational Evaluation and Policy Analysis, 15*(1), 34–50.

Tyson-Bernstein, H. (1988). The academy's contribution to the impoverishment of America's textbooks. *Kappan, 69,* 193–198.

U.S. Department of Education. (1991). *America 2000: An education strategy.* Washington, DC: Author.

U.S. Department of Education. (2001, August 2). *Prepared remarks of U.S. Secretary of Education Rod Paige: The nation's report card—Mathematics 2000.* Retrieved February 2, 2002, from www.ed.gov/PressReleases/08-2001/08022001.html

University of the State of New York. (1997). *Math, science and technology resource guide.* Albany, NY: Author. Available online at http://www.nysed.gov

Unks, G. (1995). Three nations' curricula: Policy implications for U.S. curriculum reform. In A. C. Ornstein & L. S. Behar (Eds.), *Contemporary issues in curriculum* (pp. 415–429). Boston: Allyn & Bacon.

Urdan, T. C., & Maehr, M. L. (1995). Beyond a two goal theory of motivation and achievement: A case for social goals. *Review of Educational Research, 65*(3), 213–242.

Vaishnav, A. (2002a, October 30). MCAS rule faces challenge. *Boston Globe,* p. B2.

Vaishnav, A. (2002b, September 13). Urban districts trailing amid MCAS gains. *Boston Globe,* p. B1.

Van Lehn, K. (1986). Arithmetic procedures are induced from examples. In J. Hiebert (Ed.), *Conceptual and procedural knowledge: The case of mathematics* (pp. 133–179). Hillsdale, NJ: Lawrence Erlbaum.

Vinovskis, M. A. (1996). An analysis of the concept and uses of systemic educational reform. *American Educational Research Journal, 33*(1), 53–85

von Glasersfeld, E. (1990). Environment and communication. In *Transforming children's mathematics education: International perspectives* (pp. 30–38). Hillsdale, NJ: Lawrence Erlbaum.

Vygotsky, L. S. (1978). *Mind in society: The development of higher psychological processes.* In M. Cole et al. (Eds.), *Mind in society: The development of higher psychological processes.* Cambridge, MA: Harvard University Press.

Wang, M. C., Haertel, G., & Walberg, H. (1993). Toward a knowledge base for school learning. *Review of Educational Research, 63*(3), 249–294.

Wasley, P. A., & Lear, R. J. (2001). Small schools, real gains. *Educational Leadership, 58*(6), 22–27.

Weinstein, R. S., Madison, S. M., & Kuklinsky, M. R. (1995). Raising expectations in schooling: Obstacles and opportunities. *American Educational Research Journal, 32*(1), 121–161.

Weinstein, R. S. (1996). High standards in a tracked system of schooling: For which students and with what educational supports? *Educational Researchers. 25*(8), 16–19.

Wells, A. S., Hirschberg, D., Lipton, M., & Oakes, J. (1995). Bounding the case within its context: A constructivist approach to studying de-tracking reform. *Educational Researcher, 24*(5), 18–24.

Wentzel, K. R. (1989). Adolescent classroom goals, standards for performance and academic achievement: An interactionist perspective. *Journal of Educational Psychology, 81,* 131–142.

Wentzel, K. R. (1993). Motivation and achievement in early adolescence: The role of multiple classroom goals. *Journal of Early Adolescence, 13,* 4–20.

Wertsch, J. V. (1979). From social interaction to higher psychological process: A clarification and application of Vygotsky's theory. *Human Development, 22*(1), 1–22.

Wiggins, G. (1989). Teaching to the authentic test. *Educational Leadership, 46*(7), 41–47.

Wiggins, G. (1995). Standards, not standardization: Evoking quality student work. In A. C. Ornstein & L. S. Behar (Eds.), *Contemporary issues in curriculum* (pp. 187–195). Boston: Allyn & Bacon.

Wiggins, G. (1996/1997). Practicing what we preach in authentic assessments. *Educational Leadership,* 54*(4),* 18–25.

Wilson, D. M., & Weiner, R. (2001, October 10). Education called key to defense. *[Rockland County, N.Y.] Journal News,* p. B1.

Wisconsin Department of Public Instruction. (1996). *Position statement on standards.* Madison: Office of Public Accountability.

Zuckerman, M. (1996, September 16). Why schools need standards. *U.S. News and World Report,* p. 128.

Index

The Corwin Press logo—a raven striding across an open book—represents the happy union of courage and learning. We are a professional-level publisher of books and journals for K-12 educators, and we are committed to creating and providing resources that embody these qualities. Corwin's motto is "Success for All Learners."